THE CROSSROADS OF JUSTICE

BRILL'S STUDIES IN INTELLECTUAL HISTORY

VOLUME 36

Pieter Brueghel the Elder: Justitia

THE CROSSROADS OF JUSTICE

Law and Culture in Late Medieval France

BY

ESTHER COHEN

E.J. BRILL
LEIDEN • NEW YORK • KÖLN
1993

Frontispiece: *Justitia* (Pieter Brueghel the Elder; photograph: Rijksmuseum, Amsterdam).

The paper in this book meets the guidelines for permanence and durability of the Committee on Production Guidelines for Book Longevity of the Council on Library Resources.

Library of Congress Cataloging-in-Publication Data

Cohen, Esther, 1947 Dec. 21-
The crossroads of justice: law and culture in late medieval France / by Esther Cohen.
p. cm.—(Brill's studies in intellectual history, ISSN 0920-8607; v. 36)
Includes bibliographical references and index.
ISBN 9004095691 (cloth)
1. Customary law—France—History. 2. Culture and law—History. 3. Law, Medieval. 4. Ritualism. I. Title. II. Series.
KJV263.C64 1992
340.5'0944—dc20 92-570
CIP

ISSN 0920-8607
ISBN 90 04 09569 1

PRINTED IN THE NETHERLANDS

IN MEMORY OF ROBERT

CONTENTS

ACKNOWLEDGEMENTS

The book was first conceived, and later written at the Netherlands Institute for Advanced Study. Twice, first in the spring of 1985 and subsequently during the entire year of 1988-89 the Institute provided me with the leisure necessary not only for writing, but more importantly, for developing ideas in the congenial company of some of the best brains in Europe and America. To all NIAS fellows, director and staff, my most sincere thanks for help wittingly and unwittingly given, information generously shared and friendship freely granted. The Institute's library and librarian, Ms. Dinny Young, deserve special thanks for locating arcane bibliographic items. Research in French archives and libraries, as well as camera-ready formatting of the book, were funded by Ben Gurion University.

My search for rare bibliographic items was greatly aided by the courtesy of many colleagues. Walter Simons helped me find material on the Ypres cat-feast, and José Goñi Gaztambide was gracious enough to part with the last offprint of his edition of Martin de Arles' work for me. Brenda Danet and Bryna Bogoch have allowed me to read and quote their unpublished work on Anglo-Saxon charters. To all of them, my thanks.

A book taking several years to gestate and write must necessarily incur considerable intellectual debts. Several portions of the book have served as bases for lectures at learned societies and other fora. Commentaries and criticisms voiced on these occasions have been most useful in further defining and sharpening the issues of the book. If any of the numerous scholars who did so, or who have patiently answered my queries over the years has now been forgotten, I apologize most sincerely. In fact, the list of my debts is as long as the list of my teachers. Bryce Lyon, with whom it was a privilege to study, opened the realm of social history of law to me. In later years numerous friends and colleagues have been my teachers in a variety of fields. Ilana Zinguer on Renaissance thought, Eli Yasif and Helmut Birkhan on medieval folklore, Kenneth Stow and the late Benzion Dagani on medieval Jewish history—all have generously shared their knowledge and expertise with me. Kenneth Stow has both read and commented upon the sections concerning Jewish history and allowed me to consult the manuscript of his forthcoming book. Clinton Bamberger introduced me to Saint Yves, and Peter Mason provided an anthropological point of view.

Special thanks are due to Mayke de Jong and Florike Egmond for reading, correcting, and commenting upon the entire manuscript, and to Arjo Vanderjagt, who urged me to write the book in the first place, providing constant encouragement and fruitful insights from his own encyclopedic knowledge of medieval philosophy and culture. All three deserve also my gratitude for their friendship and encouragement.

My sons, Shammai and Yaron, have contributed nothing of scholarly nature to the writing of the book. Nor did they carefully refrain from bothering their mother at work. To the contrary, they insistently reminded me that life and history are one, much to the long-term improvement of the book. My debt to Robert Cohen—husband, friend, colleague, trenchant critic and staunch supporter—is far too great and deep to be properly acknowledged in any public sphere. In the terrible grief and darkness of his sudden death, I dedicate this book to his memory.

ABBREVIATIONS

AN	Archives Nationales, Paris
BN	Bibliothèque Nationale, Paris
CB	Beaumanoir, Philippe de. *Coutumes de Beauvaisis*. Ed. A. Salmon. 3 vols. Paris, 1899-1974.
CF	Fontaines, Pierre de. *Conseil*. Ed. M.A.J. Marnier. Paris, 1846.
CIAM	*Coutumes et institutions de l'Anjou et du Maine antérieures au XVIe siècle*. Ed. C.J. Beautemps-Beaupré. 4 vols. Paris, 1877-97.
ESL	*Établissements de Saint Louis*. Ed. Paul Viollet, 4 vols. Paris, 1881-86.
GC	Ableiges, Jacques d'. *Le Grand Coutumier de France*. Ed. E. Laboulaye and R. Dareste. Paris, 1868.
MGH	*Monumenta Germaniae Historica* *LL - Leges* *SS Rer. Germ. - Scriptores rerum Germanicarum*
MPL	J. P. Migne, ed. *Patrologiae Latinae cursus completus*. 221 vols. Paris, 1844-64.
MSHP	*Mémoires de la société de l'histoire de Paris et d'Ile-de-France.*
RHDFE	*Revue historique de droit français et étranger.*
RHGF	*Recueil des historiens des Gaules et de la France*. Ed. V. Bouquet et al., 24 vols. Paris, 1737-1904.
SR	Boutillier, Jean. *Le grand coustumier general de praticque, aultrement appelle Somme rural*. Ed. L. Charondas le Caron. Paris, 1603.
ZRG, GA	*Zeitschrift der Savigny-Stiftung für Rechtsgeschichte, germanistische Abteilung.*

INTRODUCTION

This book is an inquiry into the socio-cultural functions of law and legal practice in northern France in the later middle ages. Lawyers studying law have always viewed their subject as an autonomous field, regardless of time and place. Be it biblical, Roman, or constitutional English law, it is studied according to issues, not contexts. The laws of persons or of property, procedures and proofs all loom as immutable categories of human legal systems.

The historian, however, should view the law as embedded within a specific temporal and geographic context. More so, within a specific social and cultural scheme. Formally legislated or not, historical legal systems were emphatically not autonomous fields. As a product of the human mind, law is an integral part of any culture. As a social mechanism, it is an expression of social structures. It is shaped at one and the same time by social realities and by the perception of these realities in contemporary minds, and in turn exercises a significant influence upon continuing social and cultural formations.[1]

The search for the cultural roots of late medieval French legal systems has taken me down a startling number of unexpected avenues. Public rituals, perceptions of the human body, contemporary medicine and theology were only a few of the fields I found myself exploring in my quest for answers. The history of a customary legal system became transmuted, in the course of writing, into the history of mentalities. But the minds I was led to explore were often not the minds of jurists or judges. They were the minds of peasants, townsmen, minor royal officials, and even criminals. Law became a many-faceted phenomenon, shifting its shape and meaning according to one's perspective.

In pursuance of this elusive social paradigm, the book emerges not as a continual, linear narrative, but as a series of different approaches circulating around the same problem. It has neither beginning nor end, in the sense that every chapter and every approach bears upon all others. Insofar as law deals with all aspects of human society, to be

[1] While this perception of law is rare among historians and jurists, legal anthropologists have always followed it. For an excellent and succinct survey of the literature see Simon Roberts, "The Study of Dispute: Anthropological Perspectives," in *Disputes and Settlements: Law and Human Relations in the West*, ed. John Bossy (Cambridge, 1983), pp. 1-24.

comprehensive the book would have had to become a total history of late medieval France. The task was not only beyond my capabilities, it was also to a great extent supererogatory. The most obvious connections, such as those between economics and law, or statecraft and law, have been long part and parcel of late medieval historiography. I have therefore chosen to concentrate upon those aspects of law and culture which, ostensibly having little to do with institutional developments, have hitherto been neglected. I have focused upon those aspects which to lawyers might have seemed most trivial, but to historians carry great import: perceptions of law and legal rituals.

Every legal phenomenon I observed seemed to reflect quite a number of cultural trends and ideas. Being unable to disentangle the different strands, I was forced to disregard the King of Hearts' excellent advice: "Begin at the beginning, and go on till you come to the end: then stop." I began instead at the end—that is, with the legal manifestations of those intermingling cultural strands. Starting with the ideas of law and justice, I attempted to find the common perceptual denominator underlying these concepts.

From the idea of law, the book moves to practice. Here again I chose to concentrate upon the cultural context of procedures particular to the time and the place: oaths, ordeals, and ritual formulae. The demise of these procedures seemed to reflect a cultural change prevalent also in other social spheres. But legal practice at the time meant more than courtroom procedures. Though the legal rituals of the courthouse provide one aspect, the greater part of the rituals I have studied took place in the streets and outside city walls. Unlike courtroom practices which spanned both civil and criminal litigation, these rituals belonged purely to the realm of punitive law. For reasons which I shall explore, ritualism vanished from civil, adversary actions while remaining in criminal prosecution.

Punitive rituals, either defamatory or capital, form the main part of the book. The search for the method behind what seems to the modern eye indiscriminate cruelty yielded the richest lodes from the mines of contemporary culture, both popular and learned. By going backwards from the rite to its roots I have learned, and illuminated, perhaps more of the context than of the legal practice. But the intimate connection between the two says a great deal about what law meant at the time to those who used it.

Thus the search for the cultural context of late medieval law led me from the theories of the jurists to the practices of the lawyers, and to the street-dramas of public executions. But it does not end there. No less than royally-staged pageants, public punitive rites were dramatic articulations of those perceptions of law and justice I began with. Ideology and practice intersected in legal rites, to create one cultural unity.

PART I: LAW

CHAPTER ONE

FUNCTIONS AND FORMS OF LAW

Legal systems serve a variety of functions. They establish, order, and define social relationships. They provide an institutional justification for society's norms and sanctions against those who transgress the established order. As societies change and evolve, it is the function of law to redefine the new relationships.[1] Embedding human ties at all their stages—initiation, severance, or mending—within legal frameworks imbues them with a certain stability. At the same time, the form legal processes assume is intrinsically tied to, and derives from a specific cultural context. For example, an act of feudal homage is essentially the legal seal of a bilateral contract. Within the context of a society that attached greater value to the spoken than to the written word, and even more merit to formal ritual gestures, the contract was 'signed' in a ceremony heavily loaded with symbolic gestures and objects. The form of the law in this case was firmly embedded within a specific cultural context, and the constant reiteration of the legal ceremony in turn reinforced the underlying cultural imperatives. The relationship of law and culture in any given society, therefore, is one of mutual shaping influences.

Human beings had laws from times immemorial. Judging by present-day primitive societies, pre-literate social groupings in the past also had their laws long before they possessed the capacity of writing them down.[2] But laws seldom remained oral once writing appeared, and law corpora are often the most ancient documents we possess of early civilizations. From the citizens of Eshnunna, Hammurapi's Babylon and the ancient Israelites to the Salian Franks, apparently every society wrote down its laws at a fairly early stage of development.

Recent scholarship of ancient law corpora has posited the theory that most of them were no codes of law in the modern sense at all. They were quite separate from contemporary legal practice, and not meant to be implemented in court. The laws were literary traditions, a record for posterity and a mirror for any society's self-perception. This

---

[1] E. Adamson Hoebel, *The Law of Primitive Man: A Study in Comparative Legal Dynamics* (Cambridge, Mass., 1954), pp. 75-287.

[2] *Ibid.*

point has been argued convincingly about the Mesopotamian and biblical codes, the twelve tables of Rome and the Germanic law codes of the early middle ages.[3]

Indeed, in these texts the borderline between law and myth tends to blur. Most ancient law corpora are associated with the name of a mythical, or semi-mythical law-giver, not necessarily a ruler, but certainly a man (or men) of authority and wisdom. The four mythical Franks who supposedly wrote the Salic law belong much in the same category as Moses and Solon. The law-givers loom as mythical figures of origin at the source of ancient law corpora, providing them with authority and legitimation.

Furthermore, there is no hard proof that these corpora had indeed been created, either as operative codes or as literary traditions, at the time history formally dates their birth. We possess no contemporary original proof of the existence of Solon's laws, or for that matter of the law of the twelve tables.[4] The law-codes of the Pentateuch were written down centuries after the desert era. The earliest known manuscript of the Salic law, supposedly written at the beginning of the sixth century, is nowadays dated to the second half of the eighth century, and it has already been suggested that the whole is a ninth-century fabrication.[5] It is possible that all these codes did indeed exist in oral form at the time legends claim they were created, but the fact was immaterial to the people who used them in subsequent centuries. To them, the mythical source of the law was as important as its historicity. The Book of the Covenant was decreed by God at Mount Sinai, and Solon had indeed legislated for the Athenians. The mythical origin only serves to underline the extra-legal character and functions of ancient law corpora.

Why then were these law corpora written down, if not for use? If indeed they served as a literary genre, they were fulfilling an exceedingly important function. Law was and is a tool of societal self-defini-

---

[3] Meir Malul, *The Comparative Method in Ancient Near Eastern and Biblical Legal Studies* (Alter Orient und altes Testament, Kevelaer, 1990), pp. 105-107; A.S. Diamond, *Primitive Law Past and Present* (London, 1971), pp. 114-23; Patrick Wormald, "*Lex Scripta* and *Verbum Regis:* Legislation and Germanic Kingship from Euric to Cnut," in P.H. Sawyer and I.N. Wood, eds., *Early Medieval Kingship* (Leeds, 1977), pp. 105-38; but see Rosamond McKitterick, *The Carolingians and the Written Word* (Cambridge, 1989), pp. 40-60, who argues that these codes were indeed used in court.

[4] For a view contrary to Diamond's, see Alan Watson, *Rome of the XII Tables: Persons and Property* (Princeton, N.J., 1975), p.3.

[5] Simon Stein, "Lex Salica," *Speculum* 22 (1947), 113-34, 395-418.

tion, and the possession of a code based either upon custom (as in the case of feudal law) or stemming from a mythical law-giver allowed any society to perceive itself as the heir to a clearly-defined, authoritative past. It also allowed the same society to claim that it ruled itself according to the maxims and norms derived from this past. Whether it did so in actual fact or not mattered little. Hence, the writing of law codes had very little to do with functional preservation. Oral codes could operate on the purely legal level just as well as written ones. But a long-term literary tradition, designed for cultural rather than practical-legal ends, required recording. The survival of ancient codes is an indication of the very careful preservation of those same written versions, be it on clay tablets, stone, papyrus, or parchment. Like holy writings, another carefully preserved genre, law corpora were evidently accorded a great deal of physical respect, a respect based upon the authority inherent in the written text of the law.

The authority of a written law corpus could stem from the position of its eponymous author, be he a codifier like Justinian or a legislator like Solon. Those early codes of law that carried the stamp of political power probably, but not necessarily, did in the first instance derive their authority from this power. The law of the twelve tables was presumably redacted by a commission (as was the Salic law), not by political authority, yet some of its precepts, preserved on bronze tables in the Forum of Rome, were known for almost a millennium. The writing thus enhanced the authority of the law, especially when the written text (as in Rome and in Hammurapi's Babylon) was placed in a public area, becoming almost a monument. Writing and monumentality in these cases endowed the law with a quasi-sacral quality.

Beyond the literary and hieratic value of writing, it possessed the very simple value of a record. It not only enshrined memory, it ensured its survival. No codifier or legislator envisaged his work as operative in his lifetime alone. Whatever its pre-literate existence had been, once the law was written, its very authority hinged upon its power of future survival. It was written not only to serve as a memory of past oral laws, but in order to shape the memory of generations to come. Again, the writing was necessary for the sake of continuity. It is possible to forge a memory of oral laws, but it is almost impossible to ensure accurate transmission without a written text.

Once the written text became enshrined in tradition, it bound the past and the future together in a consciousness of a continuous common tradition.

> These are the commandments, the laws and the judgments, which the Lord your God commanded to teach you.... And thou shalt teach them diligently unto thy children, and shalt talk of them when thou sittest in thine house, and when thou walkest by the way, and when thou liest down, and when thou risest up. And thou shalt bind them for a sign upon thine hand, and they shall be as frontlets between thine eyes. And thou shalt write them upon the posts of thy house, and on thy gates.[6]

The legal prescriptions of Deuteronomy thus comprise the authoritative legislative source (divine in this case), the duty of oral and written memorization, and the transmission to future generations. Continuity depended upon memory, and both together were enhanced by the existence of a written record. Finally, continuity of transmission, the consciousness of an ancient and unadulterated character, bolstered the authority of any code.

The medieval West had a double tradition of written law. The Judaic one, incorporated into Christianity, and the Roman one, which affirmed the ultimate validity of *lex scripta*. This tradition was faithfully followed in the early middle ages in the various codes of the so-called barbarian nations. Most of these codes were associated with the name and memory of a codifier-ruler—Clovis, Gundobad, Alaric, or Recceswinth—but they supposedly recorded the age-old customs of the people ruled by that specific law. The authority of the law did not derive from the codifier, but from the oral tradition preceding the written text. The same holds true for the later codifications of Germanic laws dating from Carolingian times. They were presumably all records of an already existent local law, not a legislation deriving from the ruler's central authority. In fact, the rulers who ordered those codifications took good care to include only those sections of oral law that served their purposes. The following Carolingian rulers simply separated written codes from daily practice. They acknowledged the existence and validity of the various legal systems within their realm, taking care to have old codes re-edited and new ones recorded, all the while running their empire with the aid of capitularies, not laws. After their time, the writing of laws was confined to Anglo-Saxon and Norman England, while most of Continental Europe had no written codes again until the thirteenth century.

This phenomenon raises some questions. Undoubtedly, by the twelfth century the early medieval codes had ceased to carry any force

[6] Deuteronomy, 6:1-9.

at all. The operative law on both legal and literary levels in France and Germany until the thirteenth century was orally transmitted custom. The so-called 'feudal society' certainly had both the technical skills necessary for writing down the law and an awareness of its particulars. Why then, did a society in possession of writing refrain from endowing its laws with a written form, as all other literate societies had done?

The answer to this question lies in the dual nature of customary law. On the one hand it was undoubtedly a practical type of law, made in courts and used there, and no purely literary tradition. It was not a coherent corpus or a code of law, and its authority had little to do with writing. On the other hand, customary law shared with the ancient law corpora certain literary qualities:

> Based upon formula, gesture, and ritual, the procedures of the feudal court resembled more than superficially the literary performance. Both fulfilled in different ways a common purpose—the affirmation of an acknowledged set of shared beliefs and aspirations through the articulation of a collective history as prerequisite to the constitution of the legal and social community.... The feudal court and the literary performance enjoyed a common and inherently legal function, respectively the articulation and the enforcement of a sanctioned code of conduct.[7]

Until then, law had been written either because it was a literary tradition or because it had been codified by a ruler. Customary law owed its authority to no ruler, and it coalesced at a time when literary production was also orally transmitted. Consequently, either as literature or as practice there was no reason to write down the law. Furthermore, there were some very fundamental reasons that prevented the writing of customary law, reasons connected with the very perception of law and custom.

First of all, there were already in western Europe two separate codes of written law. One was the code of Justinian, and whether one considered it operative or not, it was by definition 'the law', as opposed to 'custom'. At the same time, canon law was slowly acquiring a coherent form. The work of Gratian and his successors shaped the centuries of conciliar and papal legislation into a code usable in every part of western Christendom. The existence of such prior codes was certainly a hindrance to the writing of customary law. At a time when most Roman and customary jurists agreed that the main distinc-

[7] R. Howard Bloch, *Medieval French Literature and Law* (Berkeley, 1977), p. 3.

tion between law and custom was the written character of the first and the oral form of the latter, customary lawyers had very good reasons to preserve the separateness of their system by keeping it unwritten.

Far more importantly, there was no incentive for political authorities to write the law. Law was not within the ruler's province. While the administration of justice was most emphatically a prerequisite of political authority, the knowledge of law and its dissemination were not. This knowledge resided in the memories of laymen, not necessarily literate ones at that. Long after the inquest, born in Frankish courts, had ceased to be a fact-finding practice in the Continent, it remained there as a method for ascertaining the nature of specific rulings and procedures. It was not until the administrators of law became literate that customs came to be written down. As long as the authoritative knowledge of the law remained in the hands of a largely illiterate group of people, the writing of the law was both useless and counterproductive.

The writing down of customs, begun in the thirteenth century, must be seen within the context of general cultural trends. The process of setting down in writing hitherto oral traditions, many of them literary, had assumed impetus already in the eleventh and twelfth centuries.[8] For a variety of reasons, the writing of law was a latecomer within the trend.

In the first place, the men who knew customary law were neither scholars nor clerics, but laymen with administrative and local experience. Moreover, they were keenly aware of the intrinsically oral character of their system. Customary law placed the ultimate legal commitment in the spoken word and the gesture, rather than in the written word, and it was therefore in character that the tradition remain oral. Nor did the element of orality disappear once the customs were written. It was carefully preserved within the texts of thirteenth-century customals. The lateness of customary law writing is evidence of resistance to the growing trend of literacy, a resistance born of the intrisically conservative and oral character of customary law.

[8] "The codification of feudal law is perhaps less a direct consequence of Roman influences than an aspect of the more widespread transition to literate legal institutions." Brian Stock, *The Implications of Literacy* (Princeton, 1983), p. 56. Stock, however, confuses in his analysis the private and governmental redactions of customary law.

The writing of custom, therefore, was a contradiction in terms. Nothing elucidates the ambivalent character of customary writing better than the private nature of the early texts. Unlike ancient law corpora, almost no customal was ever associated with a ruler or a formal commission of experts. Customals carried no stamp of political authority; they were private, local, consciously subjective collections, not authoritative codifications. They were written by judges and administrators with some knowledge of Roman law, who drew mostly upon their years of practical experience in court for their material. These administrators made no attempt to formulate legal principles or posit general tenets, but instead gave minute and careful descriptions of their specific area's customs.

At the same time, in addition to working within an environment of increasing literacy, they lived with the gradual encroachment of royal prerogatives and jurisdiction upon the local spheres in which they acted, and of the enhanced prestige of Roman law studies. These pressures had a double effect: on the one hand, they forced customary lawyers to define their field of expertise in a clear-cut fashion so as to avoid unconscious imitation or alterations. On the other hand, the same lawyers evinced a considerable respect for extraneous sources of authority, adopting various elements from them. The writing was thus no mere setting down of a hitherto oral tradition. All customal authors edited their material, and what they added or omitted often tells us a great deal about the forces affecting law at the time.

Until its writing, customary law was a tradition in the literal sense of the word, something handed down from one to another over a long period of time. Any tradition, legal or otherwise, is characterized by three basic elements. It stems, or is supposed to stem from the past, it carries authority in the present, and it is continuously transmitted between the past and the present.[9] In this process of transmission no tradition remains immutable. This is especially true of a legal tradition, constantly made and re-made in court.[10] All the more so when the legal tradition in question possessed no hard basis of legislation, but acknowledged precedents as the foundation for future decisions. Customary law was by its very nature processual rather than static, and this fact, coupled with the its oral nature, made it especially vulnerable to change. The writing, therefore, was a necessity for those who be-

---

[9] Martin Krygier, "Law as Tradition," *Law and Philosophy* 5 (1986), 237-62.

[10] Cf. Sally F. Moore, *Law as Process: An Anthropological Approach* (London, 1978), pp. 42-48.

lieved that custom derived its authority from its putatively ancient and unaltered character.

The incorporation of extraneous 'authoritative' matter into private customals was extremely important in ensuring their acceptance and legitimacy. The literate form, dictated by external pressures, made customary law respectable in educated eyes. At the same time, form was bound to influence matter, thus changing the custom. Though no theoreticians, the authors of customary material were forced to define in general terms the legal idea of custom, its relationship with written (i.e., Roman) law, and with political power. In general, custom was defined as legal rules deriving their authority from long, consistent, and common usage.[11] Custom originated from 'the people' not from the ruler: "Custom comes into being when the people begin to keep a certain thing with such perseverance that from then on it becomes custom, or, as others say, when it especially pleases the people that a certain thing should be henceforth kept as custom."[12] According to some authors, it was by definition oral, losing its customary character upon being written down.[13] Others, though, did not consider writing a material change in the nature of custom, merely a formal record. The writing in no way proved the validity of any custom, nor did it endow it with the position of 'written law', reserved for Roman law.

None of these ideas was born in customary circles. When in need of theory, customal authors turned to the academics and experts in Roman law. And the doctors of law from Orléans had indeed discussed extensively article 8:52 of the *Codex*, *Quid sit longa consuetudo*. The expositions of Simon of Paris and Jacques de Révigny provided whatever theoretical definitions customal authors required in order to clothe their trade in the trappings of a science.[14] They were never formally quoted, but simply used time and again. They appeared later in a practical textbook, the *Formularius* of Guillaume de Paris,

---

[11] "... la costume... vaut mels que drois, se ele est resnable et ele a esté longuement gardée..." Anonymous thirteenth-century text, published as an appendix to *CF*, p. 483.

[12] "Costume est amenée quant li peuples conmence à garder aucune chose par tel courage que ce soit d'ileuc en avant costume, ou si conme li autre dient, quant ci plest expressément au peuple que aucune chose soit gardée el tens à venir por costume." *Ibid.*, p. 492.

[13] "Cele costume qui est mise en escrit est apelée lois ou constitutions, ce est establissemens; cele qui n'est pas mist en escrit retien son nom, et est apelée costume." *Ibid.*

[14] L. Waelkens, *La théorie de la coutume chez Jacques de Révigny* (Leiden, 1984).

parts of which were eventually translated into French and used as a customal.[15]

The distinctions of law and custom in late medieval jurisprudence in no way conform to the models generated by modern anthropologists. For the modern student of primitive or developed societies, custom means a set of commonly shared norms, while the law implies the existence of coercive state power.[16] Though Roman law was defined in late medieval Europe as the written law, this fact did not endow it with any formal legal validity in customary lands. The law administered and enforced by the courts in those areas was specifically called custom and honored as such. The authority of lordship was implemented through the use and administration of custom as a coercive form of state power.

But the writing of custom did not comprise merely the record of its rules. As literacy became a cultural norm, court proceedings and other legal instruments came into existence, sometimes side by side with the spoken word and sometimes in its place. It is thus an oversimplification to identify all written legal sources with prescription, as opposed to oral practice. A written text might be one of several things, all at different degrees of distance from the spoken word. The distance between a treatise of jurisprudence and the confession of a criminal taken down in court is certainly greater than the distance between the latter and the spoken avowal. Some texts were meant to reproduce the oral reality of the courthouse, others to describe or interpret it, another kind was meant to ordain it and still another to create its theoretical basis. A verdict of a central court could and did easily carry more weight of authority than the opinion of a written customal, for the former, whether written or not, was prescriptive and authoritative, and the latter was essentially descriptive. While this trait of early customals makes them dangerous sources for generalization, it does allow one to elicit from them elements of practice. At the same time, the records of the Parlement of Paris, for example, covering as they do the appellate jurisdiction of most of northern France, occasionally pro-

[15] The section of the *Formularius* concerning custom was published as appendix I in Hippolyte Pissard, *Essai sur la connaissance et la preuve des coutumes en justice, dans l'ancien droit français et dans le système romano-canonique* (Paris, 1910), pp. 188-97. Auguste Lebrun, *La coutume. Ses sources - son autorité en droit privé* (Paris, 1932), pp. 32-33, was the first to note that the anonymous text published by Marnier was no more than a French translation of the *Formularius*.

[16] Stanley Diamond, "The Rule of Law Versus the Order of Custom," in C.E. Reasons and R.M. Rich, eds., *The Sociology of Law* (Toronto, 1978), pp. 239-62.

vide equally crucial information concerning local practices. The search for practiced law and its divergence from theory can thus be carried out on both descriptive and prescriptive levels.

The court record is the closest approximation available to an oral source. Protocols of trials, especially from rural areas, have not survived in great numbers before the fifteenth century. Nevertheless, they provide far more accurate information concerning actual practice than any prescriptive text. They repeat the depositions of litigants and witnesses alike, often using their very own words, and faithfully record judicial decisions.

The memoranda and private collections of precedents kept by jurists to use in court arguments constituted another type of record. Such a collection was extremely useful in a system that granted court decisions the status of proven custom, which could be a precedent. Several jurists in the fourteenth and the fifteenth centuries kept such records. Though considered purely private notations of no prescriptive value whatsoever, not to be adduced as proof in court, they do form a written non-authoritative source of law, quoted in later centuries as an authoritative custom.[17]

A third level is that of the non-legal text. Often practices that have vanished from legal texts survive in literature, sermons, *exempla* and proverbs. These are the ideal descriptive sources, for unlike the customals they have no ax to grind and no interpretation to enforce. More importantly, the non-legal source will often illuminate perceptions underlying specific practices far more clearly than any juridic interpretation might. Especially didactic literature drew its matter from popular sources, couching it in language intelligible to all: "The pages of popularizing medieval texts contain an ongoing hidden dialogue between official doctrine and folkloric consciousness, leading to their convergence but not to their fusion."[18] This trait is largely due to the dual character of popularizing literature, a character shared also

[17] For the fourteenth century, see Jean le Coq, *Quaestiones Johannis Galli*, ed. Marguerite Boulet (Paris, 1944), and the anonymous author of "Notes d'audiences prises au Parlement de Paris de 1384 à 1386, par un praticien anonyme," ed. Fr. Olivier-Martin, *RHDFE*, 4th ser., 1 (1922), 513-603. For the fifteenth, see Jean de Marès, *Coutumes tenues toutes notoires et jugées au Chastelet de Paris,* published by Julien Brodeau in his *Commentaire sur la coustume de la prévosté et vicomté de Paris* (Paris, 1658), and Gui Pape, *Decisiones Parlamenti Dalphinatis Gratianopolitanis* (2nd ed., Geneva, 1667). See also F. Cheyette, "La justice et le pouvoir royal à la fin du moyen âge français," *RHDFE*, 4e ser., 40 (1962), 378-79.

[18] Aron Gurevich, *Medieval Popular Culture: Problems of Belief and Perception*, trans. J.M. Bak and P.A. Hollingsworth (Cambridge, 1988), p. 5.

by the law of the time: both relied upon writing as a mnemonic and disseminatory device, but both had deep roots within oral traditions. Customary manuals were also a type of didactic literature aimed at instructing judges and litigants in courtroom activities and strategies. They also deliberately drew upon a vocabulary of perceptions beyond the purely legal-technical sphere. Very much like the popular preachers of the time, Philippe de Beaumanoir could tell the horrifying story of a pilgrim who innocently fell into the wrong company and was executed together with his casual drinking-companions, and Jacques d'Ableiges could cap it with a salacious tale of a priest who lost the privilege of high justice by farting in the royal sergeant's face.[19] The parallel dynamics of interaction between orality and literacy in both law and literature make the non-legal, literary text an excellent mirror of law before it became the province of professionals and literates.

As in the literary text, the oral element of law did not vanish with its writing, but remained firmly embedded within the written version. The ideology of law, as articulated by customals, granted orality a primary weight in court procedure. But even this ideology was no more than one private person's view of the law, be he ever so experienced. In the absence of a unified, coherent legal theory, one cannot evaluate the congruence of theory with practice. Theories belonged to other systems of law, some operative, some ideal. Customary law only developed an ideological superstructure in the sixteenth century, long after its authoritative redaction was completed. In consequence, any divergences we might find were not the common modern divergence of practical law from the legal text. Congruence and incongruence at the time were to be found between local and central practice, and between practice and extraneous theories derived from other systems. Within itself, customary law before its formal redaction was a pattern of interrelated and mutually influential local sub-systems, flimsily held together by royal legislation.

[19] *CB*, art. 1963, 2:490; *GC*, p. 639.

CHAPTER TWO

THE REALITY OF MEDIEVAL LAW AND ITS MYTHS

1. THE MULTIPLICITY OF LEGAL SYSTEMS: MUTUAL INFLUENCES AND CONFLICTS

Late medieval practiced law never formed one system. All societies are composed of sub-groups arranged in differing hierarchical orders and possessing different sets of rules. These structures might belong to a tribe, a clan, and a nuclear family, or to a kingdom, a fief, a town, and a guild, or any other configuration. But in every case the sub-groups will each have their own power structures and enforceable rules. While this statement is a sociological truism, it has rarely been viewed within the context of law, certainly not of European law. The laws of sub-groups are rarely called by that name. They are labelled statutes, ordinances, or bylaws, but they function like any other law.

In his survey of the problem, Leopold Pospisil has argued that "the tendency to dissociate law from the structure of the society and its subgroups" was rooted in a European tradition that viewed law as one universal structure. "This attitude was undoubtedly caused by the tremendous influence the well-elaborated and unified law of the Roman Empire exerted upon the outlook of the European lawyer."[1] But the impression of solid, monolithic unity projected by the Code of Justinian has little to do either with the reality of late antique Roman law or with its influence upon the judicial realities of the subsequent centuries. While every modern aspiring lawyer must learn Roman law, it is doubtful that outside Italy many practicing lawyers before the sixteenth century either possessed or needed such knowledge.

Ernst Levy has long since proven that the law practiced in the western provinces of the late Empire and during the early middle ages differed considerably from what was codified by Trebonian and his colleagues.[2] Insofar as Roman law had any immediate influence upon the early medieval Germanic codes, it was exercised by local, vulgar

[1] Leopold Pospisil, *Anthropology of Law: A Comparative Theory* (New York, 1971), p. 99.

[2] Ernst Levy, *West Roman Vulgar Law: The Law of Property* (Philadelphia, 1951).

law, rather than imperial law. The greatest influence of Roman law lay in the act of codification, which provided the impulse for Germanic leaders to ape the emperor in writing down the laws of their people.[3] In the later middle ages Roman influence upon actual practice of law was even more problematic.

The tendency to view law as a unified whole thus belongs to modern jurists. No medieval student of law could possibly have adopted this view, for the multiplicity and occasional contradictions of different legal levels was the most real and persistent characteristic of late medieval society. Consequently, Pospisil's postulated dissociation of law from society had no place in reality. To the contrary: there was hardly a period in European history when law, society and culture were more closely intertwined.

The lack of a single authoritative source of law was undoubtedly one of the main reasons, though not the only one, for this phenomenon. The very complexity and fragmentation of social and political institutions, with their concomitant systems of rules and enforcement lay at its heart. This fact was acknowledged by medieval jurists. "Even though, generally speaking, there is only one justice, stemming from God and administered by the king in this kingdom, nevertheless, it is specifically divided into several parts..." stated Jacques d'Ableiges. He then went on to divide justice into high, middle, low and seigneurial.[4] In so doing, he neglected to mention the most important division of justice at the time, namely secular and religious. This omission was not due to forgetfulness, for the chapter dealing with types of justice follows immediately upon three discussing the boundaries of lay and clerical jurisdiction. It was a deliberate statement of the origins and structure of practical jurisdiction as viewed by a secular lawyer. The existence of different levels of justice within the overall secular framework could be acknowledged in a very matter-of-fact manner, for they fitted into one consistent and unified hierarchy of justice. They did not conflict with the overall scheme. But ecclesiastical jurisdiction posed a problem. It was a rival independent system, drawing its justification and origins from alien and powerful sources. Its very existence called into question the "one justice, stemming from God and

[3] Wormald, "*Lex scripta*," pp. 125-35.

[4] "Jà soit ce que a generallement parler il ne soit que une justice qui meut de Dieu, dont le roy a le gouvernement en ce royaulme, toutesfois en especialite elle est divisee en plusieurs membres, car l'une est nommee haulte justice, l'autre moyenne, l'autre basse, l'autre justice fonciere et seigneurie fonciere." *GC*, p. 637.

administered by the king." Though fully aware of its existence, d'Ableiges could not include the justice of the church in his taxonomy.

Like many taxonomies, d'Ableiges' picture was more a statement of ideals and principles than a description of reality. The conflict of jurisdictions, lay and religious, royal and seigneurial, local and central, was a perennial feature of late medieval jurisdiction. The questions of where and how one should be tried—at the place of the crime, at the court of the plaintiff, according to one's deed, or according to one's order in society—surfaced countless times both in judicial records and in books of law. The co-existence of different levels of justice, though far from peaceful, often resulted in cross-fertilization and mutual influences which shaped the development of the various systems.

Though secular and ecclesiastical justice were theoretically two separate systems, they were in fact in constant touch. Each system recognized the inherent validity and legality of the other despite constant boundary conflicts. It was not merely a matter of practical politics, acknowledging the other's power to summon backing in case of a conflict, but an admission of principle. In this, as in many other things, canon law inherited a great deal from Roman law. The latter had always recognized the validity of customary laws, both in the codification of Justinian and in late medieval commentaries.[5] As far back as Gratian, canon law had also acknowledged the validity of custom, while customary jurists affirmed the overriding quality of ecclesiastical privilege in cases of clashes with their own system.[6]

The line of demarcation between the two jurisdictions was often unclear. Though marriage litigation and religious orthodoxy were unquestionably under ecclesiastical jurisdiction, often the problem could arise in subjects entirely foreign to proper church matters. Though debt, even to an ecclesiastical institution, was a civil affair, the church often excommunicated recalcitrant debtors. When such excommunicated debtors cheerfully persisted in their unhallowed, though solvent state (sometimes for as long as twenty years), the church turned to the secular arm, requesting imprisonment as an aid to spiritual coercion.

[5] *Corpus iuris civilis*, ed. P. Krueger, T. Mommsen, and R. Scholl, 3 vols. (Berlin, 1884-95) 1: *Digesta* 1:3:32, 2: *Codex*, 8:52. Walter Ullmann, *The Medieval Idea of Law as Represented by Lucas de Penna* (London, 1946), pp. 62-70; Idem, "Bartolus on Customary Law," in D. Segoloni, ed., *Bartolo da Sassoferrato: Studi e documenti per il VI centenario* (Milan, 1961), pp. 49-73, repr. in his *Jurisprudence in the Middle Ages* (London, 1980).

[6] Anonymous in *CF*, p. 494; Jean Masuer, *Practique*, trans. and ed. Antoine Fontanon (Paris, 1576), p. 201.

At the same time, it claimed that people sustaining excommunication *animo indurato* for more than a year were heretics, thus coming under its own jurisdiction.[7] The mixture of secular and religious offenses (debt and contempt of excommunication) countered by two systems of coercion (prison and charges of heresy) created a situation in which the boundaries of jurisdiction were extremely difficult to define. Thus the two parallel legal systems existed side by side, formally independent of each other, but in reality constantly interpenetrating and influencing each other. The very vagueness of the dividing line provided a dynamic, developmental element.

The relationship among various levels of jurisdiction within the secular system was much simpler. Rather than two competing spheres, there was a hierarchy of authority within one system. By the middle of the thirteenth century the kings of France had extended their political control over most of the land. Though feudal courts still maintained their jurisdiction within territorial bounds, keeping to their customary procedures and rules, there was no question which system carried the ultimate authority. The distinct powers of high, middle, and low justice were clearly defined. When arguments arose, they usually centered around the type of justice possessed by any specific lordship, not about what was understood by high or low justice.[8] The Parlement might hold an inquest concerning the privileges of local justices, and local people would be summoned to testify to actual cases in which high justice had indeed been exercised by a local court within living memory. Nevertheless, there was no continuous central control over local justice, and sentences of feudal or urban courts were only overturned on appeal. No procedure or decision was automatically invalidated even if it failed to accord with royal principles unless the losing party decided to question the point at a higher level.[9] By the fourteenth century the Parlement of Paris

[7] GC, pp. 611-13.

[8] The records of the Parlement of Paris for the thirteenth and fourteenth centuries are full of inquests to establish who possessed the right of justice, high or low. For example, in 1301 Pons de Castillon claimed that he had always possessed the right of high justice at Villar-Savary, and that the *bailli* of Fanjeaux had deprived him of it. According to his claim, an earlier inquest had established his right, but the documents were lost. A new inquest, ordered by the Parlement, established the king's right to high justice at the place. *Olim, ou registres d'arrêts rendus par la cour du roi*, ed. Beugnot, 3 vols. (Paris, 1844), 3:103. For a similar inquest before 1236, see *Actes du Parlement de Paris*, ed. E. Boutaric and H. Fourgeot, 4 vols. (Paris, 1863-1960), 1:ccciv-cccv.

[9] Ferdinand Lot and Robert Fawtier, *Histoire des institutions françaises au moyen âge*, 3 vols. (Paris, 1957-62), 2:340-41.

was using such appeals in order to abrogate local customs that did not fit its own ideas of jurisprudence, but a systematic examination of local customs did not take place until the formal redaction began in the fifteenth century.[10]

But the unity of western laws, as projected by the *Corpus Iuris Civilis* and imagined by modern lawyers, was many centuries away. The reality of the time was that of multiple legal systems, all affecting each other's development, defining and being defined in a constant process of formation.

2. Posited Law: Reality and the Myth of the Good Old Law

It is remarkable that such a dry topic as medieval law should have been mythologized to the extent that it was. For nineteenth-century German historians, medieval law was the living, concrete expression of the *Volksgeist*.[11] Stemming from a golden, mythological past, it was the essence of national roots and the embodiment of the people's character. One tended to lose view in all this panegyric literature of the fact that there was no such thing as 'medieval law'. There were numerous codes, customary traditions, regional and urban statutes, all of which were operative within specific areas. But any medieval jurist faced with the question "what is medieval law?" would have been sorely puzzled. No customary lawyer like Philippe de Beaumanoir or Eike von Repgow could have answered, but neither could a Roman jurist like Azo or Accursius. 'Medieval law' is a construct of the modern mind.

The general concept of medieval law continued existing even with the demise of the *Volksgeist* theory. Fritz Kern in the early decades of the twentieth century made perhaps the most perceptive comments on the subject. Medieval law, he said, was by definition old, good, and unlegislated. Properly speaking, only God could legislate, and law had come down to people through the generations from a divine source. Rulers could at best promulgate statutes which were no more than interpretations, human glosses to a higher ruling. These statutes were a continuation of God's law as long as they accorded with the original, but became an aberration when they diverged from its spirit. One

---

[10] See below, p. 69.

[11] Hermann Kantorowicz, "Volksgeist und historische Rechtsschule," in his *Rechtshistorische Schriften*, ed. H. Coing and G. Immel (Karlsruhe, 1970), pp. 435-56.

could at most restore the law to its pristine purity by such glosses and interpretations.[12]

In other words, posited law was a contradiction in terms. If human law was to carry any validity, it could not by its very nature exist independently of the general concept of law. It was only a temporal, local application of a timeless, universal, changeless system. In this, Kern was pointing to a trend consistent with medieval scholastic perceptions. Anselm of Canterbury had already noted that the principles of justice and equity governed not only people, but also the very forces of nature.[13] Thomas Aquinas followed by insisting that positive law was only an evolvement of those same basic principles.[14]

It was natural for philosophers to derive legal practices from basic principles. Kern, however, did not base his assertions upon philosophy, but largely upon German customary law. Generally speaking, historians of law have not seriously contested his claims. However, if one tries to examine these generalizations in the light of customary practice, the results raise some questions. Did practitioners and customal writers indeed hold such a very exalted view of their trade?

No legal system lives up to its ideal image in practice. This is especially true when the ideal is one of immutability while the system is inherently processual. Customary law is by definition traditional, basing its authority not upon legislation but upon the past and its memory. But memory and oral traditions change their shape constantly to fit new realities, and anthropologists have already remarked upon the relative newness of 'old' laws.[15] In fact, an old custom was one whose lifespan exceeded the lifespan of a single generation. This trait was of greatest significance while custom remained oral, dwindling into unimportance with the final, authoritative redaction of customs.

The regional customals of the thirteenth and fourteenth centuries belong to an intermediate stage between the oral and the authoritative written version. While claiming to be merely a record of existent custom, they evidence and reflect the changes it underwent in the

---

[12] Fritz Kern, *Kingship and Law in the Middle Ages*, trans. and introd. S.B. Chrimes (New York, 1956), pp. 149-80. Though Chrimes claims that Kern was referring only to early medieval law (*Ibid.*, p. xxvii), Kern's reliance upon the *Sachsenspiegel*, for example, makes this assertion somewhat dubious.

[13] *De Veritate*, ch. 12, in *Sancti Anselmi Cantauriensis Opera Omnia*, ed. F.S. Schmitt, 6 vols. (Stuttgart, 1968), 1:191-96.

[14] *Summa Theologiae* (Rome, 1886), 1a-2ae, q. 95.

[15] Michael T. Clanchy, "Remembering the Past and the Good Old Law," *History* 55 (1970), 172.

very hands of the writers. They also testify to another phenomenon. Unlike many groups studied by anthropologists, European customary societies did possess structures of political power whose members were increasingly insistent upon their right to legislate. Customary texts give ample evidence of legislative processes going on at the time of the writing, influencing and shaping the final text. Even if one labelled royal rulings *établissements* or statutes rather than laws, these rulings were acknowledged as authoritative by all subjects, including jurists. Finally, the claim that the law is good rarely surfaces in legal writings. It appears in politically-oriented texts, such as coronation oaths in which kings swore to uphold the good laws of their lands.[16] Obviously, lawyers had few illusions about goodness.

Thus, the law people lived by in the later middle ages was neither old, nor good, nor unlegislated. Moreover, jurists knew so very well. Nevertheless, Kern's definition still holds, largely because those same realists were stubbornly clinging to an ancient perception of custom. Custom derived its authority from its age, from its consistent use, and from its goodness. In the very inconsistency and contradictions of these authors lies an urgency, a sense that the writing of customs was not merely a recording of details and procedures: it was the preservation of a certain creed of practical justice, the germ of a legal theory that was only to flower in the sixteenth century with Guy Coquille and Charles du Moulin. Since the validation of writing pertained to Roman and canon law, custom could not in the thirteenth century be validated by writing alone. The legitimacy of customary law was thus sought in its traditionality, its continuity, and its practice. If the theory did not fit the facts, the authors simply left both fact and theory side by side, undisturbed by the patent contradiction. While promulgated law had to be consistent, privately written customals did not.

The co-existence of the reality and the myth in the self-same texts is in itself of extreme importance. Though logically inconsistent, it made perfect historical sense. The writing was both preservation and edition, recording and shaping. In creating a written version of the myth of the good old law, customal authors did their best to preserve their own imperfect, flawed, shifting traditions.

---

[16] In the kingdom of Jerusalem, each successive king was made to swear that he would keep "the good usages and customs of the kingdom". Jean d'Ibelin, *Assises de la haute cour*, ch. 3, in *Assises de Jérusalem*, ed. Beugnot, 2 vols. (Recueils des historiens des Croisades, Lois, Paris, 1841-43), 1:182.

3. VOX POPULI: THE POPULAR COMPONENTS OF CUSTOMARY LAW

A system of law which expressly defined itself as old and based upon continuous practice was bound to include elements of popular culture. But the cultural transitions of the thirteenth and fourteenth centuries tended strongly in the opposite direction, towards a more elitist form of law. If one were to believe most customal literature, by the fourteenth century the process of dissociation of courthouse from litigants and law from society was well under way, with the resultant alienation between the two.

Nevertheless, practices of popular origin were found in local, ecclesiastical, and even central courts. Some traces of these are left in the disapproving comments of customal authors. But for the most part these jurists, anxious for the still-precarious respectability of their new discipline, deliberately edited out discordant practices. Wishing to clothe their trade in the trappings of science, customal authors often attempted to gloss over popular practices and the existence of popular, non-professional judges. In actual fact, the professional level of most local courts hardly resembled the composition of the great central ones. Within communal and seigneurial lordships jurisdiction lay in the hands of local councillors and administrators devoid of any legal qualifications. Though the *baillis*, unlike the lay judges and jurors drawn from the community, represented the authorities, they were certainly no professional jurists. The justice they dispensed was based upon pure ignorance and arbitrariness, but also upon local traditions, were one to believe customal authors. The latter were usually a cut above them—royal *baillis* of noble origins, clerks, and Parisian practitioners. They tended to concentrate in their descriptions upon the royal, ducal or comital systems of justice, where professional standards were higher and popular practices were not allowed.

Literary and customary sources might explain certain usages, but provide no hard proof of their existence. A truer picture might be culled from the sources of practice: trial protocols and descriptions of public legal rituals in sentences or chronicles. These sources all indicate with certainty that a great deal of customary practice in the later middle ages derived from popular traditions and perceptions.

All the same, it is misleading to state in an all-inclusive manner that late medieval French law contained a considerable folkloristic element. To our great methodological confusion, nineteenth-century German historians tended to lump together all legal customs not traceable to Roman law—be they early medieval Germanic legislation, late medieval French rural traditions or sixteenth-century German town ordinances—as folklore.[17] The fact that one might find a certain belief or custom in the sixth century is no proof of its existence eight hundred years later. By the same token, there is no proof that the beliefs characterizing seventeenth-century folklore indeed have their roots in ancient traditions. Demonological witchcraft beliefs are a case in point, for they have clearly been demonstrated to form no part of late medieval peasant culture before the great wave of Inquisition trials.[18] Oral traditions are made and remade in transmission, and one cannot telescope the entire European past into one age of folkloristic beliefs.

Neither was late medieval folklore a purely rural, oral phenomenon. The distinguishing mark of much that we know about this folklore is precisely the fact that for the first time literate people took the trouble to record it. The peasant women responsible for the wisdom of the *Evangiles des quenouilles* did not write their sayings down; a 'clerk', as he styled himself, recorded them. Sometimes peasant traditions were written in order to be condemned, as in the case of Dominican thirteenth-century preaching, and sometimes in order to amuse court circles by deriding rustic simplicity, as in the case of the *Cent nouvelles nouvelles*. Such story collections, common from Chaucer's England to Boccaccio's Italy, also held much that was urban, rather than rural subject-matter. The fact remains that by the later middle ages there grew a corpus of lay literature geared largely for an urban public, recording both urban and rural customs. Insofar as judicial institutions became, with the decay of feudal justice, either a royal or an urban phenomenon, much of the folkloric influence upon them stemmed from urban, rather than rural sources. True, the distinction might sometimes be artificial. After all, rural *bachelleries* and urban *abbayes de jeunesse* were essentially one and the same phenomenon, *charivaris* were held and Saint John's fires lighted in cities and villages alike, and it is hard to tell for many places whether they were towns or villages at all. Nevertheless, it is necessary to discount, once and for

[17] See, for example Karl von Amira, *Der Stab in der germanischen Rechtssymbolik* (München, 1909), and Rudolph His, *Der Totenglaube in der Geschichte des germanishen Strafrechts* (Münster, 1929).

[18] As an example of the process of internalization of these beliefs, see Carlo Ginzburg, *The Night Battles*, trans. J. & A. Tedeschi (Harmondsworth, 1985).

all, the myth that all medieval folklore was ancient, static, immutable, Germanic, and rural.

One must, therefore, distinguish between two types of popular elements in late medieval jurisprudence. There were indeed relics of ancient beliefs that had hardened into ritualized practices and were deliberately kept intact. In the later middle ages they survived predominantly within the realm of punitive public rituals. They were preserved largely because of all legal rituals, public punishment was the most common form of government propaganda. Like all public ceremonies, public executions were based not only upon a set of shared perceptions, but also upon a set of known symbols, altered only with great difficulty. At the same time, many practices of late medieval justice were popular in origin but comparatively recent additions. They were grounded in beliefs and conceptions that had developed only during the thirteenth and fourteenth centuries. Both the old and the new were either introduced or preserved by those controlling legal rituals; this control was not, and never had been, a popular prerogative. The incentive for preserving, or actually introducing elements of popular extraction into legal practice came from those possessing justice, or in other words, those who possessed lordship.

'Justice' could mean many things, but one meaning was almost invariably present. It was a lordship, an area of jurisdiction. Thus, the monks who controlled a few blocks of Paris around the rue Beaubourg referred to their rights as the 'justice' of Saint-Martin-des-Champs. The right to exercise jurisdiction was a matter of lordship, not of community. Lordship and community only overlapped when the community possessed its own justice. Once we do away with the sentimental picture of *Volksrecht* and recognize the immanent role of lordship in the exercise of justice, we can no longer justify the considerable popular element in late medieval judicial practice (as the Romantic German historians did) by assuming that 'the people' exercised justice in their own manner. Nor can we assume that this element crept in by default of legislation. True, we have no law-writing between the Carolingian period and the beginning of customal writing in the thirteenth century, but the reason for this was not a lack of law or legal procedure, but its oral nature. The *chansons de geste*, with their constant preoccupation and reiteration of the ruler's duty to do justice in an active manner, are proof of the dynamism of the feudal system of justice. Furthermore, the customals written in the thirteenth century obviously reflect a vigorous tradition of court activity. Local lords held local power and dispensed local justice even in periods of greatest anarchy. Folkloric elements were neither the foundations of medieval legal practice, nor the result of an abdication of political power.

Though ancient, obsolete elements were often deliberately preserved by dispensers of justice for governmental reasons, there was no such reason for the introduction of living folklore. One must therefore look for an answer within the later medieval period, and not before. As we have seen, actual jurisdiction at the time was not in the hands of the lords holding the privilege of justice, but in those of administrators. A bailiff, an alderman, a royal official could all be judges, depending upon the personality of the local lord—nobleman, monastery, commune, or king. And the legal training of most administrators at the lower echelons was sketchy indeed. They rarely held a law degree, even if they did possess a university education. Anyway, a formal legal education would have been pointless, as the only kind available was in Roman law, useless for a man empowered only to administer customary law.

Nor did administrators sit alone in court. By custom and by force of ignorance they had to rely upon local experts, *turbiers* or lay judges, whose existence and power is richly evident in the writings of Pierre de Fontaines. Such men, steeped in local traditions, were bound by their oath (and often by their interest) to state and uphold the custom of the place. This they did by relying on their memory of past court cases, but also upon the entire furniture of their minds. When such jurors stated that it was the custom of the Vermandois to hold a candle next to a dying kinsman or woman, they were not making a legal statement, though their context was a legal one. As it happened, the local *bailli* recorded this statement for posterity within his customal, thus integrating folklore within law.[19]

It was by this process, the enunciation of custom by experts in tradition, that folkloric elements entered legal practice. The fact that the great age of reliance upon *turbiers* coincided with the great age of customal recording was of overwhelming significance. The growing importance of precedents and their memory was equally crucial for the role of the *turbiers*. By the thirteenth century, there was a good chance that a local man might be asked for a pronouncement con-

---

[19] Pierre de Fontaines cites, among the just causes for an adjournment of trial the case of "cil qui est là où l'en tient son père [ou sa mère] ou aucune des devant dites persones, la chandeile en la mein, por criente de mort..." *CF*, p. 19.

cerning local custom, that he would base his answer upon precedent and usage, and that his words would survive in a written customal.

CHAPTER THREE

THE REALITY OF LATE MEDIEVAL FRENCH LAW AND ITS MYTHS

The mythical and real components of medieval judicial systems stand best revealed in periods and places of legal transition. Northern France in the later middle ages was such a time and place. The customary laws (for there were many) of the different areas were transformed from oral traditions to written texts. Simultaneously, the patchwork of local practices was slowly coalescing into a rather nebulous concept of *consuetudo totae Franciae.*[1] It was not quite one structure, but the concept of a legal system distinct from other functional frameworks slowly emerged in the minds and writings of customary authors. The idea—for it was no more than that—grew largely as the result of the attempt to oppose customary law to canon or Roman law, both possessing not only the aura of intellectual backing, but also systematic coherence. Neither of these systems had posed much of a threat before the thirteenth century. It was only after the Albigensian crusades that the kings of France came to rule the lands of written law and were thus forced explicitly to distinguish between the areas where custom ruled and those where Roman law was operative. The ecclesiastical courts had of course existed much earlier, but it was only in the thirteenth century that the struggle over jurisdiction became bitter enough to force customary lawyers to draw a clear line of demarcation by producing coherent written versions of their system.

While these texts purported to preserve the old laws, much of their traditional content was altered in the process of writing to suit the intellectual and jurisprudential trends of the time. And yet, many elements of popular culture remained, to be wedded within the written text to the growing science of law. Elements which jurists condemned as irrational or unjust still survived in the practice of law. At the same time, the growth of royal power and the concomitant authority both to enforce and ordain had far-reaching effects upon the formation and the practice of customary law. Law became an instru-

[1] P. Petot, "Le droit commun en France selon les coutumiers," *RHDFE* 38 (1960), 412-29.

ment not only of intra-personal regulation, but even more so, of public order.

The four elements—the old customary tradition, the continuous popular input, the evolving jurisprudence, and the implementation by central authorities—all interacted in a flexible combination of legal mechanisms and ideas. It was a time when myths about law and justice were carefully perpetuated not as camouflage for a shifting reality, but in order to endow the same reality with a certain amount of stability. Any examination of late medieval French law, therefore, is an examination of the interaction of myth and reality.

1. THE WRITING OF CUSTOMARY LAW

French customary law at the beginning of the thirteenth century exhibited two main characteristics. It was highly fragmentary, and almost completely oral in nature. Both traits were destined gradually to fade over the following centuries, first orality and later fragmentation. The process of writing was responsible for both changes.

As the earliest thirteenth-century customals asserted, every *pays* in France had its own customs, and the area ruled by a specific law could be as small as a single castellany or as big as a whole duchy.[2] The patchwork of jurisdictions and customs was preserved through another century of intense legal changes: "There are even local customs which exist in one small enclave among several others, [different] from the surrounding *pays*, and where the custom, which is totally contradictory to this small place, has no authority."[3] The comment was made by Jacques d'Ableiges towards the end of the fourteenth century, and one can practically hear the irritation of the Parlement jurist faced with this traditional complication.

The tenacity and longevity of local customs was largely due to the transition from orality to literacy. Paradoxically enough, this transition helped preserve the archaic local structure of French customary law well into the modern era. At the beginning of the thirteenth century,

[2] "... les coustumes sont si diverses que l'en ne pourroit pas trouver ou roiaume de France deus chasteleries qui de tous cas usassent d'une meisme coustume..." *CB*, p. 5. For regional customals, see for example *Coutumiers de Normandie*, ed. E.J. Tardif, 3 vols. (Rouen, 1881-1903); *Vieux Coustumier de Poictou*, ed. R. Filhol (Bourges, 1956); *Très-ancienne coutume de Bretagne*, ed. M. Planiol (Rennes, 1896); *CIAM*; *Ancien coutumier inédit de Picardie*, ed. M.A.J. Marnier (Paris, 1840).

[3] "Et y a mesmes coustumes localles qui sont en ung petit lieu enclavé entre plusieurs aultres que au pais environ là ou coutume n'a point de lieu, et sera toute contraire à ce petit lieu." *GC*, p. 599.

barring urban communities that had received a charter of privileges recording their customs, almost all legal customs were transmitted and practiced in oral form.[4] When first written, they were recorded by local administrators intent upon setting down local practice and totally ignorant of any overall legal scheme. The plethora of thirteenth- and fourteenth-century private customals enshrined regional peculiarities for centuries to come.

Writing did not come easily to French customary law, nor was it an organic development. It was clearly the result of external pressures. For the spoken word was the main vehicle of law. Law resided not only in the memories of knowledgeable *turbiers*, but in the first instance in the words spoken by judges and litigants in the courthouse. Orality was not an external form, but an intrinsic characteristic of customary French law until the fourteenth century. The courthouse was more than the place in which law was practiced; it was where law was made and enunciated.

When the administration of justice and the formation of customary law are conjoined within a single process, both phenomena become part of a larger societal context. Sentences pronounced collectively by a group of judges and based upon communal memory must rely upon a certain consensus as to the underlying legal norms of society. The oral law of the twelfth and thirteenth centuries was based upon a sense that the law and its administration were not necessarily a coercive tool of government nor the province of learned jurisprudence, but communal property. The constant use and reiteration of oral law in court strengthened that consensus.

The first written codes began appearing by the second half of the thirteenth century. The earliest written customals of Anjou, the Orléanais, Touraine, Normandy, Vermandois and Beauvaisis date from this period.[5] One and all, they were private redactions drawn up by lawyers and administrators for the use of judges and litigants alike. This trend continued during the fourteenth century,[6] some of the customals (notably the western ones) achieving a quasi-public character.

The redaction of local customs by royal order began with the ordinance of Montilz-les-Tours in 1454. By the middle of the sixteenth century the Parlement of Paris had finished reviewing, re-

[4] For a collection of early customs, largely urban, see Charles Giraud, *Essai sur l'histoire du droit français au moyen âge*, 2 vols. (Paris, 1846).

[5] In addition to the customals cited in note 2, see *ESL* and *CF*.

[6] See, for example, the customs of Picardy, Brittany, Anjou, and Poitou in note 2.

dacting, and approving all French *coutumes*.[7] Some of them had been written before, while others were taken down from oral evidence. But the process of redaction was far more than the mere recording of legal traditions. All the approved customs were regional, thus abolishing the tiny customary enclaves noted by Jacques d'Ableiges, and all had undergone an examination by trained jurists in Paris. Customs conflicting with royal ordinances were either changed or deleted in the process. While there was no general incorporation and codification for the entire realm, a certain uniformity was stamped upon all approved customs.[8]

And yet, the basic principle that each region was entitled to be judged by its own customs was preserved. The idea of one unified code of law for the whole realm required a mental revolution alien to contemporary mentality. Until the end of the middle ages, customs were verified as Louis IX had ordered in 1270, by inquest rather than by referral to a written text.[9] The *enquête par turbe* consisted of ten or twelve men called in to give information concerning the ruling of local custom.[10] By the fifteenth century these men were usually professional lawyers, but earlier they were simply local people who 'knew the law'. The inquest, which the dukes of Normandy had used within regular trial procedure as a fact-finding mechanism, was applied throughout northern France as a tool for the establishment of custom. This measure was based upon a commonly shared perception that the people resorting to any customary tradition possessed the most authoritative knowledge of its contents and nature.[11]

The writing of customs, therefore, was achieved in two stages. First came the private redactions, paving the way for the subsequent official texts. These early redactions are a unique phenomenon in the history

---

[7] René Filhol, "La rédaction des coutumes en France aux XVe et XVIe siècles," in *La rédaction des coutumes dans le passé et dans le présent*, ed. John Gilissen (Brussels, 1962), pp. 64-66.

[8] The customs were originally published, in a somewhat incomplete form, by Charles du Moulin, ed., *Les coustumes générales et particulières du royaume de France et des Gaules*, 2 vols. (Paris, 1581), and subsequently in a complete form by C.A. Bourdot de Richebourg, ed., *Nouveau coutumier général de France*, 4 vols. (Paris, 1724).

[9] Pissard, *Essai sur la connaissance et la preuve des coutumes*, pp. 112-20.

[10] For a fifteenth-century example of an *enquête par turbe*, conducted simultaneously in Normandy and in the Paris region, see G. Fagniez, "Fragment d'un répertoire de jurisprudence parisienne au XVe siècle," *MSHP* 17 (1890), 26.

[11] John P. Dawson, *A History of Lay Judges* (Cambridge, Mass., 1960), p. 44; Yvonne Bongert, *Recherches sur les cours laïques du Xe au XIIIe siècle* (Paris, 1942), pp. 261-76.

of law, for they were neither legislation nor legal record, nor learned jurisprudence. The redactions, their authors and their relationship to the law that formed their subject-matter deserve a close examination.

Practically all early customals were written by people who practiced law and its administration. Beaumanoir in the Beauvaisis, Fontaines in the Vermandois, and later Jacques d'Ableiges in the Paris area and Jean Boutillier in the Tournaisis, to name but the best-known, were all practical lawyers setting down the customs of their *bailliage*.[12] The authors of the northern and central customals were usually royal officers —royal *baillis*, counsellors at the Parlement of Paris or at the Châtelet. Though the authors of the western customals served their ducal or comital masters rather than the king, they were also practical lawyers and administrators, not professors of law at a university.

What impelled those government jurists to undertake the overwhelming task of putting custom into an alien and artificial form? Furthermore, why did their efforts span such a clearly-defined period, from mid-thirteenth to late fourteenth century? Their reasons for doing so were usually set out in the introductions to their customals, and the similarity in those reasons is a clear indication of the trends and context of the time.

In the first place, customal authors considered their work not legal texts, but manuals for laymen. They were to be of use to readers faced with litigation, unfamiliar with the complexities of courtroom behavior and strategies. In a charming and unusual prologue to his *Grand Coutumier*, Jacques d'Ableiges dedicated his book to his nephews, claiming that while he had no fortune to leave them, his manual would ensure their success.[13] Private customals were in the nature of memoranda, a text to be referred to for information concerning material that carried its own immanent authority. In a society that often resorted to courts, but not always to the aid of lawyers (whose training was in any case doubtful), and in which the wrong form of plea could lose a case, such handbooks were extremely necessary.

[12] Jean Boutillier, a distinguished jurist of many years' experience, described himself specifically as *homme rural*. Guido van Dievoet, *Jehan Boutillier en de Somme Rural* (Louvain, 1951), p. 129.

[13] This introduction was not printed by Laboulaye and Dareste in their edition; it was later discovered and published by Léopold Delisle, "L'Auteur du Grand Coutumier de France," *MSHP* 8 (1882), 145-48; concerning the importance of d'Ableiges and his contribution to the formation of the custom of Paris, see Fr. Olivier-Martin, *Histoire de la coutume de la prévôté et vicomté de Paris*, 3 vols. (Paris, 1922-30, repr. 1972), pp. 90-101; Idem, "La coutume de la prévôté et vicomté de Paris," *MSHP* 48 (1921), 178-80.

Secondly, authors claimed that local lords using the manual would dispense better justice, more in accordance with custom. The implicit assumption here was that government according to custom was by definition good government. Pierre de Fontaines' *Conseil* was actually composed as such a guide to a local lord, at his father's request.[14] The handbook was meant to be used not only by litigants, but also by judges whose legal training was at best irrelevant and at worst non-existent.

Finally, there was a third motive: the preservation of custom in the face of change. Local customs were indeed subject to several pressures during the thirteenth and fourteenth centuries. Foremost among these were the growing prestige and influence of Roman law studies, centered at Orléans[15] and the constant growth of royal legislation. As long as custom retained its purely oral character, it remained exceedingly flexible and vulnerable to external influences. Pierre de Fontaines complained about this state of affairs in which every judge ruled according to his caprice or self-interest, so that "the land is practically devoid of custom."[16] A generation later, Philippe de Beaumanoir echoed his words: "and the truth of the matter is that customs are corrupted by young judges who do not use the old customs well...."[17] The ever-changing nature of custom made it very difficult to know what it was, and this tendency was further aggravated at a time of strong external influences. The only way to preserve custom and the practical knowledge of custom was by locking it into the written mold.

And yet these authors were no conservatives trying to halt change. As royal or ducal officers, they all welcomed the introduction of a centralized, systematic structure of jurisdiction with a hierarchy of appeal and control. Nor did they see the growth of royal justice as an encroachment upon local rights. To the contrary: it was the manifest duty of all lords, not excluding the king, to apply customary law in an

---

[14] *CB*, 1:2-3; *CF*, pp. 2-6; *GC*, pp. 4-6; *SR*, p. 3.

[15] E. M. Meijers, "L'Université d'Orléans au XIIIe siècle," in his *Etudes d'histoire du droit*, ed. R. Feenstra and H.F.W.D. Fischer, 4 vols. (Leiden, 1956-76), 3:3-148. For a survey of the earlier growth of Roman law studies, see Stephan Kuttner, "The Revival of Jurisprudence," in Robert L. Benson and Giles Constable, eds., *Renaissance and Renewal in the Twelfth Century* (Cambridge, Mass. 1982), pp. 299-338.

[16] *CF*, p. 4.

[17] *CB*, art. 1982, 2:500-501. This sentiment was still extant in the fifteenth century, as a manuscript of the *Style du Châtelet* indicates: "pour ce que memoire de home est tantost passee, afin que len se recorde et ait leu memoire du noble stille..." BN, ms. fr. 4472, fol. 1.

efficient manner. A functional network of royal or seigneurial officials provided with the correct information in the form of the written handbook, they considered, would only enhance the power of customary law.

The lawyers' efforts to reconcile their matter with the growing body of royal ordinances is understandable. The power of the Parlement of Paris as appellate jurisdiction grew considerably during the thirteenth century. It could and did on occasion declare local customs invalid when they conflicted with its own principles of jurisdiction. Though not law, royal ordinances were enacted by political authority and enforceable by its agents. The legal validity of customary law could only be preserved as long as it incorporated the principles and institutions of royal authority within its framework. It is neither chance nor lip-service that made Beaumanoir open his text with the functions of royal *baillis*. Others incorporated relevant royal ordinances into their material, as did the author of the customs of the Orléanais, who inserted into his text Saint Louis' 1260 ordinance forbidding duels in his domain.[18]

Nor were these same authors immune to the influences of learned jurisprudence stemming from universities and ecclesiastical courts. Though none of the authors boasted the title of *doctor iuris*, practically all possessed a certain amount of familiarity with Roman law. In addition, they shared with the professors the feeling that Roman law was a far superior system, of greater prestige than customary law. Consequently, different customal authors in different parts of France included a varying amount of Roman law in their writings. Pierre de Fontaines and the author of the *Livre de jostice et de plet* used Roman material extensively; Beaumanoir had little use for it, and Boutillier had occasional recourse to it. The western customals of Normandy, Brittany, Touraine, Anjou and Poitou all incorporated certain amounts of Roman legislation.[19] There does not seem to be any principle

[18] *ESL*, 2:8-10.

[19] Jean Gaudemet, "L'influence des droits savants (romain et canonique) sur les textes de droit coutumier en Occident avant le XVIe siècle," *Actas del II congreso internacional de derecho canónico, Pamplona, 1976* (Pamplona, 1979), pp. 165-94, reprinted in his *Eglise et société en Occident au moyen âge* (London, 1984), XI; Jean-Philippe Lévy, "La pénétration du droit savant dans les coutumiers angevins et bretons au moyen âge," *Tijdschrift voor Rechtsgeschiedenis* 15 (1957), 1-53; J. Bart and M. Petitjean, *L'influence du droit romain en Bourgogne et en Franche-Comté (XIIIe-XVe siècles)* (IRMA, V.4.e); Philip van Wetter, "Le droit romain et Beaumanoir," *Mélanges Fitting*, ed. E. Meynial, 2 vols. (Montpellier, 1907-1908), 2:535-82.

discernible in the spread of Roman influence. Some thirteenth-century customals testify to its power, while later ones ignore it. Nor is it a purely geographical matter of center and periphery, for Boutillier in the Tournaisis and the author of the *Très-ancienne coutume de Bretagne* also used Roman law. Obviously, the degree of influence was due entirely to the personal attitude and education of each author writing a private edition of what he considered custom worth preserving.

The most significant influences came in via canon law. Issues of marriage, dowry, legitimacy, majority, and inheritance, all of them of interest to the church, were the most clearly affected. In these cases it was probably not the author materially altering custom during the process of writing: it had already been modified by his time to suit canon law rulings, and the writer was doing no more than recording the new situation. Customary procedure too owed much to the influence of ecclesiastical courts. The introduction of the inquisitorial method of proof into secular courts, advocated by Roman lawyers, probably owed much to its practice within the church system. Proving guilt according to this method was the state's responsibility, rather than the plaintiff's. A logical corollary of this shift was that a disproved accusation no longer carried the threat of an identical punishment to the accuser. Injured people could still sue for criminal offenses, but plaintiff and defendant were no longer two equal contenders in court.[20] The transition was slow and gradual, and as late as the fifteenth century litigants still collected testimonies and evidence, or paid an official of the court to do so.[21]

The growing acceptance of written evidence and insistence upon written records were similarly modelled upon the ecclesiastical example.[22] Like the introduction of the inquisitorial method, this process was slow and uneven in different parts of France.[23] Finally, the influence of church courts was felt in material issues. The inalienability of dowries in Normandy, the rights of minors inheriting their parents' debts in Vermandois, and the introduction of the appeal

---

[20] Adhémar Esmein, *Histoire de la procédure criminelle en France et spécialement de la procédure inquisitoire depuis le XIIIe siècle* (Paris, 1882), p. 78ff.

[21] See, for example, the 1425 ordinance of the Châtelet, arts. 37, 87, establishing fixed prices for such services by court examiners and notaries. *Ordonnances des rois de France de la troisième race*, ed. E. de Laurière et al., 21 vols. (Paris, 1723-1849), 13:88-103.

[22] See, for example, Beaumanoir's insistence that oral testimony should be taken down by auditors in writing; *CB*, art. 1225, 2:132.

[23] See below, ch. 4, pp. 67-68.

against a false judgement (side by side with the old challenge of witness and judge) are only a few examples.[24] It is however hard to trace those changes directly to learned Roman traditions or to church practice.

While much ecclesiastical matter and procedures had indeed become part of custom before the writing, some elements were obviously imposed by the writers with the express purpose of 'romanizing' their material, thus making it look more respectable and learned. The newly introduced matter shows in the customals in the form of direct quotes from Justinian and references to *la loi escripte*, constituting a formal, rather than material influence. This formal effect was manifested in three fields: definition, organization, and terminology.

The abstract definitions and categories of law, justice, and right (*ius*), whenever included, were taken almost verbatim from the *Institutes*. The definition of *ius*, the different categories (natural and civil), and most of all, the definition of justice: "to live honestly, refrain from harming another, and give each his due," were repeated in many customals.[25] Customary law made very few contributions to the realm of legal definitions. The most interesting one is that of *droit haineux*, a very charged term used to describe those customary laws clashing with the written, Roman text. While the jurists were forced to admit that in these cases custom prevailed over Roman law, the very use of the term *haineux* denotes their discomfort with this maladjustment.[26]

Secondly, jurists writing the hitherto oral customs of their area often borrowed their organizational model from the Roman precedent, for they had none other. Either the *Digesta* or the *Codex* were usually the basic model. In the fifteenth century, Claude Liger organized the customs of Anjou and Maine quite openly following the rubrics of the *Codex* and naming his text accordingly, *Les coustumes d'Anjou et du Maine intitullées selon les rubriches du Code.*[27] Pierre de Fontaines used both, starting out with the structure of the *Digesta*, then going on to the *Codex*, and finally returning to the *Digesta*.

Unlike the organization of customary material, an essentially pioneer job, the borrowing of Roman terms to describe customary institutions was merely the application of high-sounding terms to the exis-

---

[24] Lebrun, *La coutume*, pp. 38-39; *CF*, p. 95; *CB*, art. 1774, 2:399.

[25] *ESL*, 2:330-31; *Li livre de jostice et de plet*, ed. Rapetti (Paris, 1850), p. 3; *SR*, p. 2; *GC*, p. 189.

[26] *SR*, p. 3; *GC*, pp. 190-91.

[27] In *CIAM*, vol. 2.

tent reality. Thus, Beaumanoir used in one and the same paragraph the customary term 'pledge' and the Roman 'caution' to describe one and the same object, while Gui Pape referred to *represalia* for the same.[28] By the same token, the fourteenth-century Poitevin gloss to the *Établissements de Saint Louis* defined an *assurement*, or the breach of a feudal peace-keeping oath as *lèse-majesté*, justifying its punishment with the citation of the *Lex Iulia maiestatis*.[29]

The imposition of Roman terminology occasionally created considerable confusion. Boasting his erudition, sometimes the author pasted in entire sections taken from Roman sources with little relevance to the law of his time. When dealing with serfdom (*servage*), Pierre de Fontaines glibly inserted the entire sections in the *Institutes* and the *Digesta* concerning slavery.[30] But when he came to treat contemporary serfdom, he resorted to the term villein, and his record of villeinage customs bears absolutely no relation to Roman tradition, only to contemporary reality.[31]

The insertion of Roman maxims, forms, and terms into customary material was a means to an end. At a time when the great Roman jurists openly looked down upon customary law as a field not fit for intellectual endeavor, the tendency to pour customary contents into a Roman mold is understandable. While customary jurists probably felt a genuine respect for the learned, written system, their writing was an attempt to preserve, rather than reform customary law. Roman elements, however irrelevant, endowed their work with a certain aura of intellectual legitimacy it had hitherto lacked. Customary authors felt this and deliberately used it. They attempted to reconcile their subject matter with Roman rulings wherever possible, dressing it in Roman verbiage. Whether relevant or not, they studded their work with numerous quotations from Justinian. By contrast, though they usually knew each other's work and borrowed a great deal from it, they never cited their customary sources. Beaumanoir was the only author to admit his debt to the customs of neighboring areas.[32] Jean Boutillier, who cheerfully used for his *Somme rural* the neighboring customs of

[28] Van Wetter, "Le droit romain et Beaumanoir;" Gui Pape, *Decisiones*, q. 22.

[29] *ESL*, 1:180-83, 2:46-47, 2:56-58, 2:423-24; "qu'il blecet le droit de la reau majesté" (cf. *Digesta*, 48:4,1).

[30] *CF*, p. 499; *Institutiones* 1,3-4; *Digesta*, 1:5.

[31] *CF*, pp. 79-80, 239, 424.

[32] *CB*, 1:3. See also Paul Viollet, "Les établissements de Saint Louis dans le Beauvoisis," *MSHP* 8 (1881), 95-106.

Artois, Orléanais, Touraine, Normandy, and Paris, never acknowledged any of the borrowed material.[33]

Oddly enough, there was also very little attempt to acknowledge the debt in the fields of family law and legal procedure, where Roman law had materially influenced custom. Possibly authors were unaware of the original source, as these elements came into custom indirectly by way of canon law. And given the constant tension between customary and canon jurisdiction, jurists were not very eager openly to acknowledge canon influences. Citing the code of Justinian was therefore both respectable and useful, while citing Gratian was neither. Thus Roman forms were used as camouflage for customary matter, while the real Roman influences were hidden behind customary forms.

Roman learning and royal centralization were intimately connected. While Roman lawyers almost never served in courts as judges or advocates, they did serve the throne well in other capacities. Many Roman lawyers in the thirteenth and fourteenth centuries spent their careers serving the royal administration and fostering royal ideologies.[34] Roman jurists clearly identified the rule of custom with an expression of popular will while viewing Roman law as a tool of royal power. Jurists on both sides of the Alps shared this view, Placentinus going so far as to place law above custom on the grounds that by granting power to the prince, the people had voluntarily abdicated their sovereignty.[35] But in practice French lawyers paid little attention to this attractive theory. No customary author ever voiced a similar proposition, or placed his material in any way in opposition to royal authority. Customals spoke of tacit consent, long usage, and common acceptance as the cornerstones of custom, admitting its popular origin, but did not consider it as an expression of popular sovereignty. Royal lawyers too ignored the theoretical aspect when it came to actual jurisdiction. The Parlement of Paris stated explicitly that Roman law carried no authority in the land of customary law.[36]

The imposition of Roman forms upon customary material and the insertion of royally-sanctioned legislation gave customal literature a semblance of permanence and structure inherently lacking in it. All customals paid attention to public as well as private law, and in so

33 Dievoet, *Jehan Boutillier*, pp. 178-86.

34 Meijers, "L'Université d'Orléans," pp. 8-24; J.A. Clarence Smith, *Medieval Law Teachers and Writers*, (Ottawa, 1975), pp. 61-70.

35 Waelkens, *La théorie de la coutume*, p. 310.

36 *Ordonnances des roys de France*, 1:313.

doing incorporated a great deal of governmental attitudes towards authority and order. Ironically, customary authors were unaware of what they had done. Since customs rather than law were in use, said Beaumanoir, it was "good and profitable" to write them down, "so that they should henceforth be immutably maintained."[37] But this very immutability was contrary to the flexible and fluid nature of custom. The transition from oral to written law was more than a formal change. As the early customals carried no stamp of approval by public authority, they did not really anchor practice at one point in time. Their influence consisted largely in imbuing customary law with a hitherto lacking intellectual content. Though the authors were no legal philosophers, their organization of the material, their attempts to emulate Roman principles, and their insistence that custom must be reasonable[38] helped change the very nature of their subject.

The process of writing down customs also brought about a gradual distancing of judicial theory from practice. During the first stage the effect was minor, for the texts were mnemonic and descriptive rather than authoritative. Written texts assumed the force of legislation only in the fifteenth century, with the appearance of authoritative compilations and redactions of local custom. The distance until then was not so much between theory and practice as between local and central rulings. Often the Parlement of Paris overturned local sentences, ruling according to its principles. Roman principles had a much greater effect in central practice than in manuals of local custom. Changes in procedure and modes of proof originated with the courts of Paris, not with the jurisprudence of local *baillis*. The direct source of change in the age of private customals was the one that had the authority to enforce its principles in lay courts.

But during the fifteenth century the new customary texts became law, written by order of the crown. Codification took the place of practice as the operative force in the development of customary law. But this codification was partially based upon private redactions. The compiling jurists consulted and cited the customs of Anjou, Boutillier's *Somme rural*, and even the memoranda of Jean le Coq and Jean de Marès.[39] They remained the cornerstone and ultimate authority of customary law, the supposedly pure, unaltered, ancient custom. In

[37] *CB*, 1:4.

[38] "...costume vaut pour tant conme ele soit resnable..." Anonymous in *CF*, p. 492; "Coustume est ung raisonnable establissement..." *GC*, p. 193.

[39] Dievoet, *Jehan Boutillier*, pp. 116-24.

fact, they were no such thing. They were an instant of development frozen in time, comprising both tradition and change, orality and literacy, the old and the new. But they represented the basis of customary law to future generations.

2. The Myth of Customary Law

French customary law, therefore, was anything but static or unaltered during the later middle ages. The ideal of a pure, old, good law could hardly have applied to France. And yet the general interplay of ideology and reality was brought perhaps into a sharper focus in France than elsewhere. The plethora of customary writings, many of them also defining custom, its nature and scope, deepened the inherent contrast. Contradictory as they were, both the ideology and the reality of custom lived cheek by jowl in the customals.

Theoretically custom serving in place of law derived its authority from its age. Many customal authors stated that custom became notorious, requiring no proof once it had been observed uncontested for forty years, or as far back as human memory went. Notorious custom was tantamount to posited law, and it prevailed even if it was odious, or in conflict with Roman law.[40] Custom, therefore, was indeed defined in terms of the ideal: old, unchanged, universally recognized and applied.

In practice, however, all customal authors were strongly conscious of the winds of change blowing about their courtrooms. But they were no hidebound reactionaries attempting to preserve a dead tradition. They knew, none better, that custom was not age-old, timeless, and of divine origin. While they might have deplored the constant shifts, they openly acknowledged that what they were recording was merely contemporary practice, not a tradition handed over from their forefathers. Furthermore, they knew very well that their writing would be outdated within a few years. Beaumanoir said as much in the conclusion to his book. Aware of the ignorance and arbitrary rulings of judges, he well knew that custom would have become unrecognizable within the span of another human life. Hence, he begged his future readers not to blame him if his customal became irrelevant: "At the

[40] *CB*, art. 683, 1:346: "... maintenue de si long tans comme il puet souvenir a homme sans debat..."; Anonymous in *CF*, p. 493; *GC*, p. 192. Cf. Lebrun, *La coutume*, pp. 51-52.

time we did it, we wrote to the best of our ability what was commonly held and had to be done in the Beauvaisis."[41]

The myth that custom was ancient did not fool the writers. They knew custom was relatively new and indeed took measures to institutionalize the introduction of new customs into practice. Side by side with notorious customs, requiring no proof since they were known 'from time immemorial' there were private customs which acquired the status of notoriety upon being proven by an inquest in court.[42] The idea that even one precedent created a custom, and that proof of a precedent in court could transform the same into a notorious one crystallized during the second half of the thirteenth and the early fourteenth centuries.[43] All authors acknowledged that custom could be created through practice, though Jehan Boutillier did warn that relying upon the proof of private customs "was highly dangerous", as inquests were unpredictable and records rare.[44] Thus custom, mythically a good old law, expressly contained within its structure the mechanism for innovation.

If the good old law was not necessarily old, was it nevertheless good? Custom, they all said, must be reasonable and consistent, but neither custom in general nor specific customs were necessarily good. Beaumanoir accused local lords of keeping iniquitous and unreasonable customs merely because they fed seigneurial cupidity.[45] Others too recorded from time to time customs of which they disapproved, such as practices contrary to the church's prerogatives. By claiming that certain customs—those contrary to natural law or the rights of church and ruler—were automatically null and void, customary authors tacitly admitted that such customs existed.[46] The assertion that the king had the duty of correcting harsh, iniquitous, and unreasonable customs carried a similar admission.[47] But the need to produce a manual describing practice was stronger than the urge to improve reality. The judges and *baillis* writing these texts were under no illusion as to the

[41] "Ou tans que nous le feismes, de tout nostre pouoir nous escrisimes ce qui tenoit et devoit estre fet communement en Beauvoisins," *CB*, art. 1982, 2:501.

[42] *SR*, pp. 5-6; Claude Liger, *Les coustumes d'Anjou et du Maine intitullées selon les rubriches du Code*, in *CIAM*, no. 1217, 2:446; *GC*, p. 192; *CB*, art. 683, 1:346.

[43] André Sergène, "Le précédent judiciaire au moyen âge," *RHDFE* 39 (1961), 224-54, 359-70.

[44] *SR*, p. 6.

[45] *CB*, arts. 387, 1944, 1:184, 2:481.

[46] Anonymous in *CF*, p. 494.

[47] Fr. Olivier-Martin, "Le roi de France et les mauvaises coutumes," *ZRG, GA* 58 (1938), 108-37.

inherent justice or equity of customs. The goodness of custom was of the same order as its great age. It was a carefully preserved myth, necessary for the common consciousness of those who lived by customary law, but openly acknowledged as a myth.

The unlegislated character of custom did not stand the test of reality any better. Authors acknowledged that if necessary rulers might either abrogate custom or actually make new laws by means of statutes. Writing in the 1280s, Beaumanoir stated that all rulers might in times of emergency or need enact statutes (such as food controls in time of famine) for the good of their people. The king could do so for the whole realm also in normal times, as long as two conditions were fulfilled. First, he must do so in the great council; secondly, the statutes had to be reasonable and for the common good. As a rule, though, it was the duty of the ruler to impose respect for customs rather than legislate.[48]

Others went even farther. The thirteenth-century author of the *Summa de legibus Normandiae* saw little difference, except in their origin, between custom and law. Custom was old, handed down from times immemorial, while law was made by rulers, and both were observed by the people. But custom too required the approval of rulers, and (as some manuscripts add) rulers could also change customs and invent new ones to fit specific situations. However, the *Summa* also distinguished between ideals and reality. Whatever it might say about *principes* in general (Roman influence being strongly visible again in the general definitions), the duke of Normandy was to keep justice and prosecute criminals, not legislate.[49] The author of the *Livre de constitucions demenées el Chastelet de Paris* (essentially a customal of Ile-de-France), was the most extreme of the thirteenth-century authors: "Custom must be created by command of the king, or the count, or the bishop, or the royal abbot, or by [the command of] whoever can or should do so..."[50]

---

[48] *CB*, arts. 683, 1511-15, 1:346, 2:262-65. S.J.T. Miller, "The Position of the King in Bracton and Beaumanoir," *Speculum* 31 (1956), 263-96.

[49] "Consuetudines vero sunt mores ab antiquitate habiti, a principibus approbati et a populo conservati.... He [*sic*, for the lords] possessiones appropriant et jura introducunt; ipsis casu mutatus jura mutantur, et variatis variantur, et innovatis innovantur.... Leges autem sunt institutiones a principibus facte et a populo in provincia conservate..." *Summa de legibus Normandiae*, in *Coutumiers de Normandie*, 3:35, 37, ch. 10, arts. 1-2; ch. 11.

[50] "Coustume doit estre faite par commandement de roi, ou de conte, ou d'evesque, ou d'abbé roial, ou de tel qui le puisse faire et doie." "Livre des

The stress on royal legislative powers increased as time went by. The early fourteenth-century gloss to the customs of Anjou restricted all legislative powers to the king: "... it is he who makes the laws and the customs...."[51] With two centuries of expanding royal power behind him, Boutillier brought the theory to its logical, extreme conclusion: "The king of France... can make ordinances that are equivalent to and take precedence over the law (i.e., Roman law)..."[52]

Was the old, good, unlegislated law of the French middle ages a figment of the historian's imagination? Not quite. By all evidence, the very people who recorded this law in France at least suffered from no such illusions. They knew that customary law was processual and shifting, that it was constantly being legislated by rulers (an innovation in which they enthusiastically acquiesced), and that goodness was largely in the eye of the beholder. They often stressed that what they recorded was neither good nor bad, merely existent practice.

It is possible that the ideal character of customary law became less and less important as jurisprudence grew and legal writings proliferated. But less important to whom? Obviously, the lawyers were interested in reality, not in myths. But they had no monopoly over the uses of law. A variety of groups, ranging from the political to the popular, used and invoked legal principles and ideals. Coronation oaths still repeated the ideals of good, old customs, and similar statements were made on other ceremonial occasions. The lay perception of what law and justice ought to be still preserved the myth, its importance undiminished by time.

3. Figures and Myths of Justice

Popular medieval culture articulated its own views on law and justice side by side with legal perceptions. These opinions were clearly distinct from the formal, legal view. Essentially, they insisted with a certain *naïveté* that law should first and foremost be just. The identification of law with justice, rather than with any kind of institutionalization is the most salient aspect of almost all lay perceptions of law. While lawyers questioned the authority of custom, searching for its

constitucions demenées el Chastelet de Paris," ed. Charles Mortet, *MSHP* 10 (1883), 55, art. 4.

[51] "...et est celuy qui fait les droiz et le coustumes..." *Les coustumes glosées d'Anjou et du Maine*, ch. 47, in *CIAM*, 1:243-44. For the dating of this text (ascribed by the editor to 1385), see Lévy, "La pénétration," 6.

[52] *SR*, p. 646. Lebrun, *La coutume*, p. 67.

roots and legitimation, the only legitimation laymen needed was that the law be just, according to their lights of justice. Beyond this demand there lay a far more complex and disenchanted view of law and lawyers in reality. Popular literature cheerfully admitted that lawyers were rarely just, also claiming that 'real' justice was often totally divorced from the law. In short, the practice of law was not considered synonymous with doing justice, nor were the dispensers of justice identified with the practitioners of law.

The centrality of the popular preoccupation with justice in the later middle ages is impossible to ignore. Literary sources ranging from proverbs to *chansons de geste* (to say nothing of didactic literature) kept harping upon the themes of justice, injustice, and their relationship with practiced law. The thirteenth-century *Dit de droit* provides perhaps the best summary of popular ideals of justice:

> Rightfulness says that one must not slander
> Rightfulness forbids all low things
> Rightfulness shows all courtesy
> Rightfulness says one must be well-behaved
> Rightfulness says that one must keep silent
> Rightfulness says that one slanderer
> Is worse than two mortal enemies.... [53]

The poem goes on, attributing a variety of proverbs and general good moral advice to *droit*. Each line begins with *droit dist*. It is doubtful that whoever composed it meant the word *droit* in the strictly legal sense. It appears to mean both a norm of conduct and a moral precept. The poem is merely a compilation of proverbial wisdom attributed to the mythical figure of *droit*. The fact that the author should have done so, rather than place the same proverbs in the mouth of *justitia* (a well-known symbolic-anthropomorphic figure), is indicative. Obviously, he considered that moral precepts did not belong to the realm of justice, but of rightfulness. Neither justice nor the law had anything to do with *droit*, a concept probably most akin to equity.

Proverbial wisdom was notoriously cynical about the processes of formal justice. "A sizeable donation blinds the judge," "Never plead or dance in a strange land," "We, the fools who plead, feed the lawyers," "Frequent plaintiffs are never rich," "Better a bad compromise than a

[53] "Droit dit qu'on ne doit pas mesdire./ Droit deffend toute vilanie,/ Droit monstre toute courtoisie./ Droit dit que l'en soit de bon aire,/ Droit dit que l'en se doit bien taire./ Droit dist qu'un mesdisant vaut pis/ Qu'avoir deux morteux anemis." A. Le Roux de Lincy, *Le livre des proverbes français*, 2 vols. (Paris, 1859, repr. Geneva, 1968), 2:290.

good trial," "Only a fool gets involved in an inquest," "Poor men present a poor plea."[54] These proverbs, ranging from the thirteenth to the fifteenth century, present a fairly coherent picture. The growing professionalization of the law, reflected in the expanding number of qualified lawyers and judges and in the increasing esotericism of practical jurisprudence, found its echo in popular comments. A single judge, employed and paid by political authorities, was probably far more amenable to bribes and pressures than a body of lay judges representing the community. The resentment towards lawyers, possessors of esoteric knowledge and power, and the conviction that they were all crooks, became a literary common-place that was to last well into modern times. Justice was for the rich and the powerful, said the proverbs, and lawyers were ignorant charlatans. Maître Pathelin, the village lawyer of a fifteenth-century farce, is depicted as barely literate but amply provided with a cynical readiness to trick laymen.[55]

According to popular literature, the best judges were not the upright, unbribeable magistrates but the clever ones who could come up with a sentence satisfying all parties or ferret the truth out of lying witnesses. The motif is fairly universal, late medieval French literature according with other wise-judge stories the world over. One narrative told of a woman who had complained of rape after being seduced and abandoned. The judge gave the defendant the choice between marriage or the payment of a fine, and the young man chose to pay. Having done so, he was told by the judge to go after the young woman and wrest his money from her. The woman resisted energetically, whereupon the judge pointed out that if she was strong enough to fight off attempts upon her money, she should probably have been able also to defend her virtue.[56] In another case, two women disputed the ownership of one skein of wool. The judge asked both how the skein was begun; one responded that it was started with a piece of black coal, the other with a piece of white cloth. Whereupon the judge ordered the skein unraveled in order to ascertain its true ownership.[57]

---

[54] *Ibid.*, 2:132, 145-46, 461; Antoine Loisel, *Institutions coutumières*, ed. Michel Reulos (Paris, 1935), p. 107.

[55] *Maître Pierre Pathelin, farce du XVe siècle*, ed. R.T. Holbrook (Paris, 1937).

[56] Etienne de Bourbon, *Anecdotes historiques, légendes et apologues tirés du recueil inédit d'Etienne de Bourbon, dominicain du XIIIe siècle*, ed. A. Lecoy de la Marche (Paris, 1877), p. 432.

[57] *La Tabula exemplorum secundum ordinem alphabeti*, ed. L.-T. Welter (Toulouse, 1927, repr. Geneva, 1973), p. 155.

Both stories, culled from the *exempla* literature, bear the unmistakeable stamp of a popular tale.[58]

Beyond stories exalting the clever, truth-finding judge lay a deeper nostalgia for the figure of the absolutely inflexible arbitrator who defended the poor, resisting all contrary pressures. Two very disparate sources linked inflexibility with the rights of the downtrodden: one judicial, concerning the manner of doing justice, and one biographical, concerning Saint Louis, the epitome of the just king. The *Très-ancienne coutume de Bretagne*, written early in the fourteenth century, made this connection. Having stated all the standard definitions of justice culled from Roman law, the author proceeded to give a definition unique in customal literature. Justice, he said, was established for charity, for otherwise the *menus giens* could not survive for the oppression of the great. Hence, justice must be rigorous in the extreme: "It must be loyal and straight, more than the rope when it is stretched, and straighter it cannot be without breaking."[59]

It is no chance that the customs of Bretagne made the express connection between inflexibility, charity, and pure justice. The patron saint of this province was a lawyer and an ecclesiastical judge, famous for both his thoroughgoing justice and his charity. Yves Héloury was born to Breton lower nobility in the middle of the thirteenth century and educated in the universities of Paris and Orléans. He spent his entire ecclesiastical career as official, first in Rennes and later in the bishop's court at Tréguier. He was reknowned throughout his life for his austerity, devotion, and justice. Saint Yves' life spanned the second half of the thirteenth century, precisely the time when the processes that were to distance common people from legal proceedings began to gather impetus. Though his career was purely within the field of ecclesiastical jurisdiction, for his contemporaries and their descendants he was the epitome of what a lawyer and a judge should be.[60]

The distance between ideal and reality was summed up in the popular doggerel: "Saint Yves was a Breton; a lawyer, but not a thief;

---

[58] Cf. P. Saintyves, *Les cinquante jugements de Salomon, ou arrêts des bons juges d'après la tradition populaire* (Paris, 1933).

[59] "... ainsi doit estre [justice] léal et droite plus que le cordel quant il est tendu, si plus droite ne pout ester sanz cliver nulle part." *Très-ancienne coutume de Bretagne*, p. 308.

[60] For biographies of Saint Yves, see Jean Le Mappian, *Yves de Tréguier* (Paris, 1981), largely based upon the older works of, and sources cited in A. de La Borderie, *Les monuments originaux et l'histoire de saint Yves* (Saint Brieuc, 1885), and A. Desjardins, *Saint Yves, avocat des pauvres et patron des avocats* (Paris, 1897).

a wonder in the people's eyes."[61] The canonization proceedings of Saint Yves, describing his saintly character, delineate the sharp contrast between the ideal jurist and ordinary judicial reality. In addition to the usual thaumaturgic miracles he performed, Saint Yves was known for his extreme professional ethics. Even after his appointment as a judge he defended the poor in court free of charge. Within the coming century both Guillaume du Breuil and Jacques d'Ableiges, scrupulous jurists by any standards, advised lawyers to concentrate first upon the cases of the rich even if they did take some cases of poor people free of charge.[62] As judge, he did all he could to settle cases amicably out of court, to the detriment of lawyers' income. In addition, he was famous for the speed with which he expedited his cases, again an unusual trait at a time when a case before the Parlement of Paris, for example, could easily last years. As might be expected, he favored no one, least of all the rich and powerful.

And yet Saint Yves was not the personification of justice, merely the patron saint of lawyers and their ideal. The king—not only Saint Louis, though he was one of the most famous kings-justices, but the ruler *per se*—was the embodiment of justice on earth. The stories relating to absolute justice were invariably concerned with a king. A clever judge could be a king, but a judge practicing absolute justice in the stories was almost invariably a king.

It is important to distinguish the myth of the just king from the myth of the lawgiver king. The latter, a founder figure who left behind a code bearing his name, was a powerful motif in late antiquity and the early middle ages. But rulers who produced coherent codes of law were probably not the dream of litigants, but of jurists. Simple folk wanted justice done, not enacted, and done to them. Thus in the later middle ages kings appeared as figures of justice, not of law-giving. Significantly, such myths rarely attached themselves to kings who did in fact a great deal of legislating in one way or another. Neither Philip the Fair nor Edward I (or even Henry II) ever achieved this distinction. In French myths, it was attached to Charlemagne, to Arthur, to Saint Louis, and to Charles V. They were just kings because they presumably dispensed justice. As Joinville related, Saint Louis sat under an oak-tree in the forest of Vincennes to hear people's complaints and try

---

[61] "Sanctus Ivo erat Brito/ Advocatus, et non latro/ Res miranda populo."

[62] "Preferas in expediendo solventes non solventibus..." Guillaume du Breuil, *Stilus curie parlamenti*, ed. Félix Aubert (Paris, 1909), p. 2; cf. *GC*, p. 399, for an almost identical phrasing.

to mediate them. Whether he indeed did so or not matters little. He was considered the kind of king whom one could approach in search of justice.

The myth of the just king was closely tied to the myth of the good old law. A king achieved the status of just ruler by applying the laws and customs of the past—the ones he shared with his people, not the ones he had invented. The importance of the king as judge, rather than legislator, is a thread running throughout the developing myths of justice and kingship.

The archetype of the just king was theoretically embodied in the biblical figure of Solomon. But Solomon was never quite justice incarnate. He was the archetypal figure of the clever, truth-finding judge. Though Solomon's fame rested upon his judgment between two claimant mothers, his greatest claim was not to justice necessarily, but to wisdom. He provided all the answers in the *Dialogue of Solomon and Saturn*, explaining the nature of the universe.[63] In a parody version of this motif, Solomon spouted proverbial clichés of wisdom, only to be countered by the real earthy wisdom of the peasant Marcolf.[64] Solomon the quasi-omniscient fount of wisdom overshadowed Solomon the judge.[65]

Mythical figures of absolute justice played an important role in popular and popular-oriented literature. The story of the ruler whose son was sentenced to be blinded in both eyes and who offered to sacrifice one of his own eyes so that his son would still see while justice remained inviolate had several popular and learned versions.[66] Another story told of the emperor who had inadvertently broken his own law by entering the council-chamber girded with his sword. Rather than break the law, he promptly had himself executed.[67]

These stories, reflecting the trends of the time, were told by thirteenth-century preachers. But the traditions linking justice and kingship in customary law go back farther in time, to the mythical heroes

---

[63] *The Prose of Solomon and Saturn and Adrian and Ritheus*, ed. James E. Cross and Thomas D. Hill (Toronto, 1982).

[64] "Dialogus Salomonis et Marcolphi," ed. Giulio Cesare Croce, *Le sotilissime astuzie di Bertoldo...* (Torino, 1978), pp. 169-206.

[65] However, in Jewish folklore Solomon remained overwhelmingly a wise judge. See Eli Yasif, "King Solomon Proverbs," [Hebrew], *Mechkaré Yerushalayim be-Safrut Ivrit* 9 (1986), 357-73; for a bibliography of Solomon legends in all cultures, see *Ibid.*, 357, n. 1.

[66] Welter, *Tabula exemplorum*, p. 34 (concerning Emperor Trajan); Saintyves, *Les cinquante jugements de Salomon*, p. 98 (concerning Zeleucus the Greek).

[67] Welter, *Tabula exemplorum*, p. 36.

of the *chansons de geste*. The mythical justice of Arthur and Charlemagne (or any other Carolingian) is problematic. It appears in the *chansons* phrased as a challenge to the king, who often does not do justice as he should. Thus, in *Garin le Loheran* and *Raoul de Cambrai*, Kings Pepin or Louis are continually addressed as *droiz emperere,* usually as a prelude to a complaint about their arbitrariness and injustice.[68] In *La mort le roi Artu* Mador, suspecting the queen of having killed his brother, practically challenges the 'just king' to do his duty: "King Arthur, if you are as just as a king should be, hold me in the justice of your court, in such a way that, if anyone has reason to accuse me, I will act justly as you please, and if I have reason to accuse whomsoever it might be, justice will be granted me as the court will decide."[69] The words *droiturier* and *droit* recur in this short declaration four times. Mador demanded a trial by duel to prove guilt or innocence, as customary law decreed.

The king in courtly literature was thus not automatically the embodiment of justice. To the contrary, on the evidence of the *chansons* he was often unjust to his vassals. The assumption was that a ruler ought to be just, and that the noble men and women of his court were entitled to demand, sometimes in very sharp terms, justice of him. Justice in this context often meant the preservation of feudal rights. Pepin might not marry Garin's betrothed, Louis was not allowed to disinherit Raoul de Cambrai, and Arthur had to investigate the accusation against his wife as though she were a stranger. Justice in these cases was due to the plaintiffs, and they demanded it of right, rather than begging for mercy.

The transition in perceptions of justice cannot be precisely dated, but it is unequivocally tied with the figure of Saint Louis. Hence, it was probably roughly contemporary with the beginnings of customary writing, and the two processes were interconnected. The picture of Saint Louis, as drawn by his contemporary and friend Joinville, clearly shows a king of justice. He was available to all and sundry seeking his help, in his bedroom in winter and under an oak-tree in the Vincennes forest in summer. There he patiently listened to simple people who begged for his justice. But there is no indication in Joinville's words

---

68 *Garin le Loheran*, ed. Josephine Elvira Vallerie (Ann Arbor, 1941); *Raoul de Cambrai*, ed. P. Meyer and A. Longnon (Paris, 1882).

69 "Roi Artus, se tu es si droituriers come rois doit estre, tien moi a droit en ta cort, en tel maniere que, se nus m'e set que demander, g'en ferai droit a ton pleis, et se ge sai que demander a ame qui i soit, droit m'en face l'en einsi comme la cort esgardera." Quoted by Bloch, *Medieval French Literature and Law*, p. 15.

that Louis as judge was applying the law. He offered the sort of arbitration and compromise that Saint Yves advocated a generation later.[70]

The words the biographer put into Saint Louis' mouth at his deathbed summarize the role of the just king. Instructing his son in the art of just government, the king made a plea for uncompromising justice: "In order to deal justly and equitably with your subjects, be straightforward and firm, turning neither to the right hand nor to the left, but always following what is just, and upholding the cause of the poor till the truth be made clear."[71] Both Saint Louis and Joinville were contemporaries of Pierre de Fontaines, Philippe de Beaumanoir, Philippe de Novare and a number of other customal authors. The times of Saint Louis and his legends were no longer the times and legends of the *chansons de geste*, and the perception of justice had changed accordingly. The image of the king who has justice reluctantly and arbitrarily wrested from him by his discontented vassals gave way to a new image in the later middle ages: the king who granted justice as a gift to all and sundry, regardless of their status.

The same motif, with one very important difference, was echoed by Christine de Pizan in her description of Charles V's justice. The justice of Charles the Wise manifested itself in two forms: first, the king always upheld the just quarrel of the lower echelons of society. He penalized a knight of his court who had struck a sergeant and even supported the just claim of a Jew against a Christian. Secondly, like Saint Louis before him, Charles V dispensed justice in person. Unlike his illustrious predecessor, he no longer did so under a tree but at the Parlement, "he in person, according to the noble ancient customs," often held a *lit de justice* in which he acted as the judge.[72] This statement implies that Charles V upheld the tradition of personal royal justice established by Saint Louis, but in a manner befitting the late fourteenth century. This was no longer a matter of personal arbitration, but of applying the good old law, as was the express duty of a

[70] Jean de Joinville, *Vie de Saint Louis*, ed. M. Natalis de Wailly (Paris, 1868), pp. 21-22; Michael T. Clanchy, "Law and Love in the Middle Ages," in *Disputes and Settlements*, pp. 52-53.

[71] "A justices tenir et à droitures soies loiaus et roides à tes sougiez, sanz tourner à destre ne à senestre, mais adès à droit, et soustien la querelle dou povre jeusques à tant que la veritês soit desclairie." Joinville, *Vie de Saint Louis*, p. 264.

[72] Christine de Pizan, *Le livre de faits et bonnes moeurs du sage roi Charles V...* (Paris, 1892), book I, ch. 16, pp. 52-54.

just king. The just king had become a judge, applying the laws of the land.

In the later middle ages the two traditions merged in an image of a king still universally available to all his subjects while applying and preserving the existent law, and whose justice was tempered with mercy. This image found its real-life expression in the king's supreme power to grant grace. Though late medieval kings no longer had any personal contact with those seeking their mercy, the overwhelming majority of remissions for crime were granted in the king's name. As the pardon formulae indicated, the king had the power absolutely to remit any punishment, pardon any crime, restore any criminal to his position, his property and his community, release prisoners, and save criminals at the very foot of the gallows.

Letters of remission were granted for a wide spectrum of crimes, but they were far from automatic. The king's mercy knew a number of normative limitations. In the first place, genuinely heinous crimes (such as parricide) neither deserved nor received pardon.[73] Secondly, grace hinged upon the verification of the petition's facts in local courts. Finally, it was very often conditional upon a prior settlement being reached between the petitioner and his victim. In other words, the king's mercy as exhibited in the letters of remission hinged not only upon truth, but also upon certain principles of equity. By contrast, on solemn occasions the king's mercy could be entirely indiscriminate and unconditional. The release of all prisoners from local jails on the occasion of the king's (or the queen's) solemn entry into a city exhibited this type of mercy. It was a fairly well-known practice for sought criminals to turn themselves in just before a *joyeuse entrée* in order to gain the blanket pardon of the occasion.[74]

Royal entries were also excellent occasions for the articulation of the king's justice in visual form. Each entry was accompanied by a series of pageants at various points along the royal route. In Paris, the spectacle exhibiting the ruler's judicial attributes was enacted at the

[73] Claude Gauvard, "L'Image du roi justicier en France à la fin du moyen âge d'après les lettres de rémission," *La faute, la répression et le pardon. Actes du 107e congrès national des sociétés savantes* (Brest, 1982), 1:169-70 claims that there were no normative limits to the power of royal grace, which could extend to the most heinous crimes. In my opinion, there were no clear-cut rules in the matter, but the frequency of certain types of crimes and criminals among the remissions, and the rarity of others, indicates a certain informal selectivity in the matter.

[74] *Ibid.*, 173-75. For the procedure of granting and registering remissions, see Natalie Z. Davis, *Fiction in the Archives: Pardon Tales and their Tellers in Sixteenth Century France* (Stanford, 1987), pp. 7-15.

Châtelet by the confraternity of law-clerks. Here the conception of justice originated neither with a feudal nobility nor with the popular elements of the city. This was the perception of the professional legal elite of the city:

> The notion of the constitutionalists that a commonwealth was composed of separate but dependent juridical estates was the theme for most of the Châtelet productions. In this view the king's role was to distribute justice to each estate; his central position called attention to his role in preserving national union and peace. In the programs the prominent position given to allegorized justice and counsel emphasized the king as judge or conservator of a preexisting order rather than as its legislator and creator.... The ideal ruler was always presented in terms of his relationship to ideal justice...[75]

The king of the jurists thus did not drastically differ from the just king of other strata. He still gave each his due, preserving concord as well as justice. He was still the dispenser, rather than the creator of justice. The jurists' pageants invariably identified justice and law with power and majesty.[76] They did not view kings as being in any way above, or dissociated from the law. In this, they were in harmony with the old tradition. The just king was neither the incarnation of the law nor the lawmaker. He was the man who applied and preserved the laws of the realm. At the time of Saint Louis these laws were still mostly oral. By the end of the fifteenth century customary law had changed into a written system stamped with the seal of royal approval, and the transition was mirrored in the shifting figure of the just king. From informal arbitrator to formal judge, faithfully following the rites prescribed by a caste of lawyers, the myth of the just king grew into its Renaissance form.

4. NORTHERN FRENCH LAW IN THE EUROPEAN CONTEXT

Up to a certain point, every legal system is a product and a reflection of the society it rules. Whether one considers English constitutional law or the customs of the Tiw tribe, laws reflect certain realities. Those are not only the social realities of the time and place, but also the cultural realities resident in people's minds. Perceptions and myths

---

[75] Lawrence M. Bryant, *The King and the City in the Parisian Royal Entry Ceremony: Politics, Ritual and Art in the Renaissance* (Geneva, 1986), pp. 178, 189-90.

[76] *Ibid.*, pp. 178-94; Joël Blanchard, "Les entrées royales. Pouvoir et représentation du pouvoir à la fin du moyen âge," *Littérature* 50 (1983), 3-14.

of law are every bit as important as social realities in the process of shaping legal systems.

The interaction of reality and myth, socio-political pressures and cultural changes stands out clearly in the development of late medieval French customary law. In theory, the law of a society endowing political authority with legislative power need not necessarily be responsive to popular, or even intellectual needs. After all, the practice of law in France had always been tied with lordship, and in the later middle ages this practice came increasingly to be held in royal hands. Furthermore, the kings of France did in fact legislate for their realm while carefully maintaining the myth of unlegislated custom. Nevertheless, one is hard put to find a legal system in which developments followed so very hard upon the heels of cultural trends. Written customals might not have been an absolutely accurate seismograph recording the tremors affecting late medieval society and culture, but in France they came very close to such accuracy.

The writing of custom is a case in point. It reflected simultaneously two contradictory trends: on the one hand, the increasing tendency to put oral traditions in writing, apparent in other fields already a century before its spread to the legal realm. On the other hand, the very delay was clear evidence of the resistance to the new form which contradicted the oral nature of the law. The intellectual climate of the thirteenth century—the growth of Roman jurisprudence, the tendency to sum up all human knowledge in *summae* of one kind or another, the fight of mendicant preachers to eradicate the so-called popular superstitions and, by contrast, the beginnings of popular literature—all these played a role in the writing of law.

Thus, the written customal became a sort of carryall in which both learned and popular practices and perceptions could be found. Both Roman tradition and customary precedents came into the new jurisprudence through the pen of practical lawyers with a modicum of Roman education. At the same time, these authors were keenly aware of their role as curators of the old law and recorders of existent practice. Therefore, they carefully preserved the popular elements of customary law. Those were not necessarily ancient relics of long-forgotten beliefs, but the living, evolving folklore of the period of writing.

There was very little conflict between the learned and the popular traditions in the customals. Many of the same perceptions surface in the words of the lawyers and in contemporary popular sources. The image of the ruler preserving and applying an existent law, enthusiastically fostered by royal biographers, was commonly shared by all strata. Practical clashes between royal prerogatives and local jurisdictions notwithstanding, the general perceptions of the just king's role seem to have been universal. The kings too were careful to preserve the myth, not only in pageants and public rituals, but primarily in court, where they produced ordinances and *établissements*, but never laws.

Consequently, while in other spheres clashes between learned and popular traditions became increasingly common in the early modern period, the realm of law exhibited remarkable cohesiveness and consensus. By the end of the middle ages France did not possess one united legal system, but within the great complex of local customs it did have a certain cultural coherence. Unlike the Holy Roman Empire, early modern France did not undergo a process of national codification and legislation in the manner of the *Carolina* or the *Theresiana*. There was no need. Local customals could function very well with the seal of royal approval, precisely because they embodied a cultural consensus lacking elsewhere. It was perfectly respectable for Antoine Loisel, learned Renaissance jurist, to include in his *Institutions coutumières* popular proverbs and traditional views of justice as legitimate sources of custom. Learned and popular traditions merged in customary law, forming a congruent whole.

The law of the time was the product of a certain cultural environment. It was an intensely physical, graphic culture. Ideas were manifested in pictures, anthropomorphic representations, and allegories. Entire conceptual frameworks were articulated in the form of ritual and pageantry. Thus law too assumed its place within the pageant of late medieval culture, internalizing the same principle. The tenets of customary law were articulated in ritual, symbolic forms. While many of these rituals took place within the courthouse, the law of the time carried the ritual element also into the streets, enacting many of its ceremonies well within public view. The ritual manifestations of the culture of late medieval law are the subject matter of part two.

PART II: RITUALS

THE JUDICIAL CONTEXT

CHAPTER FOUR

COURTHOUSE RITUALS IN TRANSITION

The ritualism characterizing medieval law found its earliest expression in court ceremonial. Though this particular trait was to disappear in time, nothing elucidates the intimate connection between contemporary culture and law better than the character and transformation of these rituals. In their original, high medieval form, they reflected attitudes towards physical gestures and spoken words, and towards the connection between the individual human and the surrounding cosmic forces. In transition, they reflected the growing reliance upon literacy and the written word. In their final stage, they epitomized the early modern breach between increasingly professional lawyers and progressively more sceptical laymen.

The writing down of customs, first by private people and subsequently by royal authority, inevitably affected both content and procedure of law. The change was part and parcel of the generally altered attitude towards the written word and its role in judicial matters. If one could write down an oral legal tradition in order to preserve it, one could also use written records in courtroom proceedings. The use of written documentation under such circumstances was bound to alter the very nature of legal proceedings, their meaning within the cultural context and their use by lawyers and litigants alike. The resultant changes went much farther than a transition from orality to literacy.

Medieval judicial procedures, especially the criminal ones, bore until the thirteenth century a markedly ritual character. Though proof by charter and testimony had never disappeared completely, trial by battle, ordeal, and oath were commonly used when other evidence was unavailable.[1] The origins of these procedures went back to Germanic

[1] See sources quoted in n. 3 below, and Charles M. Radding, "Superstition to Science: Nature, Fortune and the Passing of the Medieval Ordeal," *American Historical Review* 84 (1979), 945-69.

traditions and to late west Roman vulgar law.[2] But unlike other late antique and early medieval practices, these rituals survived the obsolescence of the Germanic codes, remaining in force until the thirteenth century. Historians have explained this phenomenon by two different theories. Peter Brown attributed the extraordinary longevity of ordeals to a certain communal consensus, typical to high medieval small communities, which surfaced in God's verdict as interpreted by the spectators-participants. Conversely, Bartlett has argued that ordeals survived due to governmental preservation and support, their disappearance being due to the withdrawal of this backing.[3] Indeed, the origins of ordeals lie in a period when jurisdiction was not yet inextricably tied in with lordship, but the preserve of communal decisions. Furthermore, their disappearance was foreshadowed by the twelfth-century judicial changes that subsumed all justice under the power of political authority.[4] These facts tend to support both social and political theses.

It is possible, however, to adduce a third, equally valid explanation—that ordeals, oaths and duels survived simply because in their ritual fashion they fitted in perfectly well with the functioning of courts in other spheres. When almost all judicial activity was conducted in a ritual manner, there was no reason to apply different standards to the law of proof. Furthermore, like all other legal rituals, duels and ordeals were firmly grounded in contemporary extra-legal culture. Both relied upon a public religious ritual for legitimacy and verification. Each ordeal was preceded first by a Mass and then by an adjuration to the trial element (hot or cold water, hot iron, etc.) to exhibit the truth.[5] It was a joint invocation of the natural and the

---

[2] See Ian Wood, "Disputes in Late Fifth- and Sixth-Century Gaul: Some Problems," in Wendy Davies and Paul Fouracre, eds. *The Settlement of Disputes in Early Medieval Europe*, (Cambridge, 1986), pp. 15-18, who argues that both oath and ordeal stemmed from late Roman traditions, while trial by battle was of Germanic origin. Cf. Bartlett's assertion that the ordeal appeared only among the Franks, while trial by battle was common to all Germanic peoples. For a legal analysis of ordeal procedures, see Bongert, *Recherches sur les cours laïques*, pp. 211-28.

[3] Peter Brown, "Society and the Supernatural: A Medieval Change," *Daedalus* 104 (1975), 133-51; Robert Bartlett, *Trial by Fire and Water: The Medieval Judicial Ordeal* (Oxford, 1988).

[4] R. van Caeneghem, "The Law of Evidence in the Twelfth Century: European Perspective and Intellectual Background," *Proceedings of the Second International Congress of Medieval Canon Law, Rome, 1965* (Ghent, 1966), p. 301.

[5] For formulae of ordeals, see *Formulae Merowingici et Karolini aevi*, ed. Karl Zeumer, *MGH* (Hanover, 1886), pp. 599-722, covering texts up to the thirteenth century, and Petrus Browe, *De ordaliies*, 2 vols. (Rome, 1933), 2:7-18.

supernatural, for justice was held to be immanent in both.[6] The ritual was conducted and centered around the officiating priest, rather than the suspect, so that the human element took second place. The suspect was no more than a witness (occasionally an unwilling one) to his own guilt or innocence. The human and the personal were so unimportant in comparison with the vindication of truth and justice, that ordeals could even be held between books of different persuasions. During a dispute concerning the use of different rites in the Spanish church in 1077, two books containing respectively the Roman and the Toledan rite were cast into the fire, and the latter "leaped out of the flames."[7] The phenomenon was repeated when Saint Dominic's writings jumped three times out of the fire while those of his heretical opponents burned to ashes.[8]

In 1215 the fourth Lateran council forbade the participation of the clergy in the ritual of ordeals. This step initiated the gradual extinction of ordeals in medieval courts, though the process lasted throughout the thirteenth century. The Parlement of Paris recorded until the end of the century both trials by water and duels, the latter sometimes being supervised by the Cathedral chapter.[9]

The duel was not an ordeal in the strict sense of the word. Autonomic ordeals were those "in which the judgment of success or failure, guilt or innocence is dependent upon involuntary responses such as scalding or blistering of the person or persons tested in the course of 'trials'".[10] In other words, the proof rested entirely in supernatural hands or rather, in the human interpretation of supernatural manifestations. By contrast, a duel necessitated the active participation of both parties (or their champions), with proof resting upon prowess. Nevertheless, ultimate victory lay in God's hands, so that late medieval duels were invested with an certain autonomic aura. This perception was acted out in the ritual preceding the duel. Vigils in church, Mass, communion, and the solemn blessing of arms by a priest who also handed each adversary his sword and shield approximated the duel to an ordeal.[11] In addition, practically all customary sources mentioning

---

[6] P. Rousset, "La croyance en la justice immanente à l'époque féodale" *Le moyen âge* 54 (1948), 225-48.

[7] *Crónica Najarense*, ed. Antonio Ubieto Arteta (Valencia, 1966), p. 49.

[8] *Anecdotes historiques*, pp. 286-87.

[9] *Actes du Parlement de Paris*, 1:12, No. 142; 1:75, No. 818; M. Guérard, *Cartulaire de l'église Notre-Dame de Paris*, 4 vols. (Paris, 1850), 3:433.

[10] John M. Roberts, "Oaths, Autonomic Ordeals, and Power," *American Anthropologist* 67/2 (1965), 187.

[11] Hermann Nottarp, *Gottesurteilstudien* (München, 1955), pp. 275-89.

duels as judicial proof stress the oaths taken before battle.[12] Though the pre-duel secondary oaths varied in formulae and content, all sources insisted that the combatants swear a primary oath to the veracity of their cause and the falsity of their adversary's.[13] The pre-duel oath, very similar to the judicial oath, thus placed the outcome of the battle beyond human endeavor. At the same time, it was not administered by a priest in church, but either in court or upon the battlefield by a judge.

In contrast to judicial oaths, though, the pre-duel oath was a mutual affair. In the formula used by the Parlement of Paris towards the end of the fourteenth century the combatants were to swear three separate oaths on three different occasions. In the first one, the plaintiff came first, alone, swearing on the Gospels to the legitimacy of his cause. While he was still present, the defendant came and repeated the opposing vow. The second oath, taken separately by both parties, swore the opponents to use no means (especially witchcraft) but legal ones in order to win the battle. Both oaths were impersonal, being phrased as statements addressed to no one in particular. The third oath was the most dramatic. It was the only one in which the opponents specifically and formally addressed each other. On this occasion both parties appeared simultaneously. Holding each other's left hands, both clasped in the judge's own fingers, and placing their right hands upon the Gospels, they took the oath, with the plaintiff taking precedence again:

> Item, at the third oath the parties return together before the judge: and they take each other by their left hands, placed in the judge's palm. And they place the right [hands] on the book. And the plaintiff swears first and says: Oh you, man whom I hold by the hand, I swear on the Holy Gospels and by the faith and baptism that I hold from God that the deeds and words that I have attributed and made [others] attribute to you are true, and I have a good and true cause to summon you, while yours is bad. And the defendant swears and says: Oh you, man whom I hold by the hand, I swear on the Holy Gospels and by the faith and baptism that I hold from God that you have a bad cause to summon me. And I have a good and loyal cause to defend myself.
>
> At the first oath, each one comes without his adversary, and the plaintiff swears first alone, and soon afterwards the other comes. At the second each one comes alone without his adversary, and they do not take their gauntlets off either at the first nor at the second oath.

---

[12] *CB*, arts. 1834-35, 2:429-30; *ESL*, 2:156-60; BN, ms. fr. 21726, fol. 189-91; "Livre des Constitucions," arts. 32, 42, 60.

[13] All secondary oaths declared that the combatant would use no unlawful means (such as illegal weapons, ointment or witchcraft) in battle.

> At the third oath the two come together before the judge and remove their gauntlets....[14]

The repetition of the exact same formula by the dissenting parties made clear the mutual and equal character of the duel. Where no other proof existed, plaintiff and defendant stood equally before God, bound to prove their words by deeds. The final oath was more than mutual. The joining of hands was a symbolic gesture commonly used in rituals cementing permanent mutual bonds between two people, whether of vassalage or of marriage.[15] While in wedding rituals the priest joined the parties' hands, here the judge had the same position of supervising authority, endowing the entire procedure with legitimacy. The joining of left hands illustrated the antagonistic nature of the bond. It was equally significant that while the first two oaths were pronounced with gauntlets on, the last one was taken with bare hands. The wearing or removal of gloves within wedding rituals also bore specific meanings.[16] It was as though two antagonistic parties were joined together in requesting a resolution of their conflict from a higher power. The oath reflected more than mutuality; it reflected a certain bonding and unanimity, a consensus necessary for all ordeals, autonomic or otherwise. The courthouse was more than a meeting-ground for disputants. It was the place and the occasion in which they were joined together, even if in mutual animosity, by the use of ritual.

---

[14] "Item, au tiers serment les parties reviennent ensemble devant le juge: et s'entreprennent par leurs mains sensetres mises en la main du juge. Et les dextres mettent sur le livre. Et jure le premier le appellant et dit: O tu homme que je tiens par la main ie iure sur les Sainctes Evangiles et sur la foy et baptesme que ie tiens de Dieu que les faits et parolles que iay proposées et fait proposer contre toy sont vrays et ie ay bonne cause et loyalle de toy appeller, et tu las maulvaise. Et l'appellé iure et dit: O tu homme que je tiens par la main ie jure sur les Sainctes Evangiles et sur la foy et baptesme que ie tiens de Dieu que tu as maulvaise cause de moy appeller. Et ie lay bonne et loyal de moy deffendre.

Au premier serment chascun vient sanz son adversaire et premier l'appellant iure seul et tantost l'autre vient. Au second il vient chascun seul sanz son adversaire, et ne ostent point leurs gantelles ausdit premier et second serment. Au tiers serment tous deux ensemble viennent devant le juge et ostent leurs gantelles..." 1386; ms. fr. 21726, loc. cit. The formula is far more complex than the one cited during the first half of the century by Guillaume du Breuil, *Stylus curie parlamenti*, pp. 114-15.

[15] Jacques Le Goff, "Le rituel symbolique de la vassalité," in *Pour un autre moyen âge* (Paris, 1977), pp. 373-74; Jean-Baptiste Molin and Protaïs Mutembé, *Le rituel du mariage en France du XIIe au XVIe siècle* (Paris, 1974); Kenneth Stevenson, *Nuptial Blessing: A Study of Christian Marriage Rites* (New York, 1983), pp. 89-90.

[16] Esther Cohen and Elliott Horowitz, "In Search of the Sacred: Jews, Christians, and Rituals of Marriage in the Later Middle Ages," *Journal of Medieval and Renaissance Studies* 20 (1990), 225-50.

Variations of formula and ritual can be found in different parts of northern France. But the mutual oath, affirming each antagonist's rightness, often while holding hands, appears almost everywhere. Various customals also add specific details concerning dress, weapons, length of hair and head covering allowed, and the maximum time-span permitted for the battle (from shortly after noon until the appearance of the stars in the sky). [17]

Since the outcome of duels depended less upon natural elements than the results of autonomic ordeals, papal and conciliar legislation had no immediate effect upon them. Saint Louis began the process of abolition by forbidding judicial duels as a mode of proof in the royal courts of his domains, substituting either written or oral evidence in their place.[18] This injunction, promulgated in 1260, had a very limited effect. Even within the royal domain, seigneurial courts were permitted to continue using duels both in civil and in criminal cases.[19] Indeed, judicial duels continued to be held in seigneurial courts both in and outside the royal domain.[20] Their popularity is attested by the fact that Philip the Fair restored the practice also to royal courts in 1306, though only for criminal cases in which there was clear indication of malfeasance and no other evidence could be found.[21]

The last judicial duel presumably fought by orders of the Parlement of Paris took place in 1386. It was a *cause celèbre*, a scandal of rape and adultery, reported in several contemporary chronicles. [22] Jacques de Gris, squire, was accused of raping the wife of the knight Jehan de Carrouges. Though Carrouges could not even put a date to the crime and the victim was ambiguous in her testimony, the Parlement decided to put the case to the test of a duel. Judicial opinion no longer believed by then that duels reflected God's justice. The defendant, van-

[17] *Summa de legibus Normandiae in curia laicali*, part 2, ch. 67, in *Coutumiers de Normandie*, 2:168-71; Du Breuil, *Stylus curie parlamenti*, pp. 111-16; Jean d'Ibelin, *Assises de la haute cour*, ch. 97. For a general description of duel procedures, see Bongert, *Recherches sur les cours laïques*, pp. 239-51.

[18] *Ordonnances des roys de France*, 1:86; *ESL*, 1:1-7.

[19] "Livre des Constitucions," 15-16.

[20] See above, n. 9; *CF*, pp. 127-28 and *passim*; *Livre de jostice*, p. 292.

[21] *Ordonnances des roys de France*, 1:435, 438.

[22] Jean Froissart, *Chroniques*, ed. Siméon Luce et al., 14 vols. (Paris, 1869-1966), 13:102-107; Jean Juvenal des Ursins, *Histoire de Charles VI, roy de France...*, ed. Michaud and Poujoulat (Paris, 1850), p. 371; *Chronique du réligieux de Saint-Denys, contenant le règne de Charles VI de 1380 à 1422*, ed. M.L. Bellaguet, 6 vols. (Paris, 1839-52), 1:462. The minutes of the case are in AN, X^{1a} 1473, fol. 145vo; X^{2a} 10, fol. 232; X^{2a} 12, fol. 238vo. The case was still common knowledge at the beginning of the seventeenth century, according to Expilly (see below, n. 25.)

quished and killed in battle, was a man of good and pious reputation, and the jurist Jean le Coq in his commentary on the case patently disapproved of both procedure and result.[23] By contrast, all the chroniclers recording the case believed despite the lack of confession that justice had patently been done, and the rapist's guilt summarily proven.

Popular opinion also concurred in supporting the efficacy of judicial duels. While no longer fought in courts, they found their refuge in the pages of literature. Arthurian romances abounded with judicial duels, usually described in great verisimilitude and in accordance with contemporary practice.[24] Perhaps the most outstanding example of a literary duel was the one fought between a man and a dog, a story repeated many times and in many versions, illustrating the duel's efficacy as a mode of proof. The dog of Montargis, so goes the story, belonged to one of Charles V's knights, Aubry de Montdidier. Another knight, Macaire, jealous of the king's preference for Aubry, lured his rival to the forest of Bondis, killing him there. There were no witnesses to the deed, save the dog who returned to court, seeking justice from the king. It displayed a marked friendliness to all, except Macaire, whom it attacked at every opportunity. This behavior, coupled with Aubry's continued absence, aroused the court's suspicions. Finally, the king ordered a test. When the dog refused food offered by Macaire, accepting it from another hand, the fact was taken as an indicator of guilt sufficient to warrant a duel. The man was provided with staff and shield (as a knight would be when fighting a villein), and the dog with a barrel. The dog won the fight, nearly strangling its opponent with its paws, and Macaire was constrained to confess the truth and suffer capital punishment. Clearly, the justice of God had worked through the dog.[25]

The tale in its original form antedates the prohibitions against duels. The original twelfth-century romance, now lost, placed the story in Charlemagne's mythical court, adding many other extraneous ele-

[23] *Quaestiones Johanni Galli*, q. 80, 81, 89, 91, pp. 95-98, 110-13. Outside Paris, duels were still fought in Arras (1430) and Nancy (1482). See Jean Gaudemet, "Les ordalies au moyen âge: Doctrine, législation et pratique canoniques," *Recueils de la société Jean Bodin XVII/2, La Preuve: Moyen âge et temps modernes* (Bruxelles, 1965), p. 131.

[24] Bloch, *Medieval French Literature and Law*, pp. 13-53.

[25] Of the numerous versions of the tale, I have deliberately chosen to repeat the one told by a professional jurist. See Claude Expilly, *Plaidoyez de... C. Expilly, conseiller du roy et son advocat général au Parlement de Grenoble* (5th ed., Paris, 1631), pp. 199-200.

ments. The attribution to the late fourteenth century and the court of Charles V first appeared only in the Renaissance. But whether the king was Charles the Great or Charles V mattered little. The story went through several translations and versions. In time, the mythical Carolingian elements disappeared, leaving only the dog and the man. What mattered was that even in the extreme case when no one would champion the dead but a dog, justice could prevail through the judicial duel.[26] Various authors from the sixteenth to the eighteenth century repeated the tale time and again, none of them doubting its historicity.[27]

Obviously, the use of ritual on so solemn an occasion was intrinsic to the validity of the procedure. One does not call upon the Almighty to pronounce sentence in a casual manner. And yet, symbolic gestures formed part also of the daily routine of the courthouse. Ritual behavior was limited neither to criminal matters nor to problematic issues of proof. It could be found in the most trivial of civil litigation. In Amiens, a man declaring bankruptcy had to throw his hat on the floor. In the Paris area, a litigant contesting the truthfulness of his opponent's witness had to hold him by the edge of his robe while challenging the testimony. In Lille, all oaths had to be taken with the right hand laid upon the saint's relics, thumb folded under the palm.[28] A deliberate, stately formalism informed all courthouse behavior and activity.[29]

This formalism can be detected beyond the realm of gestures and dramatic actions. Its most obvious expression surfaces in the most basic mode of judicial action at the time, namely in speech. Speech in a high medieval French court was strictly formulaic, any departure from its rigid rules losing the case to the litigant. Every word uttered had to be within the prescribed forms and in the prescribed order. Thus speech functioned somewhat like another gesture rather than a means of simple communication. It was supposed not only to transmit facts and accusations, but to do so within a specific form that endowed those facts with a transcendent validity.

---

[26] J. Viscardi, *Le chien de Montargis: Etude de folklore juridique* (Paris, 1932), pp. 54-61.

[27] *Ibid.*, pp. 61-118.

[28] *Coutumes locales du bailliage d'Amiens*, ed. A. Bouthors, 2 vols. (Amiens, 1845), 1:291; "Livre des Constitucions," art. 60, p. 70; *Le livre Roisin: Coutumier lillois de la fin du XIIIe siècle*, ed. Raymond Monier (Paris, 1932), p. 35.

[29] For the central importance of gestures in medieval rituals and their magic efficacy, see J.-Cl. Schmitt, *La raison des gestes dans l'Occident médiéval* (Paris, 1990), pp. 321-29.

Still, the constant use of specific speech formulae does not necessarily constitute a ritual, as these formulae did not form a prescribed and inevitable continuum of dramatic expressions charged with an unalterable symbolic meaning. Formalism limited the litigants' options in court, but did not abolish them. Thus, when faced with adverse testimony, one could challenge or accept the witness. At the same time, the specific formulae chosen for use in each case, if correctly pronounced and used, possessed an efficacy very much akin to that of many secular rituals.

While a great deal of formalized courthouse behavior passed away together with the disappearance of the ordeal, the spoken word came to replace the gesture. Speech formulae worked very much as 'audial gestures,' carrying the same efficacy as the visual acts. Not that speech formulae in court were any innovation. Like all legal rituals, their roots were deeply embedded in early medieval practice. The developments of the thirteenth century first cast speech formulae into a role of unprecedented importance, and then made them lapse into archaism and obscurity. The banning of ordeals was not the main force causing the rise of oral formalism. Paradoxically, the growth of literacy and the writing of customs worked here, as in all other realms of customary law, to preserve and enshrine the oral element. Rigid oral formalism necessarily depended upon knowledge of the myriad of existent formulae, and the appearance of vernacular handbooks listing them was essential for their effective use. Eventually the written word would replace the spoken formula, but this development was only a second stage of judicial literacy.

Formal oaths were only a small part of the overwhelming variety of formulae used in pleading during the thirteenth and fourteenth centuries.[30] The challenge to a judicial duel, or "words of battle"[31] depended upon the specific accusation, but in every case the challenge had to end with clearly-phrased formula: "And I stand ready to prove [it] by my body against his and to render him either dead or vanquished at an agreed upon time."[32] The refutation of an accusation in

---

[30] Concerning oaths, see Bongert, *Recherches sur les cours laïques*, pp. 205-10.

[31] "Verba duelli," *Summa de legibus Normandiae* part 2, ch. 67, in *Coutumiers de Normandie*, 2:168-69; "tex mots font bataille", *Livre de jostice*, bk. 19, 10:3, p. 292; Heinrich Brunner, "Wort und Form im altfranzösischen Prozess," *Sitzungsberichte der philosophisch-historischen Classe der kaiserlichen Akademie der Wissenschaften* 57 (1867), 700-701.

[32] "Je suis... prest et apareillié de mostrer li de mon cors contre le sien et de rendre le mort ou recreant en une houre dou jour," *Abrégé du livre des assises de la Cour des Bourgeois* part 2, ch. 26, in *Assises de Jérusalem*, 2:336; cf. "Je te fierai en I

Normandy was equally rigid: "I have not caused you this harm, and he who testifies to it neither saw nor heard [it], which I am prepared to vindicate."[33] Subsequently, the defendant had to disprove the charge *verbo ad verbum*, following the same order of words as the charge.[34]

Every accusation, denial, argument and counter-argument had to be advanced in a strictly formulaic manner, or the case was lost. "Often one loses his plea for speaking foolishly," cautioned the *Chronique de Bertrand du Guesclin.*[35] Beaumanoir warned lawyers that their first duty was to listen without being moved, for a man angered easily lost his precision.[36] In Normandy one was fined for foolish or wrong speech (*stultiloquium* or *mesdictum*), and in Lille an intervention (*entrepresure*) lost the case.[37]

The danger of speaking carelessly was common to all, judges not excepted. "One must take great care when rendering judgment by which words one does so," cautioned Fontaines. Indeed, if one of the judges began his verdict by the words "I say so by right" rather than "all present say by right" in the seigneurial courts of Vermandois, the losing party could challenge him with the words "and who follows you?" In which case all other concurring judges had to voice their support openly. If the judge used the second formula, tacit consent sufficed, and no challenge was possible.[38] Challenging a sentence meant challenging the judges to a duel. The judge who rashly took sole responsibility for a sentence could thus find himself as the only one facing a duel against the challenger.[39]

---

champs mort ou recreant," *Ancien Coutumier de Bourgogne*, ed. M.A.J. Marnier (Paris, 1858), ch. 3, p. 6. Though the laws of the Crusader states evolved in different directions from the original European customs, in the matter of procedure they adhered strictly to the archaic formulae. The similarity between these formulae and the ones used in France in the thirteenth century is eloquent proof of the durability of such forms.

[33] "Istam lesionem tibi non feci et iste qui super hoc testem se constituit, nec vidit nec audivit quod partus sum desresnare." *Summa de legibus Normandiae*, part 2, ch. 84, in *Coutumiers de Normandie*, 2:200.

[34] *Recueil de jugements de l'échiquier de Normandie au 13e siècle, 1207-1270*, ed. Léopold Delisle (Paris, 1864), pp. 29-30.

[35] Jean Cuvelier, *Chronique de Bertrand du Guesclin*, ed. E. Charrière, 2 vols. (Paris, 1839), 2:259, v. 20914.

[36] *CB*, art. 183, 1:92.

[37] L. Delisle, "Des revenus publics en Normandie au XIIe siècle," *Bibliothèque de l'école des chartes*, 3e ser., 3 (1851-52), 117; "... à le loy et al usage de cheste ville, en plaidiant, on piert et waigne par entrepresure..." *Livre Roisin*, p. 35.

[38] *CF*, 22:18, pp. 299-300.

[39] Jean d'Ibelin, *Assises de la haute cour*, ch. 110, in *Assises de Jérusalem*, 1:180-82.

The exact oath formula of a witness was the primary guarantee to the validity of his words. If he stumbled, his testimony lost its value.[40] As late as the latter part of the fourteenth century, Jacques d'Ableiges counselled judges to watch witnesses taking an oath: did they blanch, blush, or stammer?[41] Furthermore, the words in which the witness couched his facts could also invalidate it. Should he state "I know it" his words could be challenged: "How do you know it?" And if he answered "I have heard it said by so-and-so," his testimony was invalid. Certainly, in order to be valid eyewitness testimony had to be preceded by the words "I was present and saw it."[42]

The use and preservation of exact formulae was aided by specific mnemonic devices. Often, the words were couched in an alliterative or rhymed form. Thus, causing irreparable physical harm to someone was *fere mort ou mehaing*, and living together was living *à pain et à pot*. An accusation of deliberate murder claimed that the deed was done *par son tret et par son fet et par son pourchas...* and common knowledge was defined as being *à la veue et à la seue du commun.* Standard pairs of synonymous terms, such *tenir et garder, pouvoir et devoir, estans et manans,* served a similar function.[43] The use of binomial expressions is common in legal language, both medieval and modern, and is intrinsic to the formulaic character of written legal language as well.[44]

The basic principle behind this formalism was that the court was to go upon the spoken word, precisely as said, and not necessarily as intended. "The court must regard and recognize only the words that are said."[45] All statements in court had to end with the formal 'signature' submitting them to the court and stating that these were the words of which the court was to take cognizance. Once this was done, the words were irreversible and unalterable. Nothing could be added or subtracted from the original statement, nor could it be retracted

---

[40] Brunner, "Wort und Form," 732; *CB*, art. 1228, 2:134-35; *Ancien Coutumier de Bourgogne*, ch. 2, pp. 3-4.

[41] *GC*, p. 600.

[42] *CB*, art. 1234, 2:138-39.

[43] Leena Löfstedt, "Après une lecture des *Coutumes* de Philippe de Beaumanoir," *Neuphilologische Mitteilungen* 85 (1984), 28-30; see also Eadem, "Le verbe du droit français: Pléonasmes d'origine latine," *Ibid.* 86 (1985), 89-99.

[44] See Brenda Danet and Bryna Bogoch, "From Oral Ceremony to Written Document: The Transitional Language of Anglo-Saxon Wills," *Language and Communication*, forthcoming.

[45] "La court ne doit faire esgart ne counissance que des parolles que l'on dit." *La clef des Assises de la Haute Cour dou Royaume de Jérusalem et de Chypre*, art. 124, in *Assises de Jérusalem*, 1:588. Cf. Brunner, "Wort und Form," 661.

without incurring a fine.[46] If one attempted to deliver a second version different from the first, the first words uttered in court stood and the subsequent statement was null. The precise spoken word became the essence of the case, the point upon which all judgment revolved.

Occasionally a small mistake could cost a life. This was especially true in the kingdom of Jerusalem, where formalism survived in a much more stringent form than in Europe. In some formulae used to challenge an adversary to judicial duel, the plaintiff stated, after phrasing his accusation: "And if you wish to deny it, I stand ready to prove [it] to you by my body against yours... and to render you either dead or vanquished at an agreed upon time."[47] If the challenger said "dead *and* vanquished" instead of "dead *or* vanquished" he had to kill his adversary, not merely to vanquish, in order to win the case. More often, though, the thoughtless speaker automatically lost only the case.[48] A defendant asking for a day's postponement in 1344 without using the proper formula was fined for infraction of local ordinances and lost the case, for he was not allowed to give his answer on the following day. His automatically incriminating and informal request for a delay had decided the case against him. Technically, the judge asserted that an informal request was tantamount to a refusal to answer the charge.[49] While in this case the man was "caught by his word" (*pris à point, pris à parole*) by the authorities, opponents in court were always on the alert for mistakes one could challenge, thus winning the case on a formality.

This perception allowed the one exception within the inexorably formal development of a case. A man's fate hinged upon his own actions and words, but not necessarily those of another. While no man could 'amend' his words, those of his lawyer could be amended or changed. "He can certainly amend or disavow the word of his advocate" stated Jean des Marès.[50] The only way one could prevent one's own slips of tongue from losing a case was by retaining, at the beginning of one's plea, the right to amend one's own words, or those of

[46] "... puis les paroles sont couchies en jugement, l'en n'i puet riens metre ne oster." *CB*, art. 180, 1:91-92; Cf. *Olim*, 2:100.

[47] Jean d'Ibelin, *Assises de la haute cour*, ch. 90, in *Assises de Jérusalem*, 1:144-45.

[48] Brunner, "Wort und Form," 671-80.

[49] *Olim*, 2:771-72. Brunner, "Wort und Form," 679-80.

[50] "Cil qui parle de sa querelle, ne se puet pas desadvoüer, mes il puet bien amender ou desadvoüer la parole de son advocat," Jean des Marès, *Coutumes tenues toutes notoires*, 2:67; *CB*, art. 182, 1:92; *CF*, 9:8, p. 64. While this loophole existed already in the thirteenth century, its survival, alone among formulaic principles, a century later in the notes of des Marès indicates a growing trend of flexibility.

one's witnesses. Nevertheless, even the claim of this guarantee had to be phrased specifically: "I hold back my mistakes, and I will amend my words until the sentence." "I hold back [the witnesses'] mistakes until the oath, so that if one of them fails in his words, I would like to have license to amend them."[51]

Behind the legal principle lay a much deeper cultural perception of the importance of the word as a commitment also beyond the legal sphere. Proverbs such as "Once the word flies away, it can never be recalled"[52] were axiomatic truths in a society that equated a man's word with his honor. In court, moreover, one spoke under oath to tell the truth, so that any vacillation was akin to perjury.[53] The principle applied not only to willfully false testimony or accusation, but even to procedural errors, such as using the wrong name in an accusation or stumbling over a particle of speech. The spoken word had assumed the character of an ordeal: incorrect speech was not an accident, but once more the proof, through the immanence of justice, of the speaker's guilt.

The principle had several ramifications. The minute attention paid to the written record of the spoken word was perhaps the most important one. If the word captured the essence of the case, the word must be preserved in its exact form. By the same token, once taken down in writing, it was unchallengeable. The record stood not as a written text the authority of which derived from its literate nature. To the contrary: it was authoritative precisely because it captured the oral text. A charter produced in evidence could be challenged, the record could not: "Nothing can be done against the record."[54] Such was the insistence upon the *ipsissima verba* of the speaker in court, that more than a century after formalism had disappeared scribes were still careful to preserve the occasionally colloquial flavor of the evidence. Even in ecclesiastical courts, where the evidence heard in French was immediately taken down in Latin, we find scribes who, incapable of producing an exact translation on the spot, preferred to introduce

[51] "Je retient mon mès-dit, si amenderai adès ma paroles jusque à iugement." "Et si reting lor mesdit iusqu'au seirement. Ce est à dire que se aucuns déffailloit de sa paroles, ie vodroie havoir loisir de l'amender." *Ancien Coutumier de Bourgogne*, chs. 1,2, pp. 3-4.

[52] Leroux de Lincy, *Le livre des proverbes français*, 2:368.

[53] *CF*, 5:7; Brunner, "Wort und Form," 682.

[54] "Ne contre recort ne puet-en riens fere," *CF*, 21:33; Brunner, "Wort und Form," 664.

gallice the very words of the witness.[55] The protocol was the facsimile of the spoken word.[56]

In an age when the visible judgment of God had ceased to be an acceptable mode of proof, it was still manifested in other forms. Just as human prowess was evidence of the truth in the duel, human verbal dexterity was an audible proof of the same. The abolition of ordeals in no way excluded supernatural justice from human courts, for even an honest mistake could carry the same meaning and consequences as the loss of a trial by battle. Though the formulae in use in no way invoked heavenly intervention, justice was still immanent in the form, even after the religious element had been banned from the courthouse.

The shift in the Roman-influenced laws of procedure was crucial in changing this approach. The introduction of proof by testimony, circumstantial evidence, and confession put an end to strict formalism. It was impossible, for example, to reconcile the extraction of confessions by torture with the principle that only the first words uttered in court mattered, for the original declarations were almost invariably denials of guilt. If one compares the thirteenth-century texts with those written towards the end of the fourteenth, the diminution in the number of oral formulae is striking. Jacques d'Ableiges, whose *Grand Coutumier de France* devoted a great deal of space to procedure, reflected this trend. Some spoken formulae remained, but only in civil cases, and even then in very few and specific ones. Thus, d'Ableiges cautioned people suing at the Parlement who had more than one adversary against merely stating "I hereby present myself against all my adversaries," since this formula allowed any opponent not specifically named to insist that the speaker was in default against him.[57] By contrast, his manual could well have been used as a stock of written formulae, mostly not for the use of the litigants, but of court authorities. Specific formulae for pronouncing a sentence, for declaring an absentee in default or for banishing him and for many other purposes appeared in the text. All were to be applied in writing. By the late fourteenth century the written element in court procedure was no longer only evidence and record. The written sentence was not merely a visible facsimile of the oral verdict, but the very essence of the

[55] Thus, for example, in 1488 a witness testifying in a paternity suit related how he had found the couple together, "et dixit gallice elle est devenue rouge comme ung coq." AN, Z^{10} 19, fol. 62ro.

[56] For the close relationship between oral and written legal language, see Danet and Bogoch, "From Oral Ceremony to Written Document."

[57] *GC*, p. 689.

decision. Like a royal charter, the written word carried its own authority.

Late fourteenth-century court records verify this picture. No verbal formulae were used in the criminal cases recorded by the Châtelet of Paris between 1388 and 1392. The accused spoke in their own voices and words, occasionally using colloquial terms and explaining them to the court. A thief confessing to his activities claimed he and his band-members had gone on the road "with the intention of making a gain." The notary recording the case added "by gain he means stealing."[58]

The written word had gained added importance. Confessions were not valid until they had been written down, read aloud in court to the accused, and approved by him.[59] The Parlement of Paris at the time accepted not only confessions, but also testimony in written form. Drafts and records of inquests were accepted as evidence (though each party could still insist upon an oral examination of the other's witnesses), written exceptions, answers, and mostly, trial protocols, were all presented and accepted in court.[60] In many cases simple written reports presented by professional examiners took the place of sworn oral evidence. Royal remissions were granted and later registered in written form, and their presentation in court depended upon the production of the written document of which the pardon consisted.[61]

This development resulted from insistence upon the validity of court records. As of the second half of the thirteenth century, it became usual to base one's claims in court upon precedents. Sometime the plaintiffs would cite an actual case, but in other cases they simply maintained that 'it is the custom of this court' to judge in such a manner. As time passed, precedents became more and more specific, and it was necessary to refer to court records, still sketchy at the time, in order to verify claims to precedent. From being the replica of the oral court-case and the ultimate proof of its resolution, the record became a written basis for subsequent rulings.[62] Already the customal authors

---

[58] "... et appelle le mot de gaignier, embler." *Registre criminel du Châtelet de Paris*, ed. H. Duplès-Agier, 2 vols. (Paris, 1861-64), 1:70.

[59] "Après lesquelles confessions ainsi faites par ycellui... & recitées en la presence de lui..." *Ibid.*, 1:7; "Jehanne de Brigue... par serement... continue & persevera ès confessions par elle derrenierement faites, qui lui furent leues mot apès autre... & semblablement les autres confessions cy-dessus escriptes... lesqueles lui furent leues..." *Ibid.*, 2:310.

[60] E.g. AN X^{2a} 12, fol. 44ro. John P. Dawson, *A History of Lay Judges* (Cambridge, Mass., 1960), p. 52.

[61] For the procedure of granting remissions, see above, p.50.

[62] Sergène, "Le précédent judiciaire."

of the late thirteenth century cited precedents as the basis for general rules of jurisprudence, and by the fourteenth century jurists began keeping their own private collections of court decisions for future reference. Those of Jean le Coq in the fourteenth century and Gui Pape in the fifteenth became extremely popular among lawyers as manual collections of precedents.[63]

This trend could occasionally lower the prestige of the spoken word. In 1392 the Parlement adjudicated an appeal of a boundary dispute sentence from Tournai. The dispute between the monastery of Saint-Nicolas-des-Prés in Tournai and the lady of Ere and Rasse had originally been determined by a local form of inquest, a *cerquemanage*. According to this procedure, common in the area between Lille, Valenciennes, and Cambrai, a number of the oldest men living in the neighborhood (*circa manentes*) were asked to indicate the boundary line, without resorting to any written charter.[64] As the men of Tournai testified in Paris, "they say that according to the custom the elders place staffs and make the *cerqueminage*, and in this case it is not customary to show titles."[65] When the monastery appealed, the Parlement rejected the sentence of the *cerquemaneurs* on the grounds that written evidence must prevail over an oral statement, even that of experts.[66] Jean Bacquet related an almost-contemporary decision corroborating this attitude. In 1388 the canons of Notre-Dame-des-Champs in Paris claimed the right of medium justice. Though they had witnesses, the Parlement insisted that they produce charters to validate their claim.[67]

Finally, the one sacral object in court also assumed written form. While some thirteenth-century customals (especially the northern ones of Tournai and Lille) still specified that oaths in court were to be taken on the relics of a saint, by the late fourteenth century trial protocols

---

[63] See above, p. 13.

[64] E.M. Meijers, "Cerquemanage," in *Etudes d'histoire du droit*, 1:179-184.

[65] "Diesnt que par la coustume les anciens giettent bastons et font le cerqueminage, et en ce case n'en a point accoustume de monstrer tiltres," AN, X[1a] 1477, fol. 8[ro-vo], 19-30, 191.

[66] Two contemporary jurists related the case: Jean le Coq in Paris supported the position of the Parlement. Jean Boutillier in Tournai, though fully aware of the sentence, still included the *cerquemanage* in his *Somme rural* as a valid procedure. *Quaestiones Johannis Galli*, pp. 328-30; *SR*, pp. 366-68; van Dievoet, *Jehan Boutillier*, pp. 204-206.

[67] Jean Bacquet, "Traicte des droicts de iustice: Haute, moyenne, et basse," *Les Oeuvres de Iean Bacquet, advocat du roy...* (Paris, 1630), pp. 16-17. Interestingly enough Bacquet himself dissented, claiming that testimony concerning rights of justice and proving ancient practice from times immemorial was sufficient proof.

show that all oaths were on the Gospels.[68] One cannot connect this change with any decline in the respect accorded to relics. The change resided in the altered attitude towards the written text. Writings had come to assume a symbolic and evidentiary role parallel to that of objects and people within the courthouse in every type of procedure and process. They were proof not only of facts, but also of the immanent justice of God. Even the holy object which still endowed oaths with validity had to be a written text.

The disappearance of formalism inevitably imbued court procedure with a new content. Formalism had not been a veneer, but an integral part of court procedures. The effects of the change were to set the judged apart from the judges. The knowledge and proper use of formulae gave the speaker a certain control over his trial, a control he lost once the formulae became the property of the court alone. One could no longer, for example, abort a case by a deliberate slip of tongue, or win it by catching an opponent by his spoken word.[69] Formalism was the oral expression of courthouse rituals, and its decline heralded the gradual disappearance of the community of legal consent it had created. The courthouse was still the meeting-ground of judge and judged, but now the two spoke two different languages, one unstructured and informal, the other increasingly technical and obscure. The advocates took over as interpreters. While it was still possible to argue a case oneself by the late fourteenth century, it was becoming progressively more dangerous to do so.[70]

Professionalization affected not only the growing class of lawyers. The transition from a lay group of judges to a single, professional judge was both contemporary and intimately tied to the death of the courthouse ritual. Thirteenth- and fourteenth-century customals still spoke of local laymen acting as judges, or rather, as law-finders and appliers, who could be challenged to a judicial duel by a disgruntled litigant if they stumbled over their words, or fined if they rendered the wrong verdict. Guillaume du Breuil still referred to *homines judicantes*, as distinct from *judices* in areas of feudal jurisdiction.[71] On

---

[68] *CF*, p. 37; *Le livre Roisin*, pp. 32-37; *Registre criminel du Châtelet*, 1:137: "Lequel prisonnier... sur ce juré aus sains Evangiles de Dieu de dire verité de tout ce qui lui sera demandé..."; "laquele... ot fait serement aus sains Evangiles de Dieu que elle diroit verité..." *Ibid.*, 2:297. In other cases the record merely stated that the suspect was questioned "par serement," (*Ibid.*, 1:255 and *passim*).

[69] Brunner, "Wort und Form," 696.

[70] *GC*, pp. 399-400.

[71] *Stylus curie parlamenti*, pp. 49-50, 159-60.

the evidence of the customals, lay judges acted in two capacities. As of the middle of the thirteenth century they could be summoned to answer the *enquêtes par turbe* concerning the nature of local customs. But even earlier they actually sat in court, summoned by their lords to do court duty and judge their fellows. Their sentences were collective, both in the sense that they were pronounced in an assize rather than individually, and in the sense that they relied upon the common knowledge of local custom.

Lay judges, however, were part and parcel of the feudal system of justice, and the spread of royal authority tended increasingly to replace them with salaried professionals, often strangers to their area of jurisdiction.[72] The intimacy of a local court, where judges, litigants, and witnesses all knew each other, spoke the same language and shared the same legal tradition could not survive in the world of professional law, and this world became increasingly dominant towards the fifteenth century.

Like many other secular rituals, courthouse procedures both reflected certain perceptions and reinforced them by continual repetition. Those perceptions were neither the elitist ideas of professional jurists nor a folklorist substratum of popular belief. As noted earlier, the judges in the local courts described in customals were not a professional elite in any sense of the word. Nor were the professional administrators, employed by the crown, much better trained. Though possessing the knowledge acquired over many years of practice, none of them had any legal training setting him apart from the people he judged. As late as the fifteenth century, any man with a bachelor's degree in arts practicing the law could call himself *maître* in court.[73] Even in the Parlement, the highest court of the realm, the paramount criterion for acceptance was familial, rather than professional qualifications.[74] Only in 1499 did King Louis XII formally order that all incoming magistrates be subject to an examination prior to their admission.[75] Sitting in judgment over others, then, was not a matter of learning, but of status. Consequently, in the courts of free people there

[72] Dawson, *Lay Judges*, pp. 60-69.

[73] Concerning the training of lawyers in the late medieval northern France see Bernard Guenée, *Tribunaux et gens de justice dans le bailliage de Senlis à la fin du moyen âge* (Strasbourg, 1963), pp. 186-96.

[74] Françoise Autrand, *Naissance d'un grand corps de l'état. Les gens du Parlement de Paris, 1345-1454* (Paris, 1981).

[75] J.H. Shennan, *The Parlement of Paris* (Ithaca, N.Y., 1968) p. 136.

was often very little social and professional distance between the permanent members of the court and those present for a specific trial.

The courthouse thus expressed a certain community of consent. The role of laymen as litigants, witnesses and law-finders was often as crucial to the success or failure of a case as that of the 'professionals', if not more so. Their active participation through ordeals and spoken formulae underlined the fact that the courthouse was primarily their own tool of dispute settlement, not only the government's. Thirteenth-century customals were written as manuals for laymen wishing to manipulate the law for their own purposes, an indication of the common awareness, shared by jurists and laymen alike, of the need for such literature. The normative community remained intact as long as laymen in court took their fate in their own hands by means of positive participation.

Though this type of activity was invariably an expression of dissension—accusations, denials, and challenges—it was based upon a specific commitment to consensus. When the losing party insisted that all judges be unanimous in their sentence, offering if necessary to fight a duel against each and every one of them,[76] he was acting not only in accordance with local custom, but also with a certain feeling that unanimity was the one indisputable proof of justice. Before the middle of the thirteenth century, a witness could quite openly state before a Parlement inquest that a small-town murderer had been caught and hung "because the common knowledge of the countryside accused him."[77] The same feeling underlay the use of ordeals in small communities.[78] The intrinsic efficacy of every ritual gesture, every formulaic utterance, depended absolutely upon this accord. The insistence upon the faultless performance of these formulae, reiterated time and again, served further to strengthen the underlying demand for agreement. The form possessed its own intrinsic value, so that a flawed performance challenged the basic, universally accepted rules of the world of the court.

Finally, courthouse rituals and formalism stood as symbols of a certain perception of justice. Judicial and theological authorities made the clear distinction between human and natural law. If one's cause

---

[76] *CF*, ch. 22, pp. 285-315. cf. above, p. 63.

[77] "... quia fama patrie ipsum accusabat." *Actes du Parlement de Paris*, 1:cccv. The murderer had killed a man and his mother for love of the victim's wife, fled and was captured. There was obviously no doubt as to the killer's identity in this case.

[78] Brown, "Society and the Supernatural," 138-39.

could be vindicated by such 'objective' external pieces of evidence as the faultless recitation of an oath or the victory in a duel, justice was no longer a matter of purely human proof. The community of mutual consent was based upon a sense of all-pervasive justice that governed the human world, but stood above its petty divisions and rivalries.

The gradual disappearance of courthouse ritual and formalism was one facet of the metamorphosis of this community. The growth of royal authority, the influence of Roman and canon law, both requiring stringent professional training and relying upon a highly technical vocabulary, all served to create a gap between laymen and professionals, litigants and authorities. The sharp rise in litigation fees and costs in the fifteenth century was at one and the same time the result of this growing alienation and a furthering cause of the same process.[79]

The authoritative redaction of customary law in the fifteenth and sixteenth centuries completed the process. By stamping customs with a governmental seal of approval, the crown endowed the formal written version with an authority derived from above, and not from the consent of the judged. The power to edit, approve, or abrogate customs was not quite the power to legislate, but in practice it was closely akin to it. Henceforth, custom was determined by the written, government-approved version, and lay elements no longer contributed to its formation.

[79] For a comparison of court costs before the Parlement of Paris, see for the fourteenth century Ferdinand Lot, "Des frais de justice au XIVe siècle," *Bibliothèque de l'école des chartes* 34 (1873), 207-11, citing a 1375 case which cost in total £10 6s. 4d. *parisis*. A century later Guenée, *Tribunaux et gens de justice*, pp. 252-53, estimated the cost of a trial in the same court between £100 and £500 *parisis*. For trial costs in the early modern period, see Alfred Soman, "Deviance and Criminal Justice in Western Europe, 1300-1800: An Essay in Structure," *Criminal Justice History* 1 (1980), 10-11.

THE CULTURAL CONTEXT

CHAPTER FIVE

FOLKLORE AND SYMBOLIC FUNCTIONS IN MEDIEVAL LEGAL RITUALS

1. Popular Elements and Legal Rituals

The law of late medieval France was steeped in extra-judicial, partially popular influences. As might be expected, the same characteristics manifested themselves also in the visual, dramatic expressions of the law, namely legal rituals. It is typical of the time that while many of these rites took place inside the courthouse, many more were conducted within the public sphere of open urban spaces. Whether criminal or civil, legal rituals no less than texts reflected the culture of the time to a marked degree. They assimilated and exhibited a merging of world-views and perceptions. Legal rituals, it must be remembered, were decreed by judges carrying in their minds a double tradition of learning and practical jurisprudence. They were also staged by political authorities, be they royal or urban, with the specific aim of exhibiting the power and majesty of the law. But for these rituals to be effective, they had to take into account also two other elements. The 'participants' or sufferers, as the case may be, of these rituals had to cooperate in enacting a public drama. And the public watching legal rituals was, despite its ostensible passivity, perhaps the most important element in the entire picture. Unless the spectacle spoke the language of the audience, used its symbols and cultural perceptions, the entire purpose of the exercise was lost. The judge in his gallery viewing a stage set at his orders and the spectator in the crowd looking, jostling and being jostled, shouting assent or dissent, were both participants in the legal drama.

By the same token, the line demarcating judicial folklore from institutional justice can be vague indeed on occasion. This vagueness did not result from inadequate documentation. In many cases the 'doing of justice' was not a matter for professionals or magistrates alone. Local communities could sometimes formally act as plaintiffs, though very often they represented the normative consensus rather than one side in an adversary action. The fissure ran not between judges and judged, but between those within the pale, judges and plaintiffs alike, and those beyond it. The very responsibility for justice could become a communal enterprise. Sometimes the formal authorities stood aside, as in the case of a *charivari*, letting village justice take its course. But more often judges and community could work together, expressing shared values and norms through legal rituals.

As in the case of law, the folklore integrated in legal rituals was twofold. On the one hand, there were the relics of ancient beliefs preserved like fossils in the rock of usage. On the other, the living folklore of the later middle ages played a central role in the formation of many legal rituals. Clearly, one cannot lump the tradition of hanging a thief, going back to Tacitus' Germans, with the tradition of suing noxious pests, first apparent in the late fourteenth century. In the eras that passed between the emergence of one and the other the first became translated into a governmental gesture, while the second was still largely a matter of popular initiative in the sixteenth century.

Thus, legal rituals in the late middle ages were neither a tool of 'authorities', nor simply a relic of earlier 'popular' traditions. They were based upon a whole stratum of commonly-held cultural associations pertaining to the human body, human society, nature, and the universe. Hence, they could and were used to enunciate, in a visual, dramatic way, extra-legal norms and beliefs in all those fields. The sum total of these norms could serve as a framework for the articulation of any micro-society's self-perception, regarding its own structure and place within the larger configurations of humanity and the world. By fashioning its justice, by including specific elements and spectacularly excluding others, each community shaped and re-shaped itself with every public punitive ritual. Thus, legal rituals based upon certain deeply-rooted ideas concerning the nature of justice had to reflect those same ideas in a visible form. The enunciation of norms, the definition of the boundaries of the normative community, and the ostentation of justice might not have been the declared aims of the system, but they were certainly its result. Given the nature of the structure, it was an inevitable consequence.

There was a certain tension within this triad of trends. Self-definition, based upon standards deriving from commonly shared societal norms, was by its very nature an introspective exercise. The drawing of boundaries inevitably left certain categories outside the normative community. Whether these categories belonged to people born outside, such as women or Jews, or to those who had extraneity forced upon them, such as heinous criminals, mattered little. They were outside, beyond the pale of the normative community. By contrast, the perception of justice as a universal force tended to draw all of nature into one framework. The boundaries of this conceptual structure were coterminous with the limits of existence, sometimes stretching even beyond the realm of biological life. No one—not a Jew, not a bee, not even a ghost—was beyond the reach of this type of justice. Nor was this an abstraction born out of folk-legends. Trials of animals and of dead people did take place in human courts, very much in the same manner as the trials of living human beings.

The simplest way of resolving the tension between limitation and universalism is to ascribe each trend to a different cultural tradition. As all its manifestations show, the perception of all-encompassing justice obviously drew its life from a popular source. At the same time, the trend of circumscription, of boundary-drawing, of turning inwards was closely tied to thirteenth-century intellectual endeavors and to their gradual enforcement upon popular strata. Unfortunately, the judicial evidence does not fit this theory, as many legal rituals aimed at segregating categories and separating criminals from society can be traced to popular, non-scholastic sources. Furthermore, we have seen already that scholastic philosophy enthusiastically accepted the premise that justice affected also the non-human physical universe.[1] Nor can a case be made for a chronological development, from an earlier popular approach to a later learned one. Both trends were fed by learned and popular attitudes alike, and both were very much in evidence during the fourteenth and fifteenth centuries. In actual fact, they did not contradict one another. To the contrary, they complemented each other, and the tension between them is largely a matter of faulty modern perception.

A great deal of the cultural content of late medieval legal rituals did not originate necessarily from popular strata, but from a merging of popular and elite perceptions. Often both learned and popular manifestations sprang from the same set of social and economic circumstances. In this sense, it is impossible to dissociate the courthouse, the pillory and the gallows from either pulpit or marketplace, for the former so often served as a link between the two traditions that one

[1] See above, p. 20.

cannot disentangle the different strands. This melding of cultural trends can be found also outside the scope of attitudes towards socially extraneous elements. There was a mixture of traditions, of classical anatomy and late medieval physiological perceptions even in simple punitive acts, such as the horrifyingly common lopping of ears.

It was precisely this intermediate character of legal rituals, composite creations of the interactions of cultures and people of different strata, that made them so effective. The reliance upon a living cultural background that was neither learned nor popular, but both, was just as important as the preservation of ancient symbols. If court activity exhibited justice as a universal power, and this power could legally be claimed by those who held lordship, the equation could very well serve the authorities. In an age when kings were as busy defining the boundaries and identities of their kingdoms as any small community might be concerned with its own borders, the extrusion of alien elements suited both rulers and ruled.

Self-definition, whether on a national or a communal level, was hardly a function of law alone. But law and legal rituals were not separate from all other developments of the period. They were part of state-building and institutional growth, but they were also part of an entire cultural context expressing all strata and groups of society. Furthermore, within this context legal rituals served a number of socio-symbolic functions. They worked in the two opposite directions we have mentioned: they were ejective, liminalizing forces, and at the same time, integrative powers.

2. Legal Rituals and Their Functions

A. Liminalization

Ritualism and symbolic functions were an intrinsic part of European law as far back as the sixth century. Though found everywhere within the early medieval codes, the example of the *Chrenecruda* perhaps best illustrates this trait. According to the earliest version of the *Lex Salica*, a killer unable to compensate his victim's kindred was made to perform a symbolic ritual of divestiture. He was to enter his own house and collect in his fist mud from the four corners. Then he had to stand on the doorstep, facing inwards, and throw the earth with his left hand over his shoulders on those of his kindred who would have to bear the burden of compensation. If any of those was even poorer than the killer, he had to throw the mud back. After this, the

Chrenecruda, as he was called, had to jump out over a fence in his shirt, beltless and unshod, carrying a staff in his hand.[2]

What puzzles the modern legal historian in this ritual is the futility and senselessness embodied in the gesture. It neither ensured compensation for the victim's kindred nor directly punished the offender. Nevertheless, if we look at the procedure not as a failure to pay compensation, but as a ritual of divestiture of personality, transferring responsibility from a guilty individual to a kindred, it begins to make sense. As symbolic behavior, it possesses a clear-cut purpose.[3] While we are no longer able to interpret the meaning of every symbolic element in this legal ritual, it clearly dramatizes the social and moral imperatives at stake. The *Chrenecruda* first divested himself of the identity of his house, transferring it to his kindred and transmitting to them the responsibility for the *wergeld* he could not pay. But having done so, he also lost his identity within the community. The divestiture of outer clothing and shoes indicated his changed status, while the staff, often a symbol of authority and of the legal community, was in this case the mark of exclusion. The staff commonly appeared as the embodiment of the kindred in other Salian ceremonies of severance.[4] Finally, the excluded person literally put himself beyond the pale, by jumping over the fence with his staff, or kindred-symbol, in hand.

[2] *Pactus Legis Salicae*, ed. K.A. Eckhardt, *MGH LL* 4:1 (Leges nationum Germanicarum, Hanover, 1962), art. 58. For the relevance of this ritual in Merovingian times, see Franz Beyerle, "Über Normtypen und Erweiterungen der Lex Salica," *ZRG, GA* 44 (1924), 220-25; Ruth Schmidt-Wiegand, "Chrenecruda. Rechtwort und Formalakt der Merowingerzeit," *Festschrift für Gustaf Klemens Schmelzeisen*, ed. Hans-Wolf Thümmel (Stuttgart, 1980), pp. 252-73; Ekkehard Kaufman, "*Quod paganorum tempore observabant*. Ist der Titel 58 der Lex Salica (Pactus) eine Neuschöpfung der Merowinger?" *Sprache und Recht. Festschrift für Ruth Schmidt-Wiegand*, ed. Karl Hauck et al., 2 vols. (Berlin, 1986) 1:374-90.

[3] "[Der Missetäter] gab jedem einzelnen seine Persönlichkeit voll und ganz preis," Hans Fehr, "Über den Titel 58 der Lex Salica (De Chrene cruda)," *ZRG, GA* 27 (1906), 166. For an analysis of the *Chrenecruda* symbolism, see Emil Goldmann, *Chrenecruda. Studien zum Titel 58 der Lex Salica*, Deutschrechtliche Beiträge 13:1 (Heidelberg, 1931), esp. ch. 4, pp. 131-84.

[4] Thus, he who wished legally to cut himself off from his kindred had to appear in court (the *mallus*), break four alderwood staffs over his head, and throw the pieces to the four corners of the courtroom, declaring that he wished to dissociate himself from the oath, the inheritance, and all the interests of his kindred. *Lex Salica*, ed. K.A. Eckhardt *MGH LL* 4:2 (Leges nationum Germanicarum, Hanover, 1969), art. 94; See also art. 81, in which the appointment of an heir is done by throwing a staff at him in court. Ernst v. Moeller, "Die Rechtssitte des Stabbrechens," *ZRG, GA* 21 (1900), 28. For the general meaning of the staff in Germanic law, see von Amira, *Der Stab*.

The *Chrenecruda* was thus a man shorn of familial and communal identity. In the language of anthropology, he was a liminal figure, assuming this status through the intervention of the law. The tendency to use liminalization either as part of a criminal penalty or as the very essence of punishment is a constant in medieval law. As present-day medievalists have discovered, liminal states carried great significance in the community-conscious societies of the middle ages.[5] The legal use of liminality in punitive law, however, is probably the most salient of these phenomena.

Liminality, as defined by van Gennep and analyzed by Turner, is the central part of any rite of passage from one stage of life to another. It comes after the ritual subject has already been separated from society in his previous stage, and before his or her re-integration into the new role. It is an in-between stage, characterized by inversion, ambiguity, humility, and occasionally nakedness.

> The liminal state has frequently been likened to death; to being in the womb; to invisibility, darkness, bisexuality, and the wilderness. Liminars are stripped of status and authority, removed from a social structure maintained and sanctioned by power and force, and leveled to a homogeneous social state through discipline and ordeal. Their secular powerlessness may be compensated for by a sacred power, however—the power of the weak.... In this no-place and no-time that resists classification, the major classifications and categories of culture emerge within the integuments of myth, symbol, and ritual.[6]

Thus Victor Turner, summarizing his own perception of liminality. In so doing, he described many of the characteristics forced upon medieval criminals in the course of their punishment. Coercive pilgrimages were used as penal measures in northern France and the Low Countries in the later middle ages, for pilgrimage and punishment shared those traits pertaining to the state of liminality. According to the laws of many cities, criminals guilty of anything from homicide to false charges could be sent on a pilgrimage for a prescribed period, to a specific shrine. In order to ensure compliance, they were to bring back from the shrine a certificate of pilgrimage. Significantly, there was no

---

[5] See, for example, Patrick Geary, "L'humiliation des saints," *Annales E.S.C.* 34 (1979), 27-42, and Caroline W. Bynum, "Women's Stories, Women's Symbols: A Critique of Victor Turner's Theory of Liminality," in *Anthropology and the Study of Religion,* ed. Robert L. Moore and Frank E. Reynolds (Chicago, 1984), pp. 105-25.

[6] Victor Turner and Edith Turner, *Image and Pilgrimage in Christian Culture* (New York, 1978), pp. 249-50; See also Victor Turner, *The Ritual Process* (Chicago. 1969), pp. 94-96; Idem, *Dramas, Fields and Metaphors* (Ithaca, N.Y., 1974), p. 259.

correlation between the crime and the shrine of destination. What mattered was not how far one had to wander before expiating one's fault, but the duration of liminal time spent as punishment.[7]

The majority of criminals, however, were punished locally in a public ritual. Liminality played a central role in their drama even without resorting to geographic mobility. Divested in the end of clothes, symbols of office and status, reduced to the basic common denominator of Christians facing death, and reputed to possess an ambiguous supernatural power, they fitted remarkably well into Turner's scheme. Nor did the liminal status end with death, for the executed criminals remained unburied, thus also unintegrated even within the community of the decently buried dead. The use of symbolism, ritual, and common myths to articulate societal divisions is overwhelmingly clear in the public penal systems of late medieval Europe.

Whether temporary or permanent, the liminal status imposed upon offenders was a means of demarcating the boundaries between the normative community and those who had offended against it. Like any other mechanism of social control, legal processes could and did use imposed, coercive liminality. The purpose was twofold: the liminalization of an offender not only lessened his danger to normative society; it also drew by contrast the boundaries of the established community. But the offender's impact upon society did not cease once he was publicly branded as liminal. The very stance of humility and rolelessness, noted Turner, carried within it a power of its own. This power was no longer that of individual identity and actions, for the liminar became part of the ritual, his forces channeled into his role. His physical presence in the community's midst sharpened the ceremonially marked differences between him and them, his otherness emphasizing the moral and social coherence of all those within the pale of the normative community.

In this sense, the symbolic function of legal rituals stands out even more clearly than their social role. What mattered was not merely society's retribution, or even the redress of the balance of justice, for both could easily be privately achieved. The public, ceremonial character of medieval punitive law hinged not only upon its governmental

[7] Etienne van Cauwenbergh, *Les pèlerinages expiatoires et judiciaires dans le droit communal de la Belgique au moyen âge* (Louvain, 1922); Jan van Herwaarden, *Opgelegde bedevaarten: Een studie over de praktijk van opleggen van bedevaarten in de Nederlanden gedurende de late middeleeuwen* (Assen, 1978). For an anthropological interpretation of pilgrimages in general as liminal, see Turner and Turner, *Image and Pilgrimage*, pp. 1-39.

and coercive role, but also, on a deeper level, upon the fact that much of the punishment meted out by this law was also a transition into liminality. It was therefore publicly celebrated like any proper rite of passage. Publicity and liminality were inextricably tied together and mutually influential, for without a public ceremony one could not impose liminality. The very punitive value of liminality hinged upon its public character.

Legal rituals achieved this state by several means, the most common and recurrent of them being symbolic role inversion. Inversions appeared in a variety of punitive rituals. They set the tone of public executions, equally as important as the symbolism of state. They also informed a number of other public rituals of shame—the *amende honorable*, the pillory, and even the popular justice of the *charivari*.

> Symbolic inversion may be broadly defined as any act of expressive behavior which inverts, contradicts, abrogates, or in some fashion presents an alternative to commonly held cultural codes, values, and norms be they linguistic, literary or artistic, religious, or social and political.[8]

Anthropologists have already noted that inversions are a central feature of the liminal period in rites of passage.[9] Insofar as many punitive rituals were indeed rites of passage, inversions came to play a crucial role within them. The most common inversion motif, the 'world upside down' recurred often in late medieval art and literature. Built upon the reversal of hierarchical opposites, it depicted children disciplining parents, women ruling men, hares hunting people, people pulling carriages driven by horses, and fishes flying in the air.[10] The public acting out of such inversions as punishment, therefore, struck a familiar chord in the minds of all viewers. Like other punitive symbols, inversions relied upon already prevalent conceptions.

The impact of any inversion of roles in the public sphere relied upon deeply-embedded conceptions of societal and natural order. A man in a woman's position, a human in an animal's, a reversal of the normal upright, forward-looking stance of people—all of these could only convey a message of liminalization when highlighted upon the background of the normal and the normative. The function of these

[8] Barbara A. Babcock, "Introduction," in Barbara A. Babcock, ed., *The Reversible World: Symbolic Inversion in Art and Society* (Ithaca, N.Y., 1978), p. 14.

[9] *Ibid.*, p. 24.

[10] David Kunzle, "World Upside Down: The Iconography of a European Broadsheet Type," in Babcock, *Reversible World*, pp. 39-94.

inversions was not to disrupt order and hierarchy, but to the contrary, to strengthen and emphasize them by contrast.[11] They placed the subjects undergoing the ritual apart from the normative community, beyond its pale, and they did so by clearly drawing the moral boundaries of the community.

Inversion was not necessarily a punishment *per se*. Rather, it was a visible articulation of liminal status. Nevertheless, in legal rituals it invariably carried an association of degradation which must certainly have endowed it with a punitive impact, both for its subject and for the surrounding community. The infamy resulted from the fact that every inversion relied not upon a pair of equally valid categories, but upon hierarchical opposites. Thus the inversions invariably placed their subjects, whose original position was within the superior category, in the subordinate position. For example, in no case did legal rituals place a woman in a man's position. They invariably relied upon the degrading effect of the opposite procedure. The shame was inherent in the structure of the human and natural hierarchy of categories.

In general, punitive inversions were built upon the most basic categories and divisions of society and nature. The naked and the dressed, or the marginal and the person of status were the simplest and most common of contrasts consistently employed in punitive justice. But underlying these social constructs were the more fundamental contrasts that stemmed from the basic categories of being. The difference between the Christian, member of the community of believers, and the non-Christian outsider; between man, created in God's image and woman, imperfect replica, and the inversion of both served as a basis for punitive symbolism. But the most elementary categorization was that which distinguished the human from the animal, and its reversal was reserved for crimes meriting the severest of infamies.

Ritual punitive inversions served a triple purpose. By placing their subject in a liminal position, they not only highlighted the special, extra-societal stance of the criminal, but once more affirmed the boundaries of the normative. By applying procedures associated with one natural or social category to another, they stressed the differences between the two. By borrowing from the permanently liminal to characterize the newly (and sometimes temporarily) liminal they did not merge the two in contrast with the normative, they only clarified

[11] Natalie Z. Davis, "Women on Top," in *Society and Culture in Early Modern France* (Stanford, 1975), pp. 130-31.

the hierarchical structure linking all three. The normative, the liminalized, and the permanently liminal were all carefully graded.

B. Integration

Two of the most salient features of medieval legal rituals were their quasi-universality and their immutability. Compared to the rarefied—and horrifying—forms of death and suffering that the ancient world inflicted upon its criminals, medieval justice was remarkably uninventive. As the infliction of pain was not their aim, medieval jurists and judges wasted no time whatsoever in devising new and horrible penalties for criminals. They persistently stuck to the old forms, not out of simple conservatism, but thanks to a certain underlying perception of justice. It had little to do with learned jurisprudence. Rather, it was more a feeling that permeated and shaped legal practices than a clear-cut theory of law. Broadly stated, it was a conviction that justice was universal, changing neither to accommodate life or death, human or animal conditions, or the passage of time.

In other words, justice was not limited to human beings, or to the living. This perception allowed medieval courts to treat as legal personalities not only the dead, but also pigs, horses, cows, and dogs. In this, the popular view of justice was completely opposed to learned taxonomies. While theologians affirmed time and again that only God could try the dead and the non-human, jurists were faced with the simple reality that both categories were in fact tried in court and punished. In order to justify human jurisdiction over transcendent categories, jurists invoked the divine origin of all law.

But it was not enough to subject the dead and the animals to human justice. The universal validity of human jurisdiction had to be expressed in the forms of judicial ritual. Just as specific rituals were designed to alienate distinct human categories from the general community, other rituals were aimed at doing the exact opposite: the incorporation of the human and the non-human within one community of justice. When a court pronounced a death sentence against a dead man or a homicidal pig, using the exact formula employed in the case of a living human murderer, it was doing more than making a statement concerning the universality of justice: it was placing the subject of the sentence within one category with all subjects of the court. The formalistic conservatism of the ritual employed in all cases, regardless of the culprit's nature, underscored this characteristic. "There is but one justice, and it stems from God," affirmed d'Ableiges in the face of the patchwork of jurisdictions existent at his time.[12] Jurisdiction could belong to tiny enclaves or great duchies, but justice was universal.

The old dictum, repeated again and again in the wake of Justinian, that justice meant giving each his due, was not quoted merely because it was a convenient definition. Unlike other forgotten and neglected maxims of the *Corpus*, the definition of justice fitted medieval judicial reality very neatly. On the one hand, each person was tried according to a variety of criteria, socio-legal status being one of them. On the other, he or she or it deserved justice not as a privilege, but as something due, regardless of status. Legal rituals were the means for translating this perception into a visual form. A noble murderer would die on the gallows in a manner different from a simple man, and a murderous animal otherwise from a human being, but they all ended up in the same place, suffering the same fate for the same deed.

[12] *GC*, p. 637.

CHAPTER SIX

THE RITUALS OF EXCLUSION: WOMEN AND JEWS

1. ANALOGIES OF LIMINALITY

While even the simplest of legal rituals was firmly embedded within a specific cultural context, it is easiest to perceive and analyze this trait on flamboyant public occasions. As the geologist finds it simpler to note the occurrence of a major convulsion of the earth in past eons than to follow the slow shifting of strata over millenia, so it is easiest for the historian of culture to follow those rituals and cultural phenomena that expressed very powerful, deep-seated emotions. Anti-Semitism and misogyny were two such forces in the later middle ages, their translation into the language of legal rituals forming clear evidence of the interaction between justice and culture. Both groups were perceived as outsiders within male, Christian society, and both groups were made to dramatize their difference in legal rituals.

The perception of Jews and women as liminal in late medieval society requires some elucidation. Neither femininity nor Judaism were temporary conditions connected with any rites of passage. Furthermore, neither group could have been said to lack a clear-cut, well-defined position within creation. How could they possibly be seen as liminal? Nevertheless, both women and Jews were perceived as being not only marginal to established society, but also outside the very notions of human and social structure. In the first place, both groups were associated with sin: women with original sin, or the fall of the first Adam, and Jews with the rejection of Christ, or the death of the second Adam. The sin in question in both cases was more than an individual aberration: it had cosmic consequences, disrupting the ideal progress of history. While Christ's death redeemed Adam's sin, his ultimate return hinged upon the conversion of the Jews.[1] The link

[1] This position, first taken by Saint Paul and subsequently developed by Saint Augustine, was to shape papal attitudes towards Jews throughout the middle ages. See Kenneth R. Stow, *The "1007 Anonymous" and Papal Sovereignty: Jewish Perceptions of the Papacy and Papal Policy in the High Middle Ages* (Cincinnati, 1984), pp. 9-21; Idem, "Hatred of the Jews or Love of the Church: Papal Policy

between the two was the connection of two dissonant elements in the progress of human history.

Both Jews and women, as might be expected, exhibited some of the most common elements of liminality. They were both forced into a stance of humility and passivity, but like all other liminars, their very weakness contained their strength. It was a strength derived from supernatural, unholy sources. Both Jews and women were exposed to accusations of magic and sorcery, for supernatural powers, holy or otherwise, are invariably connected with liminal states.

Women and Jews shared one outstanding characteristic: uncleanliness. The Jew was often associated with stench (the *foetor judaicus*) and impurity. While during the middle ages this stench was supposed to disappear automatically at the baptismal font, by the seventeenth century it clung also to converted Jews, a quasi-genetic rather than religious characteristic.[2] As for women, the belief in the dangers inherent in a menstruating woman (and her blood), or even one lying in childbirth are a constant in medieval science. Menstrual blood could kill plants, rust metal and harm animals. Hair and nails of menstruating women could also be used for the perverted generation of noxious beasts. Due to the poisonous emanations of her body, the look of a menstruating woman tarnished mirrors. In this women resembled the fabulous basilisk, half-snake and half-cock, whose look was deadly and who could be killed only by having its image presented to it in a mirror.[3] These strains were neatly tied together in the belief common in medieval France that among Jews both men and women menstruated. This was not seen as a normal menstruation, but as a genetic disease,

---

Towards the Jews," [Hebrew] *Antisemitism Through the Ages*, ed. S. Almog (Jerusalem, 1980), pp. 91-111.

[2] Caesarius of Heisterbach, *Dialogus miraculorum*, ed. Joseph Strange, 2 vols. (Köln, 1851), 1:95-97, tells of a Jewish girl converted to Christianity who perceived the "Jewish stench" of her relatives for the first time after conversion. For the stench in the seventeenth century, see Gilbert Dahan, "Contre un Juif. Trois poèmes inédits du XVIIe siècle," *Archives juives* 16:1 (1980), 5-9.

[3] Plinius Secundus, *Naturalis historia*, ed. H. Rackham (London, 1961), 7:64, pp. 548-49; Bartholomeus Anglicus, *De rerum proprietatibus* (Frankfurt, 1601, repr. 1964), bk. 4, ch. 8, p. 105, citing Isidore of Seville; Danielle Jacquart and Claude Thomasset, *Sexualité et savoir médical au moyen âge* (Paris, 1985), pp. 103-106. For the basilisc, see Florence McCulloch, *Medieval Latin and French Bestiaries* (Chapel Hill, 1962), pp. 93, 199-200, and L. Tolmer, *Folklore et biologie: les oeufs de coq et basilic* (Bayeux, 1928), pp. 16-24.

closely tied with other sicknesses of which Jews were supposed to suffer.[4]

Both Jews and women were thus humans who lived within Christian society, whose existence had theological and natural justifications, but who posed a constant threat. Despite their humiliation and subjection, they possessed power, but mostly to cause harm. Moreover, they possessed the malignant will to hurt. These parallels are not a figment of the modern imagination. They were drawn in the fourteenth century by the Franciscan friar Alvaro Pelayo in his *De planctu ecclesiae*, containing a long and involved diatribe against women. The litany of women's faults and vices ends with the statement that women hide an incorrigibly proud temperament under a humble exterior, in which they resemble the Jews.[5] The association of both women and Jews with the devil was articulated in eccleasiastical iconography in the motif of the backwards ride upon a goat. The goat was one of the specific beasts associated with the devil, and hence with his closest allies, namely women and Jews. The motif of a Jew mounted upon a goat and a woman mounted upon the same beast, both riding backwards, recurs with great frequency.[6]

But there the similarity ended. Jews and women might both have been 'others' in the eyes of clerical culture spokesmen and in popular perceptions, but there are many kinds and degrees of alterity and liminality. While both Jews and women fell short of the ideal of humanity, there were some very basic differences. Oddly enough, though Judaism is an alterable condition and the feminine sex is not, the distance between the Christian man and the Christian woman was far less than the distance separating both of them from the Jew. When all was said and done, women were Christian souls with a chance of salvation. Though the cult of the Virgin had probably done nothing to alter the condition of flesh-and-blood women, it did exist as a permanent reminder that women could be holy. The number of women saints, visionaries and mystics throughout late medieval Europe is clear evidence of the fact that women themselves did not see their sex as an impediment on the road to sanctity. A hindrance perhaps, but nothing

---

[4] Joshua Trachtenberg, *The Devil and the Jews*, (New Haven, 1943, repr. Philadelphia, 1983), p. 50.

[5] Cited in Jean Delumeau, *La peur en Occident* (XIVe-XVIIIe siècles) (Paris, 1978), pp. 317-20.

[6] Delumeau, *Le peur*, p. 313; Trachtenberg, *The Devil and the Jews*, p. 45.

a determined woman like Julian of Norwich or Catherine of Siena could not deal with.

Thus, while women were often perceived as flawed, closer to the devil than their male counterparts, Jews were "the perennial opposite, the contrary, and the inverse. The Jew was injustice incarnate..."[7] Jews were thus a far more serious threat to Christian society than women could ever be. And the difference in perception was articulated in legal rituals. Both groups, when facing death at the hands of the law, died in a manner different from that of the Christian man, and this difference was visibly and symbolically acted out. Legal rituals translated into ceremonial language popular perceptions of the nature of Jews and women.

2. Jews: The Human 'Animals'

The clearest expression of the liminal status of Jews emerges from the animal symbolism attached to them. Animals, omnipresent and carrying a rich associative and cultural legacy, served as symbolic vehicles for human qualities. As people differed, so did the associations of specific animals, and animals associated with negative qualities and vices—willful blindness, greed, luxuriousness—were useful symbolic vehicles of liminality. Animalization was a common way of placing criminals in a liminal position, and much the same set of symbols was used for Jews.

Other than the previously-mentioned goat, monkeys and owls were also symbols of Judaism. Occasionally religious art symbolized Jews by picturing a monkey riding a goat backwards, holding an owl upon its wrist.[8] Here the animal symbolism and the backwards ride merged into one conceptual framework. The owl, a nightbird flying in the dark, consistently symbolized the blind Jews refusing to see Christ. The monkey was far more interesting. The similarity to man, never destined to achieve identification, troubled late medieval commentators. It was seen as a distortion of humanity, an unsuccessful replica of a unique, never-to-be-replicated creation. The Jew, too, was not-quite-human, but the very close similarity was disturbing. Riding backwards in this context assumed added significance. No longer merely an

[7] Kenneth R. Stow, *Alienated Minority: The Jews of Medieval Latin Europe*, New Haven, 1992, forthcoming), ch. 11.

[8] Ruth Mellinkoff, "Riding Backwards: Theme of Humiliation and Symbol of Evil," *Viator* 4 (1973), 170-71.

infamy inflicted upon a human, but a reversal of the naturally forward-looking stance of humanity.

Church dogma most certainly did not concur with this view. The clerical elite, anxious to convert the Jews, naturally assumed their humanity and salvability. But the perception of Jews as semi-animals did not exist within the province of popular ideas only. An eminent fourteenth-century French jurist clearly stated that a Christian who had had sexual relations with a Jewish woman should be burned at the stake, because his act constituted a mixture of natures (*commixtio nature*), likely to generate monsters and legally tantamount to copulation with a dog.[9] This legal opinion was still quoted three centuries later as a precedent in Italy and Germany.[10]

Jean le Coq did not approximate Jews to dogs by chance. Indeed, Jews were most commonly associated with pigs and dogs. The pig was undoubtedly the most significant of all the animal associations of Jews. The connection was drawn on both learned and popular levels. In the learned world of bestiaries, the Jew was associated with the pig because the latter symbolized the vice of greed, *luxuria* or *gula*. The identification goes back to late antique interpretations of the Psalms. The verse reading "from men of the world... whose belly thou fillest with thy hidden things; their children are sated, and leave the rest to their babes" (Psalms 17:14) was rendered in Greek (and subsequently in the Vulgate) as "... they are sated with swine's flesh" (*porcina*). Both Jerome and Augustine were aware of the Greek, not Hebrew source of this interpretation, but both mentioned the two versions, one of them speaking of pork. Thus far, the Greek had merely taken an obscure verse (apparently concerning those blessed by the Lord), turning it into a condemnation of the impure and the rich. There was no association between those filled with swine's flesh and the Jews until the sixth century. In his own exegesis of the Psalms, Cassiodorus was the first explicitly to connect those rich with hidden things with the Jews.

Three centuries later, Hrabanus Maurus made the transition from exegesis to contemporary physical science, incorporating the connection into his bestiary:

> The pig similarly signifies the unclean and the sinners of whom it is written in the Psalm: 'Their belly is full with Your hidden things.

[9] *Quaestiones Johannis Galli*, q. 403, p. 482.

[10] Salo W. Baron, *A Social and Religious History of the Jews*, 2nd ed., 18 vols. (New York, 1952), 11:80, 320-21, n. 4; Jacob Döpler, *Theatri poenarum suppli-*

> They are sated with swine's flesh and they leave what is superfluous to them for their children.' (Ps. 17:14) He says the Jews [are full] of unclean things because what is hidden by the Lord is known to be forbidden. By swine's flesh he means polluted things which are named unclean among other precepts of the Old Testament.[11]

The shift from biblical exegesis to bestiary literature was extremely important. A theological interpretation had been transformed into a physical fact. It was no longer merely a question of understanding an obscure passage in the Scriptures, but of perceiving the universe, and in this universe pigs and Jews shared an essential uncleanliness. Furthermore, bestiary literature reached a much wider readership than exegesis, being on the borderline between the purely learned and the popular.[12] The work of Hrabanus Maurus enjoyed great popularity, being still copied as late as the fifteenth century.[13]

Whether the popular tradition stemmed from the learned or grew autonomously is unclear. One cannot date precisely the legend explaining why Jews avoided eating pork which gave rise to this connection, but it was current all over Europe in the later middle ages in various versions. According to this legend, Jesus was challenged by a Jew to guess at the contents of a barrel (or trough). The Jew knew there was a slaughtered pig in it, but did not know that his children were also inside. When Jesus answered that the man's children were in the barrel, he was mocked and told that there was a pig inside. "Let them be pigs then" answered Jesus, and the Jew's children were promptly transformed into piglets.[14] From that day henceforth, tells the tale, the Jews avoid eating pork, because for them that would be cannibalism.

---

ciorum et executionum criminalium, oder Schau-platzes derer Leibes- und Lebens-Strafen (Leipzig, 1697), 2:157.

[11] "Porcus similiter immundos significat et peccatores: de quibus in psalmo scriptum est: 'De absconditis tuis adimpletus est venter eorum: saturati sunt porcina, et relinquentur, quae superfuerant parvulis suis' (Psal. xvi). Judaeos dicit de immunditiis, quae a Domino abscondita, id est, noscuntur esse prohibita." Hrabanus Maurus, *De universo*, in *MPL*, 111:206A-207A. Quoted in Isaiah Shachar, *The Judensau: A Medieval Anti-Jewish Motif and its History* (London, 1974), pp. 6-8.

[12] The bestiary literature, suppressed in the sixth and seventh century due to its pagan origins, began reviving in Carolingian time, reaching great popularity in learned circles by the twelfth century. During the later middle ages it was no longer the province of learned circles. See Claude Lecouteux, "Paganisme, Christianisme et merveilleux," *Annales, E.S.C.* 37 (1982), 700-16.

[13] Shachar, *The Judensau*, p. 11.

[14] Oskar Dährnhardt, ed., *Natursagen. Eine Sammlung naturdeutender Sagen, Märchen, Fabeln und Legenden*, 3 vols. (Berlin, 1907-10), 2:102-107, 279-81.

The difference between the learned and the popular traditions is clear. While the former identified pigs as symbols of uncleanliness, and by extension of Jewishness, the latter version made a total connection. Jews were pigs, not symbolically, but in reality. With this legend in the background, it is easy to understand the story of a Jewish woman who had given birth to two piglets, current in sixteenth-century Germany.[15] The pictorial translation of this motif was the *Judensau*, a highly scatological depiction of an enormous sow, simultaneously suckling and defecating upon several Jews. A Jew is also depicted as riding the sow backwards in a number of these paintings.[16] The motif was current mainly in Germany, where it was translated also into dramatic language. Carnival plays had Jews tied beneath sows, sucking their teats or having their faces pushed under the beasts' tails.[17]

The *Judensau* was rare in France. Only two instances are known, both pictorial and both in Alsace, where their appearance was undoubtedly due to German influence.[18] Still, the idea that Jews were pigs, that they belonged to the sow and the sow belonged to them, was firmly grounded also in French popular culture. Claudine Fabre-Vassas has collected an impressive corpus of French popular expressions linking Jews and pigs, arguing that a peasant economy highly prizing the pig as a domestic edible animal could not explain the avoidance of its meat by any other theory. The act of circumcision, a Jewish custom which frightened Christians very much and probably gave rise in part to the myth of ritual murder, became associated with the practices of castrating and bleeding pigs.[19]

The myth of ritual murder was closely tied to both pigs and bleeding. Often the accusation specifically mentioned that the Jews, needing the kidnapped Christian child's blood for ritual purposes, had bled it to death.[20] The body of Simon of Trent, pierced and bled like a pig by

---

[15] Trachtenberg, *The Devil and the Jews*, pp. 46-52. The author records also the belief that Jews descended from the tribe of Naphtali have pigs' teeth, ears, and stench.

[16] Shachar, *The Judensau*, plates 30, 36b, 52, 56.

[17] B. Dagani, "Carnival Plays and Satyric Literature as a tool of Anti-Semitism in the Fifteeth and Early Sixteenth Centuries," [Hebrew], in *Uma Ve-Toldoteha* (Jerusalem, 1983), pp. 252-54.

[18] Freddy Raphaël, "La répresentation des Juifs dans l'art médiéval en Alsace," *Revue des sciences sociales de France de l'Est* (1972), 26-42.

[19] Claudine Fabre-Vassas, "Juifs et Chrétiens. Autour du cochon," *Recherches et travaux de l'Institut d'ethnologie (CH-Neuchâtel)* 6 (1985), 59-83.

[20] Thomas of Cantimpré, *Miraculorum et exemplorum sui temporis libri duo* (Douais, 1605), pp. 304-305; Cesáreo Bandera, "From Mythical Bees to Medieval

Jews wearing badges of boars, sometimes appeared on the same picture as the *Judensau*.[21] The pig in this perceptual scheme was both the Jew and the child-victim of the Jews. While hardly logical, the idea made perfect sense within peasant society. The pig was often a domestic pet, carrying its own name and eating in the house. But when the time came, this same pig was slaughtered and bled. It thus made sense to identify the pig and its death with a child, and to transfer the guilt for the death to people identified collectively with pigs.

German culture translated this perception into legal language, demanding that Jews take their oath standing barefoot upon the skin of a sow. According to the *Sachsenspiegel*, the skin had to belong to a sow that had whelped during the previous fortnight, and her skin spread so that her teats were displayed. A late fourteenth-century ordinance of Berlin further specified that the Jew must stand upon the sow's teats while taking the oath.[22] According to Shachar, the use of the pigskin was a thirteenth-century innovation. Its conceptual ties with the *Judensau* are clear in the emphasis that both motifs placed upon the sow's maternity and the Jew's contact with her teats.[23]

The identification of Jews with dogs was far less evident in art, but more clearly apparent within the judicial context. The inverted hanging with the accompaniment of two dogs, originally reserved for traitors, was identified by the fourteenth century as the 'Jewish execution,' being practiced in the later middle ages throughout both northern and Mediterranean Europe. The Jewish execution in Germany has been thoroughly studied by G. Kisch, who has argued convincingly that neither the inverted hanging nor the stringing up of dogs or wolves beside the victim were particularly Jewish punishments during the high middle ages. They first appeared as Jewish punishments in

---

Anti-Semitism," in *Violence and Truth: On the Work of René Girard*, ed. and trans. Paul Dumouchel (Stanford, 1988), pp. 209-26.

[21] For the martyrdom of Simon of Trent, see P. Baudot and P. Chaussin, *Vie des saints et des bienheureux selon l'ordre du calendrier avec l'historique des fêtes*, 13 vols. (Paris, 1935-59), 3:532-35; Shachar, *The Judensau*, pp. 57-61 and pl. 33.

[22] Guido Kisch, *Jewry-Law in Medieval Germany: Laws and Court Decisions Concerning Jews* (New York, 1949), pp. 51, 97.

[23] Shachar, *The Judensau*, p. 14. The entire phenomenon deserves a special study, beyond those of Kisch and Shachar. Economically speaking, it is highly unlikely that a sow was slaughtered every time a Jew in northern Germany had to present himself in court and take an oath, especially since the death of a newly-delivered sow would have meant also the death of all piglets. Thus far, all the evidence presented for this custom comes from prescriptive sources, but I would postulate that this was the type of legislation meant to affirm the Christian community's theoretical identity rather than actually be implemented in court.

Germany only towards the end of the thirteenth century, never being recognized as exclusively Jewish penalties.[24]

In France the inverted, animal-associated hanging came to be connected with Jews by the later middle ages. The inverted hanging of Jews is specifically mentioned in the old customs of Burgundy in the context of animal hanging.[25] The custom, dogs and all, was still in force in Paris shortly before the final expulsion of the Jews in 1394.[26] Nevertheless, Jews executed in the Papal state of Avignon during the fifteenth century hung by their necks like everyone else.[27]

Whether originally Jewish or not, the inverted execution was firmly perceived as both Jewish and animal by the later middle ages. When the Basel authorities exhorted a condemned Jew "not to die like an animal" but to convert, they were putting in words a parallel that any spectator to the ceremony could see.[28] When Shakespeare's Gratiano accused Shylock of being the transmigrated soul of a wolf executed by hanging for homicide, he was making the same connection.[29] The Jew was seen as a creature of doubtful humanity, closely associated with the animal world and with specific, symbolic animals in it. His dying quite literally "like a dog" or a wolf was no more than another expression of justice, for the punishment had to suit not only the crime, but also the criminal.

---

[24] Guido Kisch, "The Jewish Execution in Medieval Germany," *Studi in memoria di Paolo Koschaker*, 2 vols. (Milan, 1954), 2:65-93, attributed the identification of inverted, animal-associated hanging with Jews to the growing influence of Roman law.

[25] *Coustume et stilles de Bourgoigne* (1270-1360), art. 197, in Giraud, *Essai sur l'histoire du droit*, 2:302.

[26] *Registre criminel du Châtelet de Paris*, 2:52.

[27] Jacques Chiffoleau, *Les justices du pape. Délinquance et criminalité dans la région d'Avignon au XIVe siècle* (Paris, 1984), p. 237. It is not clear how common the inverted execution was in the lands of Roman law. It was practiced in Spain and Majorca, for example, but was unknown in Italy. Elena Lourie, "Complicidad criminal: un aspecto insolito de convivencia Judeo-Cristiana," *Actas del III Congreso Internacional, "Encuentro de las tres culturas" Toledo, 15-18 October, 1984*, ed. Carlos Carrete Parrondo (Toledo, 1988), p. 102.

[28] Rudolf Glanz, "The 'Jewish Execution' in Medieval Germany," *Jewish Social Studies* 5 (1943), 4.

[29] "Thou almost mak'st me waver in my faith,
To hold opinion with Pythagoras,
That souls of animals infuse themselves
Into the trunks of men: thy currish spirit
Governed a wolf, who, hang'd for human slaughter,
Even from the gallows did his fell soul fleet,
And, whilst thou lay'st in thy unhallow'd dam,
Infus'd itself in thee."
The Merchant of Venice, Act IV, scene 1.

Much farther south, in Malta, the stone of Saint Paul in the grotto of the same name was said to protect all baptised creatures and animals, except dogs, pigs, and Jews from poison, rabies, and incantations.[30] The juxtaposition of Jews with two types of domestic animals, close enough to arouse human feelings but distant enough to be absolutely removed from the realm of humanity was thus deeply embedded in European popular culture, both northern and southern. Not surprisingly, it found expression in legal practices.

3. WOMEN: THE HUMAN OTHER

In contrast to Jews, women were too close to the human norm to be viewed as animals. True, according to all medical and legal authorities they were imperfect humans, physically, mentally and morally weaker than men. Late medieval misogynistic literature depicted them as corrupt and corrupting, lascivious, inconstant, impure and disloyal, but not as inhuman.[31] Sermon and *exempla* literature, far more sympathetic to women, left no doubt as to its position. Women possessed souls as fully capable of salvation as men. The same sexless souls appeared as revenants in dreams to request help in reaching perpetual rest, regardless of the defunct person's gender.

And yet, it is perhaps the very closeness of women that aroused the greatest hostility. As students of alterity have pointed out, it is easy to adopt a detached attitude concerning the 'other' who is far removed—the Mongols, the American Indians, or the inhabitants of any faraway, fabulous land described by travelers. It the 'other within' who inspires horror because of his very closeness and similarity.[32] Women, human but imperfect, part of society but liminal to its structures, were most clearly alterity within the gates. Even Jews, who lived among Christians, could be marked by distinct clothing, segregated in ghettos, avoided and expelled. But women were indispensable, not to be excised from the body social. Even monasticism was no refuge from them, for they too demanded their spiritual freedom from the bondage of their sex within the monastic orders.[33]

---

[30] Ariel Toaff, *Il vino e la carne* (Bologna, 1989), p. 152; Stow, *Alienated Minority*, ch. 11.

[31] See, for example, Jean de Meung, *Roman de la Rose*, ed. Félix Lecoy, 3 vols. (Paris, 1966-70), 1:221-52; Delumeau, *La peur*, pp. 305-45.

[32] Francis Affergan, *Exotisme et altérité* (Paris, 1987), pp. 11-12.

[33] Karl Büchner, *Die Frauenfrage im Mittelalter*, 2nd ed. (Tübingen, 1910); H. Grundmann, *Religiöse Bewegungen im Mittelalter* (1935, repr. Hildesheim, 1961); M. de Fontette, *Les religieuses à l'âge classique du droit canon* (Paris, 1967).

It was easy to exclude women completely from the perceptual structure of society in the twelfth century, when the tripartite division of those who fight, those who till the land, and those who pray still held some real meaning. Especially for the warrior, woman as *imbellis* did not constitute a category that need be considered. Late medieval reality changed this blithe disregard. The categorization of society embodied in the dance of death did include women, creating a special dance for them. There the queen, the abbess, the nun, the knight's wife and the peasant's all took part in the dance, holding hands with death.[34] The great equalizer let women and children in through the back door.

But the perception most relevant to understanding the legal rituals concerning women is derived not so much from learned discomfort as from popular ideas. In northern French rural culture women possessed great powers. They not only transmitted peasant wisdom, they also controlled much of it. Again, one finds the recurring theme of the magical powers inherent in the human body, dead or alive, and in its emanations. The fact that women exuded milk and blood in addition to the usual emissions common to all humans made them not only unclean, but also powerful and dangerous. They controlled both the knowledge and the means of affecting various phenomena. The milk of a nursing mother could make the pigeons in the coop multiply, but the hair of a menstruating woman could kill snakes.[35]

Women therefore were the most common victims of sorcery accusations. In the learned tradition of witchhunting they assumed the far more dangerous role of Satan's accomplices. Here indeed we do find quite often the woman-witch transformed into an animal in preparation for her night-flight to a Sabbath.[36] But animal or not, women were unquestionably the prime suspects of an overwhelming majority of witchcraft accusations.[37] The most charitable explanation of the

[34] "La danse macabre des femmes," in *La danse macabre de Guy Marchant (1406)*, facs. ed. (Paris, 1925).

[35] *Le Grand et le petit Albert*, ed. Bernard Husson (Paris, 1978), pp. 95, 110-11. Cf. Robert Muchembled, *Popular Culture and Elite Culture in France, 1400-1750*, trans. Lydia Cochrane (Baton Rouge, 1985), pp. 66-83.

[36] On night-flight and animalization, see Carlo Ginzburg, "Presomptions sur le Sabbat," *Annales, E.S.C.* 39 (1984), 341-54.

[37] For statistics summarizing this phenomenon, see Robert Muchembled, "Satan ou les hommes? La chasse aux sorcières et ses causes," in M.-S. Dupont-Bouchat, W. Frijhoff, and R. Muchembled, *Prophètes et sorciers dans les Pays-Bas, XVIe-XVIIIe siècle* (Paris, 1978), p. 17; for an interpretation, see Clarke Garrett, "Women and Witches: Pattern of Analysis," *Signs* 3 (1977), 461-70, and Claudia Honegger, "Comment: Women and Witches," *Ibid.* 4 (1979), 792-98.

early modern period was that women, by reason of their weakness, were more susceptible to the devil's wiles. Less benevolent attitudes accused women straightforwardly of hatred towards men and a wish to harm them. Women were witches not because they were weak and gullible, but to the contrary, because they were strong, dangerous, and intentionally malicious. Not the devil's dupes, but his willing associates.[38]

This perception was transmuted in legal rituals into specific actions. If women were by nature impure and dangerous, any woman criminal was in consequence far more dangerous than her male counterpart. In order to be effective, her punishment had to act as a ritual extraction of evil and communal purification. Once dead, she was highly likely to come back as a maleficent revenant, intent upon harming the living. Hence, any physical remains of an executed woman criminal had to be thoroughly disposed of. The principle of apotropaeics, or the removal of the harmful dead, was clearly articulated in women's sentences. The real meaning of live burial as a female sentence can be seen in the German custom of either laying thorns upon the body before covering it up, or driving a stake through the woman's body, thus impaling her to the ground. The same procedure of the stake had been in use already in the eleventh century in the burial of women who had died of childbirth.[39] Women criminals were even more dangerous, for the record of their lives predisposed them to try and cause the living as much damage as possible after their own demise. In Germany women criminals were often drowned, so that the purifying force of the water carried the corpse away.[40] The dunking of errant wives in the village fountain was common practice at the time in many parts of rural France. The drowning of witches according to a court sentence belongs to a later period, but might well have been carried out informally at an earlier time.[41]

---

[38] The literature linking women with witchcraft is too extensive to be cited. It begins with the *Malleus maleficarum* (see esp. part 1, q. 6), and goes on in full force well into the seventeenth century with Jean Bodin and Pierre de Lancre, all of them espousing the more hostile view of women. For a summary of the learned attitudes towards women and witchcraft, see Delumeau, *La peur*, pp. 323-35.

[39] Burchard of Worms, *Decretum*, XIX, 5, 179ff., quoted in H.J. Schmitz, *Die Bussbücher*, 2 vols. (Düsseldorf, 1898), 2:448.

[40] Folke Ström, *On the Sacral Origin of the Germanic Death Penalties* (Stockholm, 1942), pp. 171-78.

[41] Concerning the custom of dunking faithless wives in northern France, see AN, JJ 142, fol. 160$^{ro\text{-}vo}$. Concerning the use of water in testing and punishing witches, see, among others, Henri Boguet, *An Examen of Witches*, trans. E.A. Ashwin, ed. M. Summers (London, 1929), appendix, art. 15.

The most common deaths inflicted upon women in France were either burning or live burial. The cases of women hung before the sixteenth century were few and far in between indeed.[42] The sixteenth-century jurist Bartholomé Chassenée, who argued that one law should apply to both men and women, admitted that usually women were not hanged "because such a punishment does not fit the feminine sex."[43] This statement was taken to mean that modesty forbade the display of the female body.[44] The interpretation, however, owes far more to post-Victorian perceptions of the human body and its display than to late medieval awareness. Not modesty, but fear prevented their public hanging. Even in the case of male criminals, the hanged man was not considered really dead for a long time. And dead women were far more likely to become revenants and to cause harm precisely because of their powers and malice.

Public nudity was neither unusual nor particularly shocking in late medieval society. Though men and women commonly bathed together in the public baths, these were indeed often barely-disguised brothels, and the behavior of people in them was not regulated by public authorities. Still, the naked female body was accepted far more matter-of-factly at the time than in later centuries. In public judicial rituals female nudity, like its male counterpart, bore all the significance of shame and deprivation of identity, not of lascivious stripping.

Indeed, the punishment of women was consistently just as public as that of men, and just as immodest. Publicity of punishment was not reserved for 'public' women, or whores. Female forgers, minor thieves and other petty offenders could easily find themselves displayed for public contempt on the pillory. Numerous sentences condemned women offenders to be whipped naked through city crossroads. In 1373 a prostitute guilty of forgery was sentenced to be paraded throughout Paris and to stand for two hours on the pillory wearing nothing but a parchment proclaiming her crime, and in 1489 a widow who had deserted her child was condemned to be whipped naked through the crossroads of Paris.[45]

---

[42] J. Gessler, "Mulier suspensa: à délit égal peine différente?" *Revue Belge de philologie et d'histoire* 18 (1939), 974-88.

[43] "Talis poena non congruat sexui mulieris," Bartholomé Chassenée, *In consuetudines ducatus Burgundiae, fereque totae Galliae, commentarii amplissimi* (Paris, 1552), fol. 40a.

[44] Gessler, "Mulier suspensa," 975.

[45] BN, ms. fr. 21731, fol. 84ro; M.B. de Saint-Edmé, *Dictionnaire de la pénalité dans toutes les parties du monde connu*, 5 vols. (Paris, 1824-28), 4:473-74.

Finally, the executions of women, though ending in a manner that left no body hanging on the gallows, were just as public as those of men. Both burning and live burial took place at the same spots of execution reserved for men. In fourteenth-century Paris, a procuress was burned at the stake in the market-square and a sorceress at the pig-market, both the standard locations for the pyre.[46] In Amiens and in Paris women thieves who were buried alive suffered this fate at the foot of the gallows upon which their male counterparts hung.[47] Thus they obviously went through the same process of exclusion that marked the dying men, exposed to all eyes, very much in public. The public character of their deaths left many traces in contemporary chronicles.[48] In short, the eradication of the female criminal's body had nothing to do with modesty. The live body was callously displayed for deliberate shame, and no sensitivity protected the dead body of the same woman.

The hanging of women criminals became gradually more common during the early modern period. It is unlikely, however, that this development indicates any disappearance of old beliefs. To the contrary, all records point to a great recrudescence of apotropaeic fears at the time. Furthermore, it is highly doubtful that conscious apotropaeic beliefs motivated the sentences of fourteenth- and fifteenth-century judges. The reason that judicial authorities continued employing the same specific means of execution for women was the same as the reaon for the preservation of all judicial ritual. They were a set of commonly-recognized and shared symbols. Their strict repetition enhanced their meaning in the viewers' eyes. Any deviation alien to the cultural context voided the entire ceremony of its content.

The reason for the change in practice must be sought partly in the evolution of Roman-influenced jurisprudence, which insisted on the same punishment for both sexes, but more so within the context of contemporary reality. During the fifteenth and sixteenth centuries burning ceased to be the punishment of women. Technically, it had al-

---

[46] *Registre criminel du Châtelet*, 1:47, 363, 2:342.

[47] *Ibid.*, 1:327; 2:393, 436; Jacques Hillairet, *Gibets, piloris et cachots du vieux Paris* (Paris, 1956), p. 36. A. Dubois, *Justice et bourreaux à Amiens dans les XVe et XVIe siècles* (Amiens, 1860), p. 5.

[48] *Chronique parisienne anonyme du XIVe siècle*, ed. A. Hellot (Nogent-le-Rotrou, 1884), pp. 147-48, 161-62; Michel Félibien, *Histoire de la ville de Paris*, 5 vols. (Paris, 1725), 2:845; Jean de Roye, *Journal, ou Chronique scandaleuse, 1460-1483*, ed. B. de Mandrot, 2 vols. (Paris, 1894), 1:4-5 and *passim*; *Journal d'un bourgeois de Paris*, ed. A. Tuetey (Paris, 1881, repr. Geneva, 1975), pp. 389-90; Jean Chartier, *Chronique de Charles VII*, ed. Vallet de Viriville, 2 vols. (Paris, 1858) 2:67-69.

ways been the penalty for witchcraft and heresy, but until the fifteenth century such cases were fairly uncommon. The great witch hunts and the prosecution of heretics changed this picture. Early modern audiences were increasingly exposed to a hitherto unusual spectacle: that of men undergoing what had always been a predominantly female penalty.

By the same token, categories of female criminality became equally blurred. Audiences watching a woman being led to the pyre no longer knew whether she had merely killed her infant or performed witchcraft. In the need to distinguish between witches and other women criminals, authorities in France, the Low Countries, and Germany began applying the execution of men also to women. While woman as an abstract concept might have been associated with witchcraft, not every flesh-and-blood woman who stood on the dock was necessarily connected with any kind of maleficent magic. Two centuries of burning witches had firmly associated the pyre with the devil's collaborator, a far more dangerous criminal than the female arsonist, thief or murderer, and a far more dangerous potential revenant. It was therefore imperative both to burn the witch (thus completely eradicating her body), and to make her punishment clearly distinct from that of any other criminal or crime. Apotropaeic justice did not disappear. It was merely focused where most needed and effective.

Rituals of justice thus excluded Jews before their death, by turning them into animals, and women after their death, by eradicating their bodies. While the parallels in popular perceptions of women and Jews are significant, so are the differences. Why was there never any indication of apotropaeic fear of the Jews? Surely the devil's prime associates would have been likely to haunt the living? Yet in all the rich Anti-Semitic literature of the later middle ages, with all the fantastic accusations proffered against Jews, this one did not surface. Was it because Jewish communities faithfully reclaimed the bodies of their dead, burying them in communal cemeteries? It is not very likely that simple people would have been aware of this fact, or even considered it a proper apotropaeic measure. It is far more probable that law and popular culture followed here the same logic. Jews were animalized, and animals did not haunt. Once dead, they stayed that way. Women, by contrast, were human before and after death, and therefore dangerous in both states. When it came to exclusion, justice and popular beliefs were merely two sides of the same coin.

CHAPTER SEVEN

THE RITUALS OF INCLUSION: ANIMALS

The rituals of exclusion were one facet of legal symbolism. A considerable portion of legal rituals was devoted to the opposite process, that of inclusion. Just as rituals of exclusion served to mark the pale of the normative human community by expelling certain elements from it, so rituals of inclusion created a universe of justice that transcended the human community by imposing its normative boundaries upon the whole world. Nowhere is this trend clearer than in the custom of placing criminous animals on trial before a human court. This custom, which has aroused a great deal of controversy and interest, was clearly embedded in a specific cultural matrix.

1. THE ANIMALS

Late medieval societies had many cultures, each articulating a whole spectrum of attitudes towards animals. The variations were largely dictated by the level of coexistence specific social groups had with different animals. Clerics wrote of the pelican as a symbol of charity, noblemen judged their peers' position by their horses and hounds, town authorities complained of loose pigs in the streets, and peasants shared their real and imaginary lives with chickens, pigs, goats or sheep. A society in which animals were omnipresent naturally had many views of animals.

Legal culture was no more than another reflection of the same ubiquitous presence. The role of animals in late medieval law cannot be defined in any narrow sense, for animals possessed within this realm as many meanings as they did in other cultural manifestations. Domestic beasts were property, but also a form of life, and thus could not be severed from the dynamics of human existence. The problem of noxious animals and the extent of their or their owners' responsibilities is age-old.[1] Wild creatures in royal forests were also property, but of a different kind, and wild animals elsewhere fitted in no proprietary category whatsoever. One cannot speak of legal attitudes towards all animals in a society that so relied upon the animal world for its wealth

[1] J.J. Finkelstein, *The Ox that Gored* (Philadelphia, 1981).

and existence. Different laws in different economic structures concerned horses, pigs, sheep, deer or wolves.

Nevertheless, there was a certain broad duality in evidence. While the law of property considered animals chattels in every sense, criminal law treated them as sentient, punishable beings. This duality persisted throughout the lands of customary law, where the criminal prosecution of homicidal and noxious animals prevailed. The ambivalence towards animals in legal proceedings was no more than a reflection of the multivalence of cultural attitudes, ranging from the clear-cut theological perception to the numerous and often vague articulations of popular stances.

Perhaps the most common perception of animals in western learned culture was based upon the story of creation. Nature was conceived prior to man, as preparation for his existence. Man was the crown of creation, destined to rule over nature and use it for his own ends. Thus the prevailing taxonomy of the natural world, summed up in the thirteenth century by Bartholomeus Anglicus, was both functional and anthropocentric. In modern terms, animals were divided into food, work-beasts, pets, parasites, and predators. Deer and cattle were given to man for consumption; horses, donkeys, oxen and camels, in order to help him; monkeys, song-birds and peacocks, to amuse him. A fourth category, containing fleas, lice, and the like, was created to remind man of his fragility, and a fifth, comprising bears, lions, and serpents, existed in order to frighten man and remind him of God's power. Finally, many animals were created so that their bodies might be used to alleviate human sicknesses, for the lion's hairs cured hemorrhoids, and the bear's eye was good for quartan fever.[2]

This functional view implied the existence of a natural hierarchy placing man above animal. Humanity was measured in its distance from the animal, and the lower man sank, the closer he was to the animal world. The search for perfect humanity consisted in extending as far as possible the distance from the animal. Human soul, destined for an afterlife and capable of salvation or damnation, was something that animals did not possess. Nor did animals have the gift of reason and thought. The animal was therefore not only inferior to man in a

[2] "Omnium animalium tam iumentorum quam reptilium & bestiarum genera creata sunt propter optimum hominis usum... sunt insuper creata animalia ad sublevandam multiplicis infirmitatis humanae necessitatem..." Bartholomeus Anglicus, *De rerum proprietatibus*, Bk. 18, pp. 985-86.

hierarchy of government, but also farther removed from divinity.[3] The Aristotelian teaching attributing a reasonable soul to man alone fitted well with the Christian tradition.

The hierarchical view was reinforced in the thirteenth century by a strong taxonomical trend. The scholastic authors of the great *summae* were embarking upon a major attempt not only to codify, but more so, to classify all human knowledge and experience under specific categories. By the same token, the physical and metaphysical worlds were also organized in clear-cut divisions. There was little difference between types of angels, stones, or laws. All had to be firmly classified and placed within one major hierarchy.

The approach was not limited to schoolmen and philosophers. The aims of Vincent of Beauvais or Bartholomeus Anglicus when writing their compendia were more modest. Indeed, they also refrained from using the philosophical term *summa*. Still, the purpose was the same: to summarize all that they knew of man, or nature, or morality, or theology, and to do so within clearly set categories. Animals were defined as distinct from human beings, and any attempt to breach the impassable theological and physical barriers between categories awoke all the associations of impurity commonly attendant upon such blurrings of boundaries.[4] In learned tradition, the animal kingdom was thus inferior to man, at his use, and unalterably different.

But even scholars, of all people of their time most distant from animals, displayed a greater complexity of attitudes. There was a clear distinction within the learned tradition between the overall view of the animal kingdom, opposed to the essence of humanity, and the perception of individual animals, all of them possessing symbolic, transcendent characteristics. The latter enjoyed a special proximity to human beings by virtue of embodying specific human and metaphysical traits. The attribution of such meanings to animals was central to the tradition of bestiaries, based directly upon the *Physiologus* of Smyrna and indirectly upon Pliny's writings. Here every animal possessed specific moral and symbolic qualities derived from and transcending its physical attributes. The otter, for example, was reputed to be the enemy of the crocodile, attacking it in its sleep. Since the crocodile resembled

[3] The functional approach was carried to the extreme in the Judaic tradition. Thus, Rabbi Sa'adia Gaon (9th c.), claimed that the natural world had been destroyed in the flood because it had lost its purpose with the disappearance of man. See V. Aptowitzer, "The Rewarding and Punishing of Animals and Inanimate Objects," *Hebrew Union College Annual* 3 (1926), 118, n.2.

[4] Mary T. Douglas, *Purity and Danger* (London, 1966).

the devil, the otter was perceived as the type and image of the Savior.[5] Preachers used such traits either as warning or as an example. The dove, faithful to her mate and inconsolable as its death, was presented as a model for widows who should not remarry.[6]

Though the theological significance of each animal was undoubtedly of learned origin, the principle dictating an individualized attitude towards every creature may well have come from popular origins. Certainly the preachers relying upon the individual symbolism of each animal in their exhortations were deliberately trying to bridge the gap between their theories and their audiences. "There is a kind of frog which, when placed in a dog's mouth, silences it. Similarly, gifts placed in the hands of a judge silence him and make him avoid true judgment."[7] Parables culled from the animal sphere were sure to appeal to people whose lives were surrounded by animals. In the *exempla* literature they were also indices of piety. Etienne de Bourbon tells of storks who deserted their nest on top of an excommunicated man's house, returning only when the excommunication was lifted.[8] The use of animal symbolism here had nothing theological about it. It was an effort to bridge the distance between two perceptual schemes by the use of familiar examples. At the same time, the preachers yielded nothing when it came to the actual confusion of categories. Etienne de Bourbon fulminated against the cult of the hound Saint Guinefort, and Caesarius of Heisterbach warned that a dog baptized during a children's game immediately became rabid.[9]

The *exempla* literature was one of the means by which animal lore flowed from learned to popular strata and vice versa, merging into one tradition. Perhaps the best example of this merging is the anonymous fifteenth-century *livre du roy Modus et de la reyne Racio*,[10] in which Queen Reason posited a taxonomy of the animal world manifestly based upon everyday familiarity. Animals, quite simply, were divided into sweet [-smelling] beasts and stinking beasts. But smell in this context meant more than the purely olfactory sensation produced by proximity to a byre or a dunghill. The hart headed the list of sweet

[5] *Der Physiologus*, ed. Otto Seel (Zürich, 1967), p. 23.

[6] Michael Zink, *La prédication en langue romane avant 1300* (Paris, 1976), p. 405.

[7] Welter, *Tabula exemplorum*, p. 133.

[8] *Anecdotes historiques*, p. 255.

[9] J.-C. Schmitt, *Le saint lévrier. Guinefort, guérisseur d'enfants depuis le XIIIe siècle* (Paris, 1979), pp. 15-17; Caesarius, *Dialogus*, 2:249.

[10] *Le livre du roy Modus et de la reyne Racio* (Chambéry, 1486).

beasts mainly because of its religious symbolism and role in saints' legends. The pig was first on the list of smelly beasts not only because of the physical facts, but due also to its symbolic associations. Predatory animals—the wolf and the fox—were also considered smelly.

Late medieval popular culture was more than familiar with the specific characteristics and properties of each animal. Generalizations and theological symbolism had little meaning for people living in daily contact with animals. Folklore was far more prone to attribute human qualities to them. Hunting-dogs stood for pride and arrogance, pigs for gluttony, lions and cocks for courage.[11] But it was not enough to know that the lion symbolized courage; it was necessary to find a way of transmitting this courage to human beings. True, it was believed that wearing a belt of lion's pelt, or carrying on one's person the lion's eye or heart achieved this end, but lions were notoriously scarce and dangerous. The far more common dunghill cock, however, was equally useful, for even lions were known to fear roosters.[12] It was thus possible for people lacking courage to infuse this quality into their spirits by carrying a cock, or some parts of a cock's carcass. Women used to carry the womb of a barren bitch, or expose their genitals to the smoke generated by burning the hoof of a mule (sterile by its very nature) as contraceptive measures.[13] Any quality sought could be achieved by the use of the appropriate organs from the appropriate animals.[14]

Animals did more than embody specific human traits; they often came to symbolize specific types of human beings. The anthropomorphic tradition of the beast epics, in which animals stood for human types, was part of a rich folkloristic stratum of animal lore common to the entire Indo-European world.[15] Here the lion ceased to be a symbol of courage, becoming king of the beasts, parallel to and parody of the human ruler. The wolf, the camel, and most of all, the fox, evolved full human personalities in the beast epic. Notably, the central characters of these tales were not the domestic animals familiar to late medieval peasants from everyday life. The pig, the hare, and the ple-

[11] Schmitt, *Le saint lévrier*, pp. 87-88; Lazar Sainéan, *Les sources indigènes de l'etymologie française*, 3 vols. (Paris, 1925, repr. 1972), 1:61-66.

[12] Johannes Hambroer, "Der Hahn als Löwenschreck im Mittelalter," *Zeitschrift für Religions- und Geistesgeschichte* 18 (1966), 237-54.

[13] Sylvie Laurent, *Naître au moyen âge. De la conception à la naissance: La grossesse et l'accouchement (XIIe-XVe siècle)* (Paris, 1989), pp. 33-34.

[14] *Le grand et le petit Albert*, pp. 153-71.

[15] Joseph Bédier, *Les fabliaux: études de littérature populaire et d'histoire littéraire du moyen âge*, 6th ed. (Paris, 1969).

beian dog (as opposed to the aristocratic hound) played a very minor role in the beast epics. Wolves and foxes were probably far more familiar than lions and camels, but all of them lived beyond the control of the domestic sphere. They were convenient subjects for allegorical representation precisely because they did not share in everyday human life.

Animals in fables acted in all human spheres, and in a manner hardly complimentary to humans. The anthropomorphic perception of animals is central especially to the Renard beast epics.[16] The wily fox appeared there in several human roles, including that of a Jacobite pilgrim. The legal motif, embodied in Renard's trial before King Lion for raping Hersent the she-wolf, played an important role in these epics. Various branches of the tale followed each a different legal procedure: the German *Reinhardt Fuchs* satirized imperial justice, while the northern French *Roman de Renart* and the Flemish *Van den Vos Reynaerde* adhered strictly to local feudal law.[17] But whatever the procedure, the issues were fairly universal: lineage loyalty, vendetta, fraud, and honor.

Animals were thus symbolic surrogates for people, a mirror held to humanity's face and a vehicle of human self-perception. Consequently, the use and inclusion of real and figurative animals within public rituals aimed at shaping societal self-perception was an obvious development. One of the greatest feasts medieval Paris ever witnessed provides a striking illustration of this trend. When Philip the Fair knighted his sons in 1313 all orders of society competed in adding their own contributions to royal magnificence. Within the space of two days, the city's guilds erected over the Seine a new wooden bridge, exhibiting a series of pageants. In the weavers' procession Renard the Fox, sandwiched between Herod and Caiaphas on one side and Adam and Eve on the other, appeared first in the guise of a doctor and later as a chanter. Renard was the only non-biblical personage in the pageant except for Hersent the she-wolf. The tanners, not to be outdone, included a whole biography of Renard:

---

[16] O. Jordogne, "L'anthropomorphisme croissant dant le *Roman de Renart*," in E. Rombauts and A. Welkenhuysen , eds., *Aspects of the Medieval Animal Epic* (Louvain, 1975), pp. 25-42.

[17] Sigrid Krause, "Le *Reinhart Fuchs*, satire de la justice et du droit," in Danielle Buschinger and André Crépin, eds., *Comique, satire et parodie dans la tradition renardienne et les fabliaux* (Goppingen, 1983), pp. 139-51; Guido van Dievoet, "Le *Roman de Renart* et *Van den Vos Reynaerde*, témoins fidèles de la procédure pénale aux XIIe et XIIIe siècles?" in *Aspects of the Medieval Animal Epic*, pp. 43-52.

The life of Renard in detail
Despoiler of poultry without fail,
Here Master Renard passed as bishop,
Also as pope and archbishop.
In all his disguises he showed
Just as his life has told.[18]

Other crafts apparently had other animals in their own processions, "in which the individual animals depicted fulfilled specific functions."[19] The chronicler thus describing the feast summed up in one sentence the role of literary animals both in public ritual and within the cultural context. The individuality of animal symbolism was its central characteristic.

This trait spanned both popular and elitist views of animals. Few ceremonies could qualify as more intellectual than the pageant planned in 1389 (probably by Philippe de Mézières) for the solemn entry of Charles VI's bride, Isabel of Bavaria. Though staged by the Châtelet confraternity of legal clerks, it spoke for all the jurists of Paris. The pageant presented, quite literally, a *lit de justice*—a royally furnished bed-chamber, in which Saint Anne (always a symbol of justice) rested. Into this chamber came, from an adjoining garden, a white hart from one side, a lion and an eagle from the other. Twelve maidens with unsheathed swords protected the *lit* and the hart from the other two animals. The white hart, associated in the bestiaries with Christ, had come to symbolize by the late fourteenth century both parlementary justice and the person of Charles VI.[20]

The symbolic animals on these occasions were, of course, people in animal guise. But live animals were also included in public ceremonies. Animal processions took place in several cities of France and the Low Countries.[21] Late medieval Ypres institutionalized the 'cat feast', celebrated until today, on the second Wednesday of Lent. The feast, joined by the whole city, consisted originally of a procession, followed

[18] "La vie Renart sans faille / qui mengeoit et poucins et paille [poules] / Mestre Renart y fut evesque / Véu et pape et archevesque /Renart y fu en toute guise / Si come sa vie le devise." Geffroi de Paris, *Chronique rimée*, in *RHGF* 22:137-38.

[19] "... processionem vulpis, in qua singula animalia effigiata singula officia exercebant." Jean de Saint-Victor, *Memoriale historiarum*, *RHGF* 21:656-57. For a modern description of this feast, see Jean Favier, *Philippe le Bel* (Paris, 1978), p. 61.

[20] Bryant, *The King and the City*, pp. 178-80.

[21] For animal processions, especially cat-processions and their sculptures in Strasbourg and Aix, see Hans A. Berkenhoff, *Tierstrafe, Tierbannung und rechtsrituelle Tiertötung im Mittelalter* (Strasbourg, 1937), pp. 72-73.

by the throwing one or three cats from a tower.[22] The cat-burning ceremony, held each year in Paris on the eve of Saint John's day as part of the traditional bonfires, was even more cruel. Like the Ypres procession, it was a city-wide celebration. The pyre was erected in the Place de Grève, and one or two dozen cats in bags with an occasional fox added, were hung on it. The king and nobility watched the holocaust from specially-erected galleries, and the cat-burning was followed by a public feast at the king's expense. Similar cat-burning feasts were held on Saint John's eve also in Metz and Saint Chamand.[23]

Was the maltreatment of the cats merely public sadism? The fact that it invariably took place within a public ritual indicates otherwise. Animals, especially domestic ones, were sometimes the mirror image of the human community and the bearers of its guilt. The idea that the public death of an innocent animal can cleanse the community is age-old, emerging already in two ritual biblical practices: the beheaded heifer and the scapegoat. Whenever a dead man whose killer was unknown was found, the elders of the community were to behead a heifer never previously put to the yoke on the spot and wash their hands over its body, declaring their community clean of the spilled blood.[24] Once a year, at the ritual atonement of the entire people's sins, the high priest was to take two goats, sacrifice one and place upon the other's head the sins of the whole people. The scapegoat, carrying those sins, was then sent into the wilderness.[25]

Except when transmuted into Christian perceptions, biblical rituals had little significance in medieval culture. But Christianity had so far internalized the atonement through animal sacrifice as to name Christ dying for people's sins *agnus dei*. This was no mere figure of speech, as the prevalence of the mystical lamb motif in late medieval iconography shows. A sacrificial victim was invariably perceived in animal terms. The dying animal had to be pure and blameless, so that its public ritual death could cleanse the guilty community. Very little indeed of this solemn ritual survived in the public killing of cats, except for the fact that it was timed to coincide with periods of cleansing. This was either

[22] H. Viaene, "Kattedag te Ieper," *Biekorf* 45 (1939), 47-52.

[23] Alfred Franklin, *Paris et les parisiens au seizième siècle* (Paris, 1928), pp. 508-509; Robert Darnton, "Workers Revolt: The Great Cat Massacre of the Rue Saint-Séverin," in his *The Great Cat Massacre and Other Episodes in French Cultural History* (New York, 1984), pp. 83-84.

[24] Deuteronomy 21:1-9.

[25] Leviticus 16:5-22.

the Christian purification of Lent or the bonfires lighted on Saint John's eve, a leftover of the summer solstice celebrations.[26]

The public efficacy of the ritual was based upon a layer of folkloristic belief. The animal procession of 1313 took place on Pentecost, which fell on June 6 that year, only two weeks away from Saint John's feast. Though named for a saint, this festival had its roots in traditions far older than Christianity.[27] Herbs gathered on the eve of Saint John's were considered useful for a variety of magical purposes, from poisoning to verifying pregnancies.[28] And Saint John also associated the human and the animal in some curious ways. He was the patron of epileptics, those who suffered from Saint John's disease. It was believed in some parts of northern France that three successive acts of bestiality would cure epilepsy.[29] Saint John, and by extension his day, were thus associated with the merging of the human and the animal. The bonfires of Saint John's and the idea of animal sacrifice were thus joined in the public cat-burning ceremony.

Renard was different. In the first place, here was no flesh-and-blood fox, but a human being dressed as an animal dressed as a human being: doctor, chanter, bishop, even pope. Rather than a generalized scapegoat, he personified specific, essentially human traits superimposed by popular imagination upon the characters of the beast epics. Unlike the hapless cats, he did not suffer for his or anyone else's misdeeds, but got away with them. Thus, public rituals articulated both the aspect of animals assuming human guilt and punishment in their own form and animals aping humans and getting away with it.[30]

Of course, both symbolic and sacrificial animals appeared at carnival time, when all barriers fell and all categories were inverted. Carnival was connected with specific animals, also sometimes sacrificed at the end of the ceremony, or with people disguised as animals. Foremost among these were the creatures denoting virility (or, for that matter, cuckolding): the cock and the horned hart. Many confraternities of fools dressed up in the costume of a cock, and a 'king cock'

---

[26] Roger Vaultier, *Le folklore pendant la guerre de Cent Ans d'après les lettres de rémission du trésor des chartes* (Paris, 1965), pp. 73-79.

[27] Gustave Cohen, *Le Théâtre comique au moyen-âge*, 2 vols. (Paris, 1941), 2:86.

[28] *Les Evangiles des quenouilles*, ed. P. Jannet (Paris, 1855), p. 154; Vaultier, *Le folklore*, loc. cit.; Muchembled, *Popular Culture*, pp. 84-85.

[29] Vaultier, *Le folklore*, pp. 77-78.

[30] Cf. Jawaharlal Handoo, "Cultural Attitudes to Birds and Animals in Folklore," in *Signifying Animals: Human Meaning in the Natural World*, ed. Roy Willis (London, 1990), pp. 37-42.

symbolized also the king of the carnival.[31] Other carnival animals, such as the ass (used for parading humiliated husbands) or the horse were associated with rituals of shame and punishment. But often the symbolism of carnival animals was far more individual. During the famous carnival in Romans (1580), which ended in riot and bloodshed, the bourgeois of the town used in their parade and costumes the cock, the eagle and the partridge. The artisans, relying upon older popular traditions, expressed their collective consciousness in parading as bears (symbol of spring), sheep, hares, capons (not exactly cocks!), and of course, as asses. The higher classes deliberately chose to identify with aerial animals of strong sexual and virile associations, while the poor were identified by terrestrial animals, some of them castrated (the capon), and others of no particular sexual connotation.[32]

Carnival was a time of inversions, serving largely to strengthen preexistent categories by the very attempt to ridicule them. The assumption by human beings of an animal guise in public rituals was not necessarily a humiliation. It depended not only upon the animal chosen, but also upon the situation. At a time of total (though temporary) structural breakdown, the choice of an animal dress was a statement of identity, not its loss. But this sort of symbolic character could only function in a society possessing a rich and permanent vocabulary of animal associations and representations. The animal's cultural context mattered more for the ritual than its physical presence.

Animals, collectively and individually, meant different things to different socio-intellectual groups. Clerical culture attempted as far as possible to distance the human from the animal, using the latter to symbolize not people, but abstract concepts and characteristics. Both courtly and popular lay culture consistently attributed to animals human traits, actions, modes of thought and of feeling rather than symbolic values. Furthermore, often the value of specific animals to human beings lay precisely in this similarity of characteristics. Whenever animals appeared in public rituals, with one notable exception, it was in the role of human surrogates. They were there mostly as scapegoats, the archetypal animal figures to assume human characteristics and more so: human sins, crimes, and punishments. In symbolic terms, it made perfect sense for the blameless cats to suffer, while the guilty fox remained unscathed, for he was too culpable to carry any but his own blame.

---

[31] Claude Gaignebet, *Le Carnaval* (Paris, 1974), pp. 133-35.
[32] Emmanuel Le Roy Ladurie, *Le carnaval de Romans* (Paris,1979), pp. 240-41.

The exception consisted of a third category of animals involved in justice and punishment, next to the felonious literary animal escaping retribution and the blameless beast suffering in the place of the guilty humans: those that stood trial in actual fact, enduring punishment for their own misdeeds. Unlike the first two categories, these animals were no human substitutes. They were emphatically non-human, their incorporation into human legal rituals being no attempt to gloss over their nature. Nevertheless, like all other rituals involving animals, these too were meant to affirm the perception of justice in the universe.

The maxim that justice meant giving each his due was based upon the assumption that, according to his or her status within a specific hierarchy, each recipient had a different due. Within the hierarchy of the universe, animals occupied a lower rung than humans, and therefore any damage by an animal to a human being was an offense against justice. It was therefore necessary to try offending animals and punish them, not so much as individual retribution against the specific beast, but far more as a gesture restoring the balance of justice.

2. THE TRIALS

The trials of animals deserve attention within a study of human justice precisely because, as in all other rituals, animals mirrored the human world. The manner in which they were placed before human courts may shed a great deal of light also on the attitudes of people towards justice in general.[33] The trials were held before all types of courts: royal, urban, seigneurial and ecclesiastical. Nevertheless, there were only two distinct procedures, secular and ecclesiastical. While the former was used to penalize domestic beasts that had mortally injured a human being, the latter was employed to rid the population of natural pests that could not individually be punished. The two types were clearly distinct, both in development and in procedure, and therefore require separate description.

A. *The Secular Trials*

Though animal trials were held all over Europe, their origin was clearly French. Secular trials were first recorded in the thirteenth century in Burgundy and in the Paris area, whence they spread first to all of northern France, as far west as Normandy and Brittany, and subse-

[33] Esther Cohen, "Law, Folklore, and Animal Lore," *Past and Present* 110 (1986), 6-37.

quently to the Low Countries, to Germany and to Italy.[34] Technically, secular trials followed the inquisitorial procedure strictly according to human rules. As in any human case of homicide, the crown or town authorities prosecuted the case, presenting the complaint and summoning the witnesses. The guilty beast, most often a pig or sow (but possibly also a cow, horse, ox, or dog), was placed in prison. Thus, when three sows attacked and killed a child at Saint-Marcel-les-Jussey in 1379, the town mayor promptly arrested the entire herd. Elsewhere, the gaoler of Pont-de-Larche charged the same *geôlage* for a porcine prisoner as for a human one.[35] Once the trial began, it was conducted along precisely the same lines as the trial of a human killer, with one exception. There is no evidence that anywhere in France the animal in question was actually brought into court. For the rest, the prosecution was represented by professional lawyers and all relevant witnesses could expect to be summoned. Though Jehan Bailly's sow and her six piglets had been caught in the act of killing the five-year-old Jehan Martin, the prosecution summoned several witnesses, eight of them personally named in the protocol, in order to prove the sow's guilt. Five other witnesses were summoned to testify in the subsequent trial which exonerated the piglets.[36]

Like human killers, animals could evade punishment by receiving a remission. The herd of swine arrested in Saint-Marcel-les-Jussey were formally pardoned by the duke of Burgundy at their owner's request.

---

[34] For a general overview of animal trials, see Karl von Amira, "Thierstrafen und Thierprocesse," *Mitteilungen des österreichischen Instituts für Geschichtsforschung* 12 (1891), 545-601; Berkenhoff, *Tierstrafe*; Edward P. Evans, *The Criminal Prosecution and Capital Punishment of Animals* (London, 1906, repr. 1987), and the bibliography therein [unless otherwise specified, references are to the 1987 edition]; Gérard Dietrich, *Les procès d'animaux du moyen-âge à nos jours* (Lyon, 1961); for trials in specific areas see Benno J. Stokvis, "Bijdrage tot de kennis van het wereldlijke dierenproces in de noordelijke Nederlanden," *Tijdschrift voor Strafrecht* 41 (1931), 399-424; A. van Praag, "Het strafproces tegen dieren," *Themis* 93 (1932), 345-75; K. Wehrhan, "Ein Detmolder Tierprozess von 1644 und die Bedeutung des Tierprozesses überhaupt," *Zeitschrift des Vereins für rheinische und westfälische Volkskunde* 1 (1904), 65-77; A. Sorel, "Procès contre les animaux et insectes suivis au moyen âge dans la Picardie et le Valois," *Bulletin de la Société historique de Compiègne* 3 (1876-77), 269-314.

[35] Evans, *The Criminal Prosecution*, pp. 292, 294-95. Berkenhoff, *Tierstrafe*, pp. 118-19. For other cases of imprisonment in Meulan (1403), in Laon (1494), and in Moyen-Moutier (1572), see Evans, *The Criminal Prosecution*, pp. 290, 306, and Berkenhoff, *Tierstrafe*, p. 124.

[36] The full text of the trial has been published by J. Berriat-Saint-Prix, "Rapport et recherches sur les procès et jugements rélatifs aux animaux," *Mémoires de la société royale des antiquaires de France* 8 (1829), pp. 441-45; Evans, *The Criminal Prosecution*, pp. 298-303; Berkenhoff, *Tierstrafe*, pp. 120-23.

The language of the remission clearly indicates that this was no farce, and that the arrest was no miscarriage of justice. The mayor had arrested the pigs "in order to execute reason and justice in the proper manner." Nevertheless, since only three sows were guilty, the owner requested that "while justice was done to the three or four said pigs, the rest should be released."[37]

Despite the strict adherence to legal procedure and phraseology, it is possible to detect the underlying ambivalence. The sentences pronounced against animals reveal in their phrasing a deeply embedded anthropomorphic attitude, coupled with the uncomfortable awareness of the very basic differences between human and animal culprits. Any local jurisdiction pronouncing a death sentence upon an animal had to state within the sentence that it possessed the privilege of high, or capital justice, just as it would have had to do before passing such a sentence upon a human malefactor.[38] In each case the wording stressed that the sentence had been passed after due deliberation, consultation with experts in customary law, and proper procedure: "... also [having taken] counsel with wise men and practitioners of law, and also considering in this case the usage and custom of the *pais* of Burgundy..." "according to the duty of justice, following consultations in the said procedure... I have just consulted with these good men, and here is our sentence, which I have had inscribed upon this paper..."[39] Furthermore, again as in the case of a human killer, the sentences took trouble to imply, though they did not openly say so, malicious intent. The sow tried in Savigny was "taken *en flagrant délit*, having committed and perpetrated... murder and homicide." Another had "killed and murdered" its victim, and yet another one had displayed "cruelty and ferocity" in killing a child.[40]

Nevertheless, occasionally the simple physical facts hindered a completely anthropomorphic application. The abbot of Moyen-Moutier had possessed from time immemorial, in addition to the privilege of high justice, the right to deliver his sentenced prisoners absolutely naked to the town gallows. But pigs being less amenable than human beings, they had to be led there with a rope. Thus, when a pig at Moyen-Moutier had killed the baby daughter of Claudon François, its

---

[37] "... arresta tous lesdits porcs pour en faire raison et justice en la manière qu'il appartient" "... en faisant justice de trois ou quatres desdits porcs le demeurant soit delivré." *Ibid.*, p. 119.

[38] E.g. *Ibid.*, p. 124.

[39] *Ibid.*, pp. 121, 124.

[40] *Ibid.*, p. 120; Evans, *The Criminal Prosecution*, pp. 288, 309.

sentence specified that though the culprit would be led to the gallows tied with a rope, this case would *not* serve as a precedent for human executions.[41] The physical differences between human beings and animals probably also accounted for the fact that in many cases the beast was hung upon a tree with thick, sturdy branches rather than a gallows.[42] Even so the execution paralleled the human ritual. Sometimes the animal was actually dragged prior to the hanging, like a human murderer, while on other occasions it was carried in a cart.[43] When a homicidal horse escaped, its effigy suffered the execution—again, as in the case of a person.[44] Wherever the hangmen's bills are extant, they closely resemble those presented for human executions.

Beyond the purely technical exigencies of animal anatomy, there lingered a perception that the killing of a human being by an animal was not quite the same thing as the killing of one person by another. It was indeed an unnatural act, a breach of the hierarchy of the universe. This perception probably lay at the roots of the northern French and Burgundian practice of inverted hanging of animals, as a sign of special infamy. The feeling also remained embedded in the language of the sentences. A sow was punished "due to the heinousness of the crime," a bull sentenced "in detestation of the said crime of homicide," and a pig "in detestation and horror of the said deed."[45] The last sentence added immediately after the visceral reaction of horror the words "and in order to make an example and guard justice." The same insistence upon justice was echoed also in other sentences: "In the said case we wish to proceed as justice and reason desire and require."[46] Thus, the phrasing both juxtaposed and identified the preservation of the universal hierarchy with the maintenance of justice. Justice thus assumed the proportions of supra-human, universal law, beyond the simple mechanisms of human relationships.

---

[41] Berkenhoff, *Tierstrafe*, p. 125.

[42] Evans, *The Criminal Prosecution*, p. 300, 307, 309; Berkenhoff, *Tierstrafe*, pp. 15-24, 121.

[43] *Ibid.*, pp. 24-40; Evans, *The Criminal Prosecution*, p. 290; E. Agnel, *Curiosités judiciaires et historiques du moyen âge. Procès contre les animaux* (Paris, 1858), p. 13.

[44] *Registre criminel de la justice de Saint-Martin-des-Champs à Paris au XIVe siècle*, ed. Louis Tanon (Paris, 1877), pp. 227-28.

[45] "pour l'esnormité du cas," Berkenhoff, *Tierstrafe*, p. 123; "pour la detestation du crime d'iceluy homicide," Evans, *The Criminal Prosecution*, p. 311; "... en detestation et horreur dudit cas" *Ibid.*, p. 307.

[46] *Ibid.*, p. 306.

The secular trials are proof of the fact that the writing of law, even when meant to be descriptive, is never an accurate mirror of practice. While quite a common usage, the custom of trying and executing homicidal animals received scant mention in written customals. For example, there is ample evidence for animal trials in Normandy and Brittany, but the customals of both areas make no mention of them.[47] The main reason for this silence is neither negligence nor ignorance. The writing of customary law came as a reaction to the changes which the system was undergoing in the thirteenth and fourteenth centuries, especially the introduction of Roman law. Even in areas in which Roman law carried no authority, it was always considered by jurists as an ultimate standard of legislative perfection to be emulated and cited as much as possible. Seen in this light, animal trials presented a rather difficult problem. Roman law included no such practice, specifically enunciating the principle of *noxae deditio* which stated in cases of animal damage that the offending animal be turned over to the injured party.[48] While this principle did assume that the consequences of the deed were to be borne by the offending agency, these consequences were in no way punitive. Rather, the injured party was compensated by a transfer of property. The animal was therefore viewed not as a sentient being, but as chattel. Prescribing animal trials would thus mean supporting what Pierre de Fontaines had termed *droit haineux*, or custom contrary to Roman law.

Consequently, the best-known customal authors evinced an ambiguous attitude in the matter of noxious animals. Roman influences notwithstanding, anthropomorphic elements appeared in an attenuated form in several customals. The author of the *Vieux Coustumier de Poictou* ordered the incarceration of animals straying into other people's fields.[49] Even more interesting is the comment of the *Livre de jostice et de plet*, emanating from the Orléanais:

> If your horse or your beast, your ox, your cow, your sows cause me damage, are you responsible? Not unless it has done so by my negligence or your poor watching; but the beast is responsible.... At all times that a four-footed beast or a private bird causes damage... the beast or private birds are responsible.

---

[47] J.-P. Leguay, *Un réseau urbain au moyen âge: Les villes du duché de Bretagne au XIVe et XVe siècle* (Paris, 1981), p. 290; for Normandy, among others Caen and Falaise, see Berkenhoff, *Tierstrafe*, pp. 16, 118; Evans, *The Criminal Prosecution*, pp. 140-41, 287; von Amira, "Thierstrafen," 552.

[48] *Institutiones* 4.9; *Digesta* 9.1.

[49] *Vieux Coustumier de Poictou*, pp. 161-63.

Nowhere did the author carry this argument further, to claim that the beast's responsibility inevitably carried culpability and punishment. To the contrary, when discussing penalties, he clearly stated that a noxious animal was forfeit to the injured party. But obviously he considered that the punishment of forfeiture was inflicted upon the animal, not the owner.[50]

Only three customals mentioned animal trials specifically. Beaumanoir, who condemned them in 1283, was probably the earliest. According to the author of the customs of the Beauvaisis, the only justification for the usage lay in the cupidity of seigneurial authorities reluctant to relinquish a profitable source of income. The practice was juridically meaningless and invalid, for all crime presupposes intent, and beasts possessing neither knowledge of good and evil nor malicious intentions could not be held responsible for their actions.[51]

If one accepted his notions of justice, Beaumanoir's criticism might have been valid from the purely theoretical point of view. The imputation of venality, however, was strictly false. Lords stood to gain only under a system by which a homicidal beast was impounded to the profit of the judicial authority. The execution of an animal was just as expensive as that of a man, especially in small jurisdictions requiring the services of hangman from another town. The hangman's travel and time costs in such a case would also have been charged to the judicial authority. While the beast's owner lost, the lord stood to gain no material profits. Beaumanoir's accusation suggests that he was familiar not only with local practice, which prescribed execution in all cases, but also with the Burgundian custom of impounding certain homicidal animals.

This distinction was made by the *Coustumes et stilles de Bourgoigne*, composed sometime between 1270 and 1360:

> It is stated according to the law and custom of Burgundy that if an ox or a horse commit one or more homicides, they should not die, nor should they be tried and executed. Rather, they should be impounded by the lord in whose jurisdiction they had committed the crime, or by his men, to be confiscated and sold for the said lord's profit.

---

50 "Et se ton cheval ou ta beste, ton buef, ta vaiche, tes truies, me font domage, i es-tu tenuz? Nenil, s'a ne l'a fet par ma négligence ou par mauvèse garde; mès la beste i est tenue... A totes les foiz que beste en quatre piez fet doumage, ou oissel privé... la beste ou li oisiaus privez i sont tenuz." *Livre de jostice*, p. 322. Cf. *Ibid.*, p. 278.

51 *CB*, art. 1944, 2:481.

> But if another animal or a Jew do it, they should be hung by their rear legs.[52]

The statement is curious enough on the face of it. This was the only customal specifically to mention the upside-down hanging, common indeed in Burgundy, though fairly rare elsewhere.[53] More importantly, the Burgundian customal distinguished between two categories: the horse or ox, which were impounded and sold, and all the rest of the animal world plus the Jews, who were executed. The differentiation makes little sense on the purely practical level, and indeed it was never honored in Burgundy in practice. In 1314 an ox was hung in Moisey-le-Temple, and in 1389 a horse suffered the same fate in Dijon.[54] Furthermore, no such distinction was ever made elsewhere in France or in the rest of Europe. One could perhaps dismiss it as a local peculiarity, were it not for the fact that animal trials very probably originated in Burgundy. Even if practice blurred the finer distinctions, the fact that the authors of the customal took the trouble to record them says a great deal about their perception of animals and animal categories. Since Jews were included as well, the custom may shed light also upon attitudes towards some human categories.

At first sight, it might be argued that sheer economic calculation could justify the difference. Horses and oxen were expensive animals, and their execution might have been considered wasteful. The economic argument, however, is not very plausible. If this were the reason, cows would have been included in the same category. Furthermore, the most common perpetrators were pigs, accounting for more than half of all recorded animal executions, and within the context of peasant economy the loss of a pig could be just as disastrous as that of a bigger animal. Most people were far likelier to own a pig, or another small animal, than a horse or an ox. Nor is it probable that the law should implicitly distinguish between animals owned by people of different classes. Given the contemporary tendency of custom to pre-

---

52 "L'on dit et tient selon droit et la coustume de Bourgoigne que se un boeuf ou un cheuau fait un ou pluseurs homicides il nan doiuent poinct morir, ne lon nen doit faire justice, feur quilz doiuent estre pris par le seigneur en qui justice ilz on fait le delit ou par ses gens, et lui sont confisquez et doiuent estre vendus et exploictiez au prouffit du dit seigneur; mes se autres bestes ou juyf le font, ilz doiuent estre pendus par les piez derreniers." *Costumes et stilles de Bourgoigne*, quoted in Giraud, *Essai sur l'histoire du droit*, 2:302.

53 Evans, *The Criminal Prosecution*, p. 300; Guy Pape, the fifteenth-century Burgundian jurist, both testified to this practice and gave it his seal of approval; Gui Pape, *Decisiones*, q. 238, pp. 254-55.

54 Berkenhoff, *Tierstrafe*, pp. 28, 32-33.

scribe in all fields explicitly different standards for people of different socio-judicial standing, such a distinction would have been openly stated.[55]

The only possible explanation lies in the special role of horses and oxen within peasant existence. Of all domestic animals, these two are the most common work animals that serve. Furthermore, they are draught-animals, working harnessed and controlled by humans, so that their subjection to man is the most clearly explicit of all animals. Most other domestic beasts serve man not by their actions, but by providing food or wool. Nor are they physically constrained to do man's will. One may harness a horse to the plough or the cart, but one cannot force the cow to give milk, or the chicken to lay an egg. The hierarchical relationship between man and the beasts of service was thus maintained by daily actions, and needed no ritual reaffirmation in cases of infraction. By contrast, man's relationship to the pig or the sheep did need such a symbolic formulation when the hierarchy was breached, largely because the relationship was not so emphatically clear-cut. The place of the Jew within this scheme is a clear indicator of the symbolic importance of the execution. The Jew was an inferior human being who refused to accept a subordinate role within what should have been Christian society. Very much like the pig that had killed a child, a Jew who had killed a Christian had committed an act so heinous, so contrary to proper hierarchical perceptions, that he had to be executed by means of the inverted hanging.

The customs of Burgundy thus implicitly provided a rationale for animal trials. Towards the end of the fourteenth century one of the most famous customal authors of the time, Jean Boutillier, provided an explicit justification. Under the rubric *De la beste tuer homme* Boutillier prescribed the execution of killer animals by virtue of the biblical injunction to kill a goring ox. However, he added, if the victim was a serf its owner must pay the serf's lord 30 *deniers* silver, symbolizing the thirty generations issued from Cham, Noah's cursed son, while the beast should still be destroyed.[56]

Boutillier did more than quote a precedent. Nowhere in other customals or in trial protocols is there any indication of a special arrangement for compensation in the case of an injured serf. The ruling

[55] Thus, the customs of Poitou clearly distinguish between the fate of an animal straying into the field of a lord possessing jurisdiction and another who possesses no such privilege. *Vieux coustumier de Poictou*, pp. 162-63.

[56] *SR*, p. 267.

concerning a serf's death was taken directly from the Bible, where it follows immediately upon that of the ox that gored: "If an ox gore a man or a woman that they shall die, then the ox shall be surely stoned.... If the ox shall push a male or female slave, he shall give unto their master thirty shekels of silver.... and the ox shall be stoned."[57] The insertion of Cham, who does not appear in Exodus twenty-one at all, and whose progeny was cursed with eternal slavery for his irreverence towards his father, merely emphasized the anti-hierarchical nature of the crime.

Boutillier was the *bailli* of the Tournaisis, and his *Somme rural* described the practice of his area. Animal trials were indeed very common there, and even an author anxious to clothe his practices with the respectability of a precedent could neither ignore nor reconcile them with Roman law. One solution was to remain ambiguous, as the author of the *Livre de jostice et de plet* had done, but another was to tag on a precedent. The great arguments concerning ecclesiastical trials, due eventually to provide a theoretical foundation for practice, were still to come, and Boutillier knew of no precedent outside customary law barring the Bible. He thus invoked the most venerable precedent he could find. In the process he also inserted some extraneous biblical matter, presumably to make his statement look more learned. His elaborations, therefore, say little about fourteenth-century perceptions of animals, but a great deal about perceptions of what customary law should look and sound like. The trend of camouflaging customary material in respectable clothing, preferably Roman but possibly also biblical, was typical of much customary legal writing.

Unlike Roman law scholars, customal writers were not much given to glossing and commenting. Nor were their texts, essentially manuals of practice, suitable vehicles for theoretical disquisitions. They meant whatever comments they introduced in their books to be acted upon, not debated. If they condemned, it was in order to eradicate a custom they considered unjustifiable. If they justified the same custom by tagging on an artificial precedent, it was in order to preserve and strengthen the custom. But there is very little evidence that either praise or condemnation influenced usage. When secular sentences of animals in France quoted any precedent at all, it was the custom of the land, not the Bible. Most significantly, the great sixteenth-century debaters on the subject of ecclesiastical animal trials were entirely

[57] Exodus, 21:28, 32.

unaware of customary opinions. The only customary authority ever quoted was Gui Pape, the fifteenth-century Dauphinois jurist who baldly supported animal trials simply because such was Burgundian custom.[58] While customary jurisprudence may provide the modern historian with an insight into late medieval attitudes towards law and animals, it did nothing to influence practice.

B. *The Ecclesiastical Trials*

Ecclesiastical trials formulated the universality of the justice meted out by human courts and the human status of non-human litigants far more explicitly than secular protocols. They belonged to an entirely different tradition of legal rituals, appearing much later than the secular cases. The earliest recorded court cases belong to the fifteenth century, originating in the border areas between France, Switzerland and Italy. Relying upon the international network of ecclesiastical jurisdiction, the usage subsequently spread much farther than secular trials ever did. Ecclesiastical animal trials spread from their original epicenter to Germany, Scandinavia, Spain, Canada, and Brazil.[59]

Unlike the secular trials, ecclesiastical ones followed a modified form of the accusatory mode of procedure. There was no one victim when the rats or the weevils destroyed the crops. Thus, entire rural communes took their natural scourges to court before the only human authority conceivably able to aid the injured party: the ecclesiastical courts of canon law. As the local commune came to represent humanity in its battle for survival within a hostile natural environment, the communal character of these trials quickly grew to symbolic proportions.

Perhaps because of their late appearance, when the science of jurisprudence had evolved to great lengths, and perhaps because of the clerical venue, the ecclesiastical trials served as scenes of extremely thorough debates concerning the roles and interchanging relationships of God, man, animals and the vegetable world that fed all of God's creatures. The range and types of sources cited in justification and rebuttal of either position goes far beyond the purely judicial. In addition to Roman law and the rare customary precedent, one finds citations of biblical cases, chronicles, and saints' lives. The seventeenth-century jurist Gaspar Bailly, who constructed an entirely

[58] See above, n. 53.

[59] For a thorough analysis of the procedure, development and spread of the ecclesiastical trials, see von Amira, "Thierstrafen," 560-72.

fictitious animal trial in order to demonstrate the proper procedure of a monitory, went so far as to cite the poetry of Ovid and Pico della Mirandola's famous oration on the excellence of man.[60] In this he followed in the footsteps of Bartholomé Chassenée, who cited the same authorities in his *concilium* on the subject of animal trials. Clearly the lawyers, judges and litigants involved in these trials took them very seriously indeed, devoting a great deal of thought to their arguments and strategies.

According to Bailly, the judge receiving the complaint first had to send someone to investigate the extent of the damage wrought by the defendants. Furthermore, ecclesiastical courts invariably demanded public processions and prayers to allay heaven's anger before the trial proper began.[61] Next, the court appointed a procurator to represent the animals. In fifteenth-century Chur this was done because the defendant beetles were pronounced minors.[62] A century later the official of the bishop of Maurienne granted both a procurator and an advocate to the flies of Saint-Julien-de-Maurienne "lest the animals against whom the action lies should remain defenseless."[63] This was no simple formality, as procurators took their job very seriously, devoting a great deal of time, knowledge and legal experience to the defense of their clients. Essentially, they could adopt one of three strategies. First, they could avoid all arguments by the use of dilatory tactics. Failing these, they could claim once the trial opened that the court had no jurisdiction over animals. If this line of defense too crumbled, they could try to vindicate their clients' actions.

The dilatory tactics common to all trials—a request of time to study the arguments of the prosecution, or to receive a proper copy of the same—were used also in animal trials. But the most important dilatory tactic was employed at the first stage, or the summons. As defendants, the pests were to be summoned three times and, failing to appear, declared contumacious. In most cases the court simply accepted the

---

[60] Gaspard Bailly, "De l'excellence des monitoires," in Evans, *The Criminal Prosecution* (1906 edition), pp. 287-306.

[61] See the letters of the bishops and officials of Autun, Lyon, and Mâcon to their parish priests, quoted in Bartholomé Chassenée, "Concilium primum de excommunicatione animalium," in his *Concilia D. Bartholomaei a Chasseneo, Burgundi iurisconsulti* (Lyon, 1588), fol. 17vo-20vo.

[62] Felix Malleolus, "Tractatus secundus de exorcismis," in his *Variae oblationes, opuscula et tractatus* (Basle, 1497), fol. 79.

[63] The entire protocol of the trial was published by Léon Ménabréa, *De l'origine, de la forme et de l'esprit des jugements rendus contre les animaux* (Chambéry, 1846), appendix, and by Evans, pp. 259-305 (1906 edition).

fact that rats or locusts were not likely to respond to the summons, considering the procurator's presence sufficient for continuing. A clever lawyer, however, could turn this absence to his profit. The leading authority on animal trials in sixteenth-century France, Bartholomé Chassenée, gained his reputation initially thanks to precisely such tactics. He was appointed as a young advocate in Autun to defend the rats laying waste the fields. The rats had indeed been properly summoned three times, but before they could be declared contumacious, their lawyer argued that the summons had not been properly served. Since "in this affair the salvation or ruin of all rats was at stake" all rats deserved to be informed, and this had not been done. At his demand, the priests of each and every parish within the diocese of Autun announced a new summons. When the rats failed once more to appear, Chassenée claimed that the time granted for their appearance was too short, especially since his clients had to avoid the ambushes laid by cats on their way to court, thus achieving another delay. Though no one had bothered to record the end of the trial, the dilatory arguments were remembered for many years, not as a brilliant *tour de force* of legal casuistry, but as a plea for "the order and forms of justice."[64]

The second line of defense, or arguments against human jurisdiction over animals, was usually grounded in Roman law. No action could lie against the senseless, lacking both reason and intention. Hence, one could neither sue, summon, nor try an animal. Furthermore, as the animal kingdom was subject only to natural law, no canon law court had any jurisdiction over it. No record remains to show whether any ecclesiastical court ever accepted these arguments. Counsel for the prosecution usually argued back on biblical grounds, though adducing also legal reasons. Even Roman law admitted that though one could not punish the insensate for former deeds, one could well take steps to restrict the same from committing any further damage, as one would do in the case of a dangerous madman. This, argued Bailly, was the aim of the ecclesiastical trials: not to penalize the animals, but to prevent their doing any further damage. The jurisdiction of canon law, affirmed Chassenée, extended to all of God's creatures, animals forming no exception.[65]

---

[64] Auguste de Thou, *Histoire universelle depuis 1593 jusqu'en 1607*, 16 vols. (London, 1734), 1:414-16.

[65] Chassenée, "Concilium," fols. 14vo-16vo; Bailly, "De l'excellence," pp. 297-98.

Once a trial had proceeded beyond this stage, the competence of the court being affirmed, the arguments tended to center around two questions. The first and most basic was the right of the animals to survive in nature. Animals, it was argued, were created before man, thus enjoying prior rights in the vegetable kingdom. Moreover, though lacking reason, animals did fulfill a preordained role within creation, so that their consumption of vegetation was fulfilling God's plan. They were well within their rights according to divine law. If this consumption reached the proportions of a scourge, it was undoubtedly no more than God's punishment for people's sins. Was it either just or useful to punish God's emissaries, asked the defense? To the contrary, an attempt to stop them would be tantamount to opposing God. It would be better to pray, repent, give alms and pay tithes more faithfully, it suggested.

The counter-arguments invariably centered around the hierarchy of creation. On cosmogonic grounds, both animal and vegetable kingdoms were created for the utility of man, any beast contravening this order by consuming man's food and causing him famine automatically going against God's will. Once more both divine and natural law were cited, this time to support the opposite point of view. Man's creation as last of all only indicated his supreme position and the subordination of all the rest to him. Furthermore, numerous precedents, both biblical and hagiographical, could be adduced to support the intervention of human beings against animals, plants, or even objects. David had cursed the mountains of Gilboa, Christ had doomed a barren fig-tree, and Saint Bernard had done the same to the flies interrupting his sermon.[66] Thus a holy man, or even simply a man imbued with God's power by reason of his office, could invoke heavenly wrath upon an animal or plant failing in its role towards human beings. The fact that even a fig tree guilty only of barrenness could incur a curse indicated that those creatures actually noxious to man could all the more be punished.

The precedent provided not only the principle, but also the means of action. If animals were to be punished at all, it could only be done by the clergy and through an ecclesiastical punitive ritual. Though the sentences speak interchangeably of cursing, adjuration, anathema, excommunication, and exorcism, all precedents concerned in actual fact only cursing. At this point, lawyers for the defense usually inter-

---

[66] Malleolus, "Tractatus primus de exorcismis," fol. 74vo; "Tractatus secundus," fol. 78vo-79ro; Chassenée, "Concilium," fols. 16vo-17ro.

vened once more, arguing that one could hardly excommunicate someone who did not belong to the body Christian to begin with, and had furthermore committed no sin. In fact, the so-called excommunications of animals were, technically speaking, no such thing. An examination of actual sentences pronounced against animals yields only one case in which the term excommunication was actually used, and rather loosely there too.[67] Usually, if the animals lost their case (and this was by no means a foregone conclusion), they were solemnly adjured to vacate the lands or vineyards they had been devastating within a given period of time, often six days. If they failed to do so, they would be cursed and anathemized, or even exorcized.

Indeed, being part of an adversary procedure, ecclesiastical sentences aimed not to exterminate or punish, but to obtain relief for the plaintiffs by getting rid of the pests. The very idea of exorcism does not imply destruction, but the removal of a noxious element. Though the anathema sentences were far more mildly phrased than the exorcisms, both insisted upon one point—that the objects of the ritual should suit their existence to human convenience: "... wherever you go, be cursed so that you may decrease from day to day, till nothing is left of you except what is needed for the use of humans... whose shape He who will judge the living and the dead by fire has deigned to assume." "I exorcize you... that you should immediately retreat from these fields... nor should you further reside there, but should move to such places where you cannot harm any of God's servants...."[68]

There was thus little difference between losing or winning a case. The pests were to be moved away either by agreement or by force of exorcism. The suggestion that the animals in question should be assigned a separate piece of land where they could live unmolested and unmolesting surfaced throughout the trials. It was a compromise suggested in one case by the plaintiffs during the trial, rejected by the animals' advocate only because the land in question was unsuitable for his clients. In another, the court itself decided upon this solution.[69] The net result was that, willingly or under ecclesiastical coercion, the animals were to be removed from cultivated to wild land.

---

[67] Mâcon, 1487, *Ibid.*, fol. 19ro.

[68] Malleolus, "Tractatus secundus," fol. 79ro; Maximilian d'Eynatten, *Manuale exorcismorum*, in *Thesaurus exorcismorum atque coniurationum terribilium* (Cologne, 1626), p. 1201.

[69] Ménabréa, "De l'origine," appendix; Malleolus, "Tractatus secundus," fol. 79ro-vo.

Throughout these trials runs a strong feeling that if animals were subject to human justice, they were just as much deserving of a full measure of justice. It was this feeling that made the Autun court accept Chassenée's claims for the rats, and what so impressed his contemporaries that when seeking similar justice from him for heretics years later, they cited the case back at him. The very appointment of a procurator for the creatures and the suggestion that they be assigned a separate piece of land reflected the same attitude. The most extreme example comes from Stelvio in Switzerland, where the expulsion sentence of the field-mice allowed the pregnant and infant rodents a longer term before vacating the fields.[70]

While there was very little congruence between practice and jurisprudence in secular cases, the contrary is true for the ecclesiastical trials. Before suing the local insects, the citizens of Beaune were willing to pay a leading jurist in the field to write a learned opinion on the subject of animal punishment. Chassenée's *concilium*, entitled "*de excommunicatione animalium insectorum*" (though hardly dealing at all with excommunication), summed up practically all the relevant arguments, and they hardly differ from or add much to those voiced in court.

Nevertheless, it was the theoretical argument that shaped the practical court-case. The reason for this odd development lay in the fact that theory preceded practice by close to two centuries, and tradition preceded theory by several more. This tradition had nothing to do with law, but with punishment. Just as the goring ox in the Bible was to be killed, not necessarily tried, thus the natural pests had been freely cursed and anathemized by biblical figures and later saints without any semblance of legal proceedings. It took the medieval legal mentality to assume that one could no more punish an animal than a human being without a proper trial.

The precedents cited in favor of ecclesiastical animal trials, therefore, had two things in common. In the first place, they dealt with cursing, not trials. Secondly, the cursing was done by a holy man, an agent of God, and in his name. While some of these precedents concerned scourges harming a community, most of them were actually the saint's personal revenge upon animals that had irritated or betrayed him. The bishop of Mâcon cursed the sparrows interrupting his sermons, so that henceforth any sparrow entering the church should

[70] Evans, *The Criminal Prosecution*, pp. 112-13, 259-60.

fall dead. A hermit cursed the fish who had betrayed his hiding-place, so that from that day they vanished from the local river.[71]

These characteristics explain why, though biblical precedents abounded, no ecclesiastical authority ever cited the ox that gored. The ox may not have been tried, but it was punished by a purely human agency in a straightforward human manner. The power of God and his role, the power of the holy man and his special role as God's representative were both entirely lacking. The simple stoning or execution were totally irrelevant within the context of cursing animals.

Indeed, the first important opinion on the subject concerned exclusively the cursing of animals, the author being interested in the subject on purely philosophical grounds. Like his lay contemporary Beaumanoir, Thomas Aquinas strongly objected to the usage. While Beaumanoir based his argument on the legal concept of intent, Aquinas centered his objections to the anathemizing of harmful pests around the philosophical idea of reason. Animals, defined as insensate and irrational, could suffer no guilt, and consequently no punishment for their actions. Curses and anathemas presupposed both the object's culpability and its amenability to punishment. Since neither quality characterized the animal world, its very nature voided and nullified the curses. Man and animal were separated by the impassable barrier of reason.

Aquinas' final argument brought the entire issue back from philosophy into the realm of theology. Like the rest of the world, animals were God's creatures fulfilling by their actions God's will. Cursing them, therefore, was more than useless: it was blasphemous. Aquinas did acknowledge that noxious animals might be the devil's emissaries rather than God's, but in that case, he pointed out, any anathema or adjuration should be addressed to the willing author of the damage rather than to his unreasoning agents. Aquinas refuted awkward biblical precedents in two ways. Either the penalized animal or object symbolized human beings, or the extermination of the animal was incidental to the relations between man, God, and the devil. Theriomorphic devils were adjured purely as Satan's servants, and real animals were killed to penalize their owners.[72]

Thomas' stature in the late medieval and early modern world of learning made it impossible to ignore his opinions. In categorical opposition to jurists' opinions, theologians repeated Aquinas' rulings

[71] *Anecdotes historiques*, pp. 256-59.
[72] Thomas Aquinas, *Summa theologiae*, 2a-2ae, q. 76; q. 108, a. 4.

in later centuries time and again.[73] The weight of ecclesiastical opinion was on the whole opposed to these trials, many bishops following the advice of the eminent Spanish theologian Martín de Azpilcueta, ordering the suffering communities to repent their sins before attempting any judicial redress.[74] Some of them were willing to admit that the animals in question might be of demonic origin, and thus worthy of exorcism, but even then they were reluctant to conduct a trial.

The one authority to combine both theological and jurisprudential eminence, the Swiss Felix Malleolus, threw his weight decidedly in favor of animal trials. Perhaps the strong Swiss tradition in this matter influenced his decision, but Malleolus, conscious of the weight of opinion against him, was still very careful. He avoided altogether the argument whether or not to try, merely citing precedents, both biblical and contemporary, and prescribing the proper procedure to be followed. This stance earned him later the strong disapproval of the Jesuit Martín Delrío, who took care in his condemnation of the trials to mention that the works of Malleolus were forbidden reading.[75]

The fact that animal trials continued to be held in ecclesiastical courts was due mainly to indirect popular pressure voiced by hired lawyers. Unlike the theologians, jurists on the whole accepted the idea that animals could and should be tried, defending it enthusiastically. Though hardly able to ignore the weight of learned opposition, they could certainly argue with it. In some cases the difficulty was solved by legal casuistry. True, animals were not amenable by their nature to cursing, but one could curse them insofar as they harmed humans. A failure to do so would cause famine, bringing death in its wake. Thus, reasoned Chassenée, not cursing the pests was tantamount to homicide, certainly a greater evil than the cursing. All the more reason to intervene if animals were simply following their nature, because in that case the crime was immanent in the criminal's disposition, and in that case even the punishment of an irrational beast was permitted.[76]

These arguments were no mere learned quibbling. Lawyers hired by rural and urban communities to prosecute animals advanced them in court in all seriousness. Whether the lawyers believed their words or merely argued for pay is irrelevant: they built a framework of ideology

[73] For a listing of theological opinions, see von Amira, "Thierstrafen," 571-72.
[74] Martín de Azpilcueta, "Consilium No. 52," in his *Opera omnia*, 5 vols. (Cologne, 1616), 3:282-83.
[75] Martín Delrío, *Disquisitiones magicarum...*, liber III, pars 2, q. 4, section 8 (Mainz, 1603), pp. 96-97.
[76] Chassenée, "Concilium," fols. 14vo, 16ro.

that firmly included animals within human justice. One must also remember that the ecclesiastical community was no ideological monolith. While eminent theologians might have disapproved, local curates and canons, and in certain areas even bishops, adopted a far more lenient attitude. There were quite enough biblical precedents for cursing to justify holding such trials when people so demanded. In fact, many bishops continued holding animal trials, cheerfully ignoring scholastic condemnations. The practice began roughly a century before the need for commissioning and writing defense literature arose, continuing despite theological condemnations throughout the seventeenth century. This could not have been done had local ecclesiastical courts not cooperated with popular demands.

The ambivalence of the episcopate found its expression in an intermediate type of literature. Based upon a mixture of theological erudition and familiarity with local practices, it sought to reconcile the two. The treatise "*De superstitionibus*" of Martín de Arles y Andosilla, canon of Pamplona cathedral and doctor of theology, was an extremely popular attempt of this type. Written early in the sixteenth century, it went during the century through five editions in France, Germany, and Italy. Nevertheless, it had little impact in learned circles. A century later Delrío alone knew the treatise, but disapproved of it. Other seventeenth-century experts on witchcraft and popular superstitions did not seem to have come across the work.[77]

Andosilla clearly reflected the position of those clergymen learned enough to know that indiscriminate cursing of animals was illicit, but close enough to their parishioners to sympathize with their needs. The only solution for the Paris-trained theologian attempting to separate licit practice from superstition was either to invent or twist the meaning of his sources. Andosilla came down squarely in favor of practice in a chapter querying whether it was permitted to adjure wolves, snakes, locusts and "other such animals". As proof he cited two authorities: one was a non-existent passage of William of Auvergne, and the other was the famous statement of Thomas Aquinas, which claimed in actual fact the exact opposite. Thomas had indeed admitted that one was allowed to exorcize devils when they entered animal bodies. Andosilla went one step further, claiming that serpents were

[77] For a full survey of Andosilla's life, the history of the treatise and a scientific edition of the same, see José Goñi Gaztambide, "El tratado *De superstitionibus* de Martín de Andosilla," *Cuadernos de etnología y etnografía de Navarra* 9 (1971), 249-322.

invariably theriomorphic devils, and therefore the divine injunction was valid against them. It was a short step from this point to the exorcism of wolves, locusts, and all other noxious animals.[78]

The growth of both literacy and anti-witchcraft literature in the sixteenth century made the rendering in learned garb of such an opinion possible. Andosilla was no Thomas Aquinas, not even an Azpilcueta. He was merely a local canon with some education trying to apply his knowledge to the problems of defining and combating superstition. In the process, he tagged a badge of respectability onto a number of practices which he considered licit, among them the exorcism of animals. His words probably did not carry enough authority to justify ecclesiastical animal trials anywhere outside Navarre, but they reflected a true picture of a parochial ecclesiastical approach alien to the rarified circles of theologians.

The ecclesiastical trials involved rural plaintiffs, clerical judges and highly trained lawyers, each group holding different views of the animal world. In this they differed drastically from the secular trials, where litigants and judges came from roughly the same perceptual and intellectual stratum, sharing fairly similar perceptions of animals. One can in consequence perceive throughout the arguments and counter-arguments a commingling of three different views of the animal world. The lawyers on both sides usually adopted the learned attitude that clearly demarcated the human from the animal. They stressed time and again that the animals in question had no reason or understanding. The right of people to try animals was not evidence of equality, or even similarity. To the contrary, it was clear proof of superiority, of the legal lordship man held over nature. Animals were subject to man, and therefore also to his judicial system. Their belonging to a different category of being made no difference, since justice transcended all categories.

This position differed subtly from that of the plaintiffs. Though by the fifteenth century litigants no longer spoke with their own voice, but employed a lawyer who used the arguments of jurisprudence, occasionally one may find their beliefs expressed in action. When the syndics and commune of Saint-Julien, dissatisfied with the leisurely pace of the case, came together offering a compromise to the flies, they conceivably considered their step a viable solution. While the lawyers repeated time and again their full awareness of the insensate

[78] *Ibid.*, pp. 290-91.

character of the animals, the people who brought the case before the court probably considered the animals as real adversaries.

The disposition to view insensate creatures as legal personalities crept also into judicial arguments. When Chassenée argued his clients' fear of the cats as the reason for their failure to appear in court, he was not only establishing a supreme standard of universal justice. While both he and the judges knew that fear of cats had nothing to do with the rats' contumacy, both sides considered the argument perfectly valid within the context of the trial. Once the issue was joined, the court acted upon the premise that the animals were like all other *justiciables*. It had to determine whether they were lay or clerical, adult or minor, capable of defending themselves or not, but all those arguments would have applied to human beings as well.

A third strain, mixing with the other two, was the ecclesiastical point of view expressed in the exorcism sentences. These resembled most closely the old motif of the holy man exhibiting God's power over nature by efficaciously cursing plants or animals. Animals were part of one conjurable universe. In this universe physical elements, food, animals, devils, and people all interacted, permeated and motivated by the same forces. Thus, counselled Girolamo Mengo, anyone wishing to exorcize a devil from a possessed person had first to verify the expelled spirit's destination. Therefore, one had first to conjure the four elements: air and water not to hold the spirit; fire, unless it be hellfire, to reject it equally, and earth, to swallow it indeed, but only in a *locus turpissimus*, probably hell. All elements were to be conjured so that they cooperate with the exorcism. Even hell was conjured to swallow back the errant spirit. By the same token, the salt, oil, and medicines employed in the exorcism were not simply blessed, like any object used in ritual. They were addressed as *creatura salis, creatura olei*, and *creatura medicinae* in the rite, thus being treated as sentient beings.[79]

The material and the immaterial, human and demonic were all placed on one level, subject to God's power as wielded by the exorcist. Animals, naturally, fitted in this scheme. If one could exorcize milk soured due to the devil's malice, one could just as easily exorcize animals. This was especially true if, like the souring agent in the milk, they were acting as the devil's emissaries. The essential question was whose agents the noxious animals were. If indeed they were sent by

[79] Girolamo Mengo, *Flagellum daemonum*, in *Thesaurus exorcismorum*, pp. 331-39, 371-88.

God, as many theologians affirmed, an exorcism would be worse than useless. But if one viewed them as demonic forces, there was every justification for an exorcism.

Were the animals in the ecclesiastical trials actually seen as theriomorphic devils? There is a great deal of evidence in witchcraft literature for the belief that devils did assume animal shape.[80] The devilish animal was closely tied to the theriomorphic human, the werewolf. The devil was addressed in one of Mengo's exorcisms as "beast, serpent, ... locust-like, scabby beast, beastlier than all beasts..."[81] Nevertheless, the sentences against pests merely stated that they were noxious to humans. The precedents quoted in sentences were invariably those of holy men cursing animal nuisances, not the exorcism of devils in animal form. While the trials of animals and witches were somehow connected, the link was never explicitly stated in the trial records. One could adjure anything damaging to man within the universe by using the techniques of exorcism, and animals were simply another exorcizeable category. Thus, the popular stance implied an equality of man and animal before justice by virtue of certain similarities, while the judicial position assumed that animals were tried before human courts by virtue of their subjection to man, and the ecclesiastical attitude claimed that animals were punished not by people, but by God acting through certain people.

All these elements—community, law, and religion—came together in the ritual of animal exorcism. A nineteenth-century copper engraving, copying a presently-vanished fifteenth-century original, shows such a scene. In this engraving Benedict of Montferrand, bishop of Lausanne, stands cursing the eels of Lake Leman.[82] The picture shows the bishop in full regalia, mitered and carrying his staff, standing on a hill next to the lake. Behind him appear all the people of Lausanne,

---

[80] See, most notably, J. Sprenger and H. Institoris, *Malleus maleficarum*, trans. M. Summers (London, 1968), *passim*; Kathryn C. Smith, "The Role of Animals in Witchcraft and Popular Magic," in J.R. Porter and W.M.S. Russel, eds., *Animals in Folklore* (Cambridge, 1978), pp. 96-110; Marijke Gijswijt-Hofstra, "Mens, dier en demon. Parallellen tussen dieren en heksenprocessen?" *Geschiedenis, Godsdienst, Letterkunde: Festschrift S.B.J. Zilverberg*, ed. E.K. Grootes and J. den Haan (Roden, 1989), pp. 55-62.

[81] "bestia, serpens... bestia eruginosa, bestia scabiosa, omnium bestiarum bestiatissima..." Mengo, *Flagellum daemonum*, p. 308.

[82] The case was quite genuine apparently, for Malleolus, Chassenée, and Théophile Raynaud had cited it as precedent. Malleolus, "Tractatus secundus," fol. 80ro; Théofile Raynaud, *Opuscula moralia* (Lyon, 1665), p. 482. Chassenée, "concilium," fol. 17ro.

witnessing the exorcism.[83] Quite clearly, the event was a public ritual in which the local commune—the plaintiffs in the trial—played an extremely important role. The sentences allowing exorcism all repeated the same motif. Even before the trial took place, the entire commune joined in processions of prayer, repentance, and charity. They proceeded to court only if this expedient failed. After the trial the procedure moved back to the public domain. The snails of Autun having lost their case in 1487, the bishop instructed the rectors of all parishes in his diocese to act in the following manner:

> We hereby order that you convoke your parishioners, one and all, of both sexes, and march in procession with holy water and the standard of the cross throughout and around the boundaries of your parishes, while sprinkling holy water within the said boundaries, chanting the litany, and exhorting your people to come with you devotedly, [carrying] burning candles, and humbly to exhort and beg of God, the glorious Virgin Mary and all of God's saints that they should deign to free them of this tribulation; and you should warn and adjure the said snails damaging the land and its fruits by virtue of our Lord Jesus Christ and his most glorious passion, and the blessed apostles Peter and Paul, that they should desist within three days' time from the destruction and devastation of the said fruits and transfer themselves to deserted places, where they shall not be able to damage creatures and the fruits of the earth, under threat of the divine majesty's anger and eternal curse. And you shall conduct such processions for three continuous days without interruption, exhorting your people to devotion insofar as possible, and thus cursing the snails, so that by God's mercy we may be freed of this scourge.[84]

---

[83] Hans Fehr, *Das Recht in Bilde* (Erlenbach-Zürich, 1923), p. 46, plate 70, and pp. 69-70.

[84] "... praecipimus & mandamus quatenus convocatis omnibus et singulis parochianis vestris utriusque sexus, cum aqua benedicta et vexillo processionaliter accedatis per & inter fines parochiarum vestrarum cum aspersione aquae benedictae in finibus praedictis, letaniam decantando & populum vestrum exhortando, quatenus cum cereis & candelis ardentibus vobiscum devote accedant, Deum, gloriosissimamque virginem Mariam, & omnes sanctos & sanctas Dei humiliter exorent & deprecentur, quatenus ab huius modi tribulatione eos liberare dignetur, dictasque limaces terrae & fructibus eius damna inferentes moneatis & iniungatis in virtute domini nostri Iesu Christi, eiusque gloriosissimae passionis, beatorumque Apostolorum Petri & Pauli, ut infra trium dierum spatium, ut a dictorum fructuum demolitione & devastatione se abstineant, & ad loca deserta, in quibus nocere non possint creaturis & fructibus terrae se tranferant sub poena indignationis divinae maiestatis, & aeterne maledictionis. Et huiusmodi processiones per tres dies continuos sine interruptione faciatis, populum vestrum, quantum vobis possibile fuerit, ad devotionem exhortando. Et limaces huiusmodi maledicendo, ut misericordia Dei praeveniente ab huiusmodi flagello liberari valeamus." Chassenée, "Concilium," fol. 19ro.

What emerges very clearly from this letter is that local communes were more than mere plaintiffs. They were active participants in the execution of the sentence. The procedure obviously stood no chance of success unless the entire community joined in processions and prayers. It was certainly not a matter of ecclesiastical excommunication, or even of an exorcist ridding a sufferer from an unwanted incubus. It was an entire commune, led by a figure of ecclesiastical authority, joining together in a communal act of purification from both pests and sins. The priest pronouncing the sentence was no more than a mouthpiece of both bishop and parishioners, anathemizing in the name of one and praying in the name of the other. The procession demarcating the boundaries of the parish and hallowing them with the sprinkling of holy water—a procedure used likewise on other occasions—marked also the boundaries between the human and the animal, the beneficent and the noxious, the identity of those protected by God and the identity of those anathemized in His name. It was a cleansing, both internal and external, an affirmation of communal identity.

C. *The Justice of the Animals*

The trials of animals are an outstanding proof of the mutual influence of jurisprudence and culture. One cannot extrapolate the belief in the universality of justice from the cultural context in order to prove the influence of culture upon law. The process was reciprocal, as the continual practice of animal trials also helped form human perceptions of the animal world. There is little doubt, however, that in no other sphere of law were jurists forced to state this principle quite so forcibly as in the field of animal trials.

The animals tried in both secular and ecclesiastical courts were real, flesh-and-blood creatures. Unlike literary animals and public scapegoats they were not considered human substitutes, but genuine offenders. Nevertheless, their trials were part of the same perceptual scheme incorporating the human and the animal into one framework of justice. Court procedure mirrored and integrated an entire spectrum of attitudes concerning animals. Time and again jurists stressed that animals possessed neither reason nor malicious intent, being equated in this sense with perpetual minors. Nevertheless, the procedures applied to animals in both secular and ecclesiastical courts evinced an ineradicable anthropomorphism. Even had they wished to, jurists could neither abolish the trials nor conceive of a new way of treating animals in law. Animals were incorporated into human categories and human arguments, and thought of as humans, precisely because they were litigants facing the law.

CHAPTER EIGHT

THE RITUALS OF THE EXCLUDED: THE DEAD

The legal position of the dead was one of the touchiest points of medieval customary jurisprudence. In theory, they had no legal personality. They could not plead, they were not required to answer accusations, they were no longer liable for their debts or misdeeds. The standard metaphor for someone devoid of legal personality was drawn from the realm of death. A novice entering a monastery was 'dead to the world' from the day of his oath. A leper was 'dead as far as the world is concerned' from the moment his disease had been diagnosed.[1] In other words, legal non-existence was defined as death.

Paradoxically, physical death was anything but legal non-existence. The belief in the continued existence and activity of the dead goes as far back as Roman times, leading to the growth of the judicial concept of corporate entities. These were first founded in order to ensure continued observance of the cult of the dead in case a kindred died out.[2] It was an inevitable development in view of the importance attributed to the cult of ancestors in Roman religion. And the role of the dead within the culture of the living was destined to grow further with the vulgarization of Roman law in the West and the introduction of Germanic traditions. Within a few centuries the dead came to occupy a considerable place within the scheme of legal life. Hagiography told again and again of holy men summoning dead witnesses from the grave. Though it is doubtful that these legends actually reflect a practice, they do evince a belief in the survival, presence, and legal personality of dead people. The cult of dead saints, taking shape in late antiquity and the early middle ages, was intimately tied to a general perception of kinship between the living Christians and the dead.[3]

In criminal jurisprudence the issue of posthumous legal existence arose in two fields: suicides and executed criminals. Were it not for

---

[1] Françoise Beriac, *Histoire des lépreux au moyen âge* (Paris, 1988), p. 222; *CB*, art. 1616-17, 2:326-27.

[2] Gabriel Le Bras, "Quelques conséquences juridiques et sociales des idées romaines sur la mort," in René Maunier, ed., *Etudes de sociologie et d'ethnologie juridiques* (Paris, 1932), pp. 5-22.

[3] Peter Brown, *The Cult of the Saints: Its Rise and Function in Latin Christianity* (Chicago, 1981), pp. 4-22.

the belief in the continued life of the dead, the subjects in both cases would apparently have been beyond the arm of the law. Judicial decisions concerning the manner of dealing with both had little to do with any learned tradition of legal studies. For centuries European courts were forced to cope with a legal problem arising from a heritage totally alien to the realm of law.

To complicate matters even further, the perception of the dead and their bodies in late medieval legal rituals amalgamated two different, often contradictory traditions. On the one hand ancient Germanic beliefs apparently carried a tacit influence, durable and vital despite its informal character. Christian tradition, on the other hand, had its own lore concerning the dead, their bodies and their souls. Both systems thus had their own reasons for prescribing specific legal rituals for suicides and executed criminals.

The Germanic system of beliefs was permeated with fear from the returning dead.[4] The conviction that the dead could rise from their graves to harass the living was still extant as late as the eighteenth century.[5] Two perceptions lay at the basis of all legal practices involving the dead. First, they were not really dead, but merely sleeping. It is no coincidence that Salic law placed the section concerning the robbery of dead bodies next to the one dealing with the robbery of sleepers, meting out the same punishment to both crimes.[6] Secondly, the abiding existence of the dead was physical, not spiritual. The dead body was the locus of this continued presence. The revenant was no ghost or wandering soul, but the same person who had lived, in his or her own body.[7] As a rule, a revenant was a malignant power whose appearance presaged further death or disaster.

Though not all the dead were likely to haunt the living, some categories were notably dangerous.[8] Foremost among them were those whose bodies remained unburied, or were improperly interred. Such cases were rarely the result of mere carelessness. The suicides, the drowned, the violently dead and the executed criminals were the likeliest candidates for the improper disposition of their remains, either as a result of punitive measures or because physical circumstances made

[4] His, *Der Totenglaube*; Claude Lecouteux, *Fantômes et revenants au moyen âge* (Paris, 1986).

[5] *Ibid.*, p. 29.

[6] *Pactus Legis Salicae*, art. 14:9-11.

[7] His, *Der Totenglaube*, pp. 4-5.

[8] Paul Barber, *Vampires, Burial, and Death: Folklore and Reality* (New Haven, 1988), esp. pp. 29-39.

burial impossible.[9] They were dangerous potential revenants, partly due to the unrecoverable condition of the body, and partly because their appointed lifespan had been prematurely interrupted.[10] Just like women dead in childbirth, they were liable to return in order to complete their lives in a malignant manner. A quarrelsome and violent life and an unresolved conflict prior to death were a third factor leading to posthumous haunting. As the dead remained essentially the same person he or she had been in life, an aggressive personality was certain to survive beyond the grave.

Executed criminals were thus dangerous thrice over, as a result of their activities in life, their premature demise, and their lack of proper burial. It was therefore necessary to take apotropaeic measures in order to ensure that the dead did not return. The steps against the return of dead women were extreme indeed, but not limited to the female gender. All over Europe the bodies of potential revenants were physically prevented from returning. The methods varied: most often they were disinterred, dismembered, decapitated, burned, and subsequently more solidly buried.[11]

This system of beliefs explains far better than any judicial theory the modes of execution employed in the later middle ages. The more frightening and heinous the crime, the more drastic the measures employed to dispose of the body. While hanging left the body in full view, as the authorities required, it also detached it from any contact with the ground. As the numerous complaints concerning the use of hanged bodies for witchcraft indicate, this procedure was felt to be unsatisfactory from the purely apotropaeic point of view. In 1408 the *prévôt* of Paris complained of the theft of corpses from the gallows for use in black magic,[12] and similar statements frequently occur in witchcraft literature throughout Europe. Dabblers in black magic were reputed to steal and use not only the bodies of dead criminals, but also pieces of rope, chains, nails, and wood from the gallows.[13] Such

---

[9] His, *Der Totenglaube*, p. 6; Barber, *Vampires, Burial, and Death*, pp. 32-37.

[10] Lecouteux, *Fantômes et revenants*, pp. 28-48.

[11] See above, ch. 6, pp. 96-99. Emile Metzger, "La mutilation des morts. Contribution à l'étude des croyances et rites funeraires des Germains," *Mélanges Charles Andler* (Strasbourg, 1924), pp. 257-67; Lecouteux, *Fantômes et revenants*, pp. 146-49.

[12] AN, X^{2a} 14, fol. 411vo; Nicolas de Baye, *Journal*, ed. Alexandre Tuetey, 2 vols. (Paris, 1885), 1:221.

[13] Döpler, *Theatri poenarum*, 2:260-62; Iohannes Georg Godelmann, *De magiis, veneficiis et lamiis recte cognoscendi et puniendi libri tres* (Frankfurt, 1591), 1:62;

objects were also considered useful for a variety of popular curative, protective and homely purposes. The bones of the dead could cure ague and soothe abdominal pain, and the rope of a hanged thief could break pots and pans. Though the parts of any dead human body would seemingly have done for beneficent purposes, those of executed criminals were obviously the most easily available.[14] The folklore of the gallows was thus charged with the supernatural, often maleficent powers emanating from the hanged bodies.[15]

The Christian tradition concerning the dead body was categorically opposed to this view. Comprehensively stated by Augustine, it postulated a total breach between body and soul. The body destined for resuscitation at the end of time was a spiritual, not a physical entity. The corpse of a dead person carried neither life nor religious significance, and any rites performed in its disposal were "an office of humanity," pious acts of respect only.[16] Thus, when dying people specified in their wills that their bodies should be eviscerated, dismembered and boiled so that different parts could be buried at different sites, the church made little objection. Boniface VIII, whose bull *Detestande feritatis* attacked the practice, led a small, dissident minority of clergymen and scholastics in this matter.[17] The church was willing to acknowledge the social importance of the dead body while denying it any religious significance.

What remained after death was the human soul, which continued posthumous life. More importantly, souls bore the burden of human guilt and punishment. The first thing a disembodied soul did was to stand trial before the ultimate judge. Even the just of the earth had to face this ordeal before reaching heaven, and the souls of criminals condemned and executed in their bodies by earthly authorities certainly underwent a posthumous trial.

This belief had two corollaries. It placed all people, whether law-abiding or not during their lives, in one category once they were dead.

Henricus Kornmann, *De miraculis mortuorum* (n.p., 1610), pt. 5, ch. 2, "De cadaveribus suspendiosorum."

[14] *Le grand et le petit Albert*, pp. 157, 164-65. See also Piero Camporesi, *The Incorruptible Flesh: Bodily Mutation and Mortification in Religion and Folklore*, trans. T. Croft-Murray (Cambridge, 1988), pp. 14-15.

[15] For modern summaries of gallows beliefs, see Ström, *The Sacral Origin*, pp. 155-61, and Hans von Hentig, "Beseelung und Tabu des Galgens," *Studien zur Kriminalgeschichte* (Bern, 1962), pp. 131- 48.

[16] Elizabeth A.R. Brown, "Authority, the Family and the Dead in Late Medieval France," *French Historical Studies* 16 (1990), 803- 805.

[17] *Ibid.*, 803-32.

Thus, while designed to humble normative society and imbue it with a sense of guilt, it also incorporated marginal elements into the same confraternity of tried souls. The acknowledgement that even condemned criminals possessed souls contradicted the ancient apotropaeic content of the executions. Like everybody else, the spirits of those hung upon the gallows stood trial before God, being no likelier to haunt the living than anybody else. The belief in the returning dead was predicated upon forces that continued residing in the body after death. Late medieval Christianity severed the connection between death and life by insisting that the dead body was completely defunct and that the living soul accomplished its destiny elsewhere. While criminals were likely to end in hell or at least in purgatory, their bodies felt no punishment and presented no threat.

And yet, the ecclesiastical tradition was by no means free of popular perceptions concerning the survival of the physical body. Even the souls of the dead were depicted in the *ars moriendi* treatises as small, naked bodies. A common *exemplum* in the later middle ages, told in order to foster prayers for the dead, illustrates the mixture of traditions. A priest who regularly said Masses for the dead was suspended from his duties by the bishop. Later, when the same bishop was passing through a cemetery, the dead rose from their graves, threatening to kill him if he did not restore the priest and his prayers. Thus far, the tale accorded perfectly with Christian tradition. But the story went on to stress that the arising dead were dressed in their everyday clothes, carrying the work-implements they had used in their lifetime. This detail, totally supererogatory and unnecessary for the story's theological argument, betrays a perception of the dead alien to the belief in souls suffering in purgatory. The same detail was repeated in another *exemplum*, telling of the defunct who rose from their graves to defend a man who had prayed for them.[18]

Obviously, even the authors of *exempla* literature could not (or would not) dissociate the dead completely from their body. True, they claimed that revenants were no more than *simulacra*, or visual tricks with no bodily substance, but they had great difficulty dealing with the idea. Most thirteenth-century *exempla* telling of revenants spoke of souls appearing in dreams or visions to their kindred in order to enjoin

---

[18] Anon. *Speculum spiritualium, in quo non solam vita activa et contemplativa...* (Paris, 1510), fols. 175vo-76vo.

prayers or the fulfillment of a vow.[19] But late medieval hell and purgatory literature was far less rarefied. It was easier to detach the idea of the revenant from its physical aspects than to separate the punishment of the dead from the same. Just as the human body in life became in the later middle ages the locus of transcendent religious experience, it was still the vehicle of pain and justice beyond the grave. Sermons and treatises described both verbally and pictorially the penalties for sin in afterlife in terms of purely physical pain. Woodcuts decorating these works showed the dead as physical entities burning in lakes of sulfur, broken on the wheel, bitten, beaten, and tortured.[20] Obviously, the penalties of the afterlife were inconceivable without an embedded assumption that the body and its sensations continued posthumously existing. By contrast, the bliss of paradise could be envisioned in purely spiritual terms.

These perceptions were quite naturally translated into legal language. For both Germanic and Christian traditions postulated that the continued existence of the dead in the world, be he physical revenant or simply a ghost, resulted from the need to redress a wrong. The dead required vengeance, payment of debts, burial, or some other act of justice. In other words, it was absolutely imperative to place the defunct within a judicial context in order to finally lay him to rest.

As might be expected, the Germanic dead played a much more noticeable role in German codes and customs than in the French ones. In some codes a murder accusation was not proffered by the dead man's kindred, but by the dead man himself, whose body or hand had to be brought to court in order to lay the accusation. Elsewhere the ordeal of the bier, in which suspects were required to swear their innocence upon the murdered corpse (which bled in cases of false oaths) was practiced as legal proof.[21]

The proof of the bier existed also in France, albeit in the form of judicial folklore. Tales of murdered bodies bleeding in the presence of their murderers appeared in chronicles as early as the twelfth century. All these tales shared a certain flavor of martyrdom rather than simple

---

19 J.-Cl. Schmitt, "Les revenants dans la société féodale," *Le temps de la réflexion* 3 (1982), 285-306.

20 *Le grant kalendrier et compost des Bergiers, avec leur astrologie et plusieurs aultres choses...* (Troyes, n.d.); *Traictié des paines d'enfer et de purgatoire* (Paris, 1492).

21 Heinrich Brunner, "Die Klage mit dem toten Mann und die Klage mit der toten Hand," *ZRG*, GA 31 (1910), 235-52; Hans Schreuer, "Das Recht der Toten," *Zeitschrift für vergleichende Rechtswissenschaft* 34 (1916), 169, 178; His, *Der Totenglaube*, pp. 15-17.

violence. Abbots murdered by their monks, a wrongly-accused bishop who had died under excommunication, and a Christian girl bled to death by Jews for ritual purposes, all bled when faced with their murderers.[22] The bleeding corpse was thus adopted in France by popularizing religion, a clear indication of the merging of Christian and Germanic traditions. The only medieval case to divorce the bleeding corpse from martyrdom was purely literary, appearing in a thirteenth-century *fabliau*, "The Sacristan". A clergyman was accidentally killed by a ram while seducing a shepherdess. His corpse, lying in church prior to its burial, began bleeding when the herd passed nearby. In consequence, all animals were paraded by the bier one by one, and only the shepherdess' explanations as to the accidental nature of the death saved the unfortunate ram from execution.[23]

The introduction of Germanic folklore in clerical garb into the legal system of late medieval France was unlikely. Indeed, none of the thirteenth- or fourteenth-century customals made any mention of such a practice in court. As late as the seventeenth century, the belief was noted in superstition manuals, such as Noël Taillepied's *Traicté de l'apparition des esprits*.[24] Oddly enough, the practice did creep indirectly into the judicial system by way of the law of proof. The introduction of torture into legal procedure was accompanied by stringent rules concerning the circumstances under which 'the question' might be applied. All authorities agreed that torture could only follow upon the prior existence of indices of guilt.[25] First in Italy and later in France the bleeding of a corpse in the suspect's presence was considered such an indication.[26]

As in the case of so many other legal rituals, the climate of the time rather than ancient relics of belief were the decisive influence. The late medieval and early modern preoccupation with death and the dead, largely shaped by contemporary mortality, transferred the bleeding corpse from the realm of stories and beliefs into the French courthouse. In a world where the living were ever surrounded by the

---

[22] For a full dossier of cases, see Henri Platelle, "La voix du sang: Le cadavre qui saigne en présence de son meurtrier," *La piété populaire au moyen âge. Actes du 99e Congrès national des sociétés savantes (Besançon, 1974)*, 2 vols. (Paris, 1977), 1:161-79. See also Thomas of Cantimpré, *Miraculorum... libri duo*, pp. 304-305.

[23] Platelle, "La voix du sang," pp. 166-67.

[24] (Rouen, 1616), p. 139.

[25] Walter Ullmann, "Reflections on Medieval Torture," *Juridical Review* 56 (1944), 123-37.

[26] Platelle, "La voix du sang," pp. 164, 167; Jean Papon, *Recueil d'arrests notables des cours souveraines de France*, 2 vols. (Paris, 1621), 2:1329.

dead—their memories, their souls craving prayers and indulgences, their kinship and fellowship, and even their bodies—the practice of law could no longer posit the legal non-existence of the same dead.

There is a great deal of extra-judicial evidence for the early modern tendency to blur the boundaries between the living and the dead. Perhaps the clearest indication comes from a highly unlikely source: the realm of royal funerary ceremonial. During the fifteenth century the display of royal effigies became customary in France. At first, the effigy was no more than a substitute for the body, which could not be properly embalmed and preserved for ostentation. By the end of the century, however, "at the occasion of the funeral of Charles VIII in 1498 this effigy was no longer only the substitute for the king's corpse: it now represented the living king."[27] It sat in state, meals were served in its presence, and the Parlement continued issuing edicts in the name of the dead king until the funeral. Furthermore, the new king absented himself from the obsequies, for it was impossible to have two kings simultaneously present. Until the moment of the funeral, then, the defunct king's effigy in the sixteenth century was the king. Though the bodies of kings and saints partook of the supernatural,[28] the idea that an effigy, a substitute corpse, could function symbolically as a living entity was clearly related to the same blurring of boundaries attributed to the corpses of dead criminals, for the latter also partook of the supernatural.

The preoccupation of early modern jurisprudence with the dead and their bodies permeated also realms of law far less dramatic than the bleeding murdered corpse. The right of any justice to try the dead was proof of its powers of jurisdiction, and therefore an important factor of lordship and power. Thus Chassenée stated specifically that *merum imperium*, the highest type of authority, extended also over the dead and their bodies.[29] He established this principle while dealing with the issue of suicides, obviously the most stringent problem in this context. Of all offenders, their posthumous punishment was of greatest necessity, as their very death was the essence of their crime. Indeed, everywhere in France suicides were publicly hung like thieves. So very important was this principle that a man who had jumped into the river was fished out and hung, rather than be allowed to stay in

[27] Ralph E. Giesey, *Cérémonial et puissance souveraine: France, XVe-XVIIe siècles*, trans. J. Carlier (Paris, 1987), p. 89.

[28] Alain Boucher, *Le sacre corps du roi* (Paris, 1989).

[29] Chassenée, *In consuetudines ducatus Burgundiae*, fol. 19ro.

the water.[30] Even when a suicide cheated the authorities by hanging him or herself, justice was not satisfied. In 1499 the Evreux hangman was paid 30 *sous tournois* for ceremoniously taking down and re-hanging a woman suicide who had hanged herself.[31] When a political prisoner of the *Cabochien* revolt committed suicide in prison rather than face a public execution, the Parlement ordered his body to be promenaded in the same procession he would have suffered alive, ending with the decapitation of the body in the market-place.[32] The only exceptions were those who gained a posthumous remission, usually on grounds of insanity. Just as most killers based their requests for grace upon claims of involuntary homicide, the kindred of the dead suicide, acting in his name, usually pleaded involuntary action.[33]

But suicides were not the only dead to suffer further penalties. The very forms of execution showed the belief that the dead body still took punishment. The fact that the dead were left hanging, or were dismembered, was a clear indication that the dead body continued to bear the penalties of the living malefactor. Villon's *Ballade des pendus* makes this point painfully clear. The dead hanging on the gallows speak the poem's words, describing their condition and begging for prayers. The poet paid very little attention to the criminals' souls. He identified with the fate of their bodies, which he considered a cause for pity. The posthumous destiny of the criminals' souls was brought up nowhere in the poem, except to state that they too went to Christ.[34] In other words, the punishment of the dead was not left in God's hands. It was the task of the civil authorities.

The early modern interest in the problem was not merely an elaboration of medieval customs, but a response to contemporary cultural and punitive trends. In the first place, the growing belief in witchcraft during the fifteenth and sixteenth centuries carried with it an interest in necromancy that strongly supported the belief in the active powers of dead bodies. Like many witchcraft beliefs, this was not a popular, but a learned phenomenon, found also among jurists. Furthermore, the early modern elaboration of cruel and slow punitive deaths, imported in the sixteenth century from Germany to France,

---

[30] AN, Y6[1], Livre vert neuf du Châtelet, fol. 45. BN, ms. fr. 21731, fol. 70ro (1458).
[31] BN, ms. fr. 7645, No. 67.
[32] *Chronique du réligieux de Saint-Denys*, 5:56. See below, p. 188.
[33] E.g. AN, JJ 140, fol. 237; JJ 142, fol. 117ro.
[34] François Villon, *L'epitaphe Villon*, in *Oeuvres complètes*, ed. Auguste Longnon (Paris, 1941), p. 215.

did raise the very real problem of the life or death of people on the gallows. People broken on the wheel or hung upside-down were known to live for days, and even those simply hung on the gallows were believed to live long after their hanging.[35] The legal problem of the punishment of the dead, therefore, became real only in early modern times.

The ever-increasing practical preoccupation with the bodies of dead criminals eventually brought about the composition of learned treatises. Jurists dealing with this problem evinced a certain ambivalence towards the legal existence of the dead. A German jurist, steeped in the Germanic tradition, could not only defend the practice of trying corpses, but also devote in all seriousness a treatise to the problem of whether it was possible to bring the dead back to life, and furthermore to consider the legal implications of such a feat.[36] But in France, where the attempts to romanize customary laws prevailed, one had to reject any legal proceedings, civil or criminal, that considered the dead a legal person. A French jurist with a romanist bend also devoted a treatise to trials conducted against "corpses, memories, brute beasts, inanimate objects and the contumacious." Significantly, the treatise was published within the framework of a book dealing with ancient Greek and Roman legal procedure as adapted to the usage of France.[37]

As a practicing judge and jurist, Pierre Ayrault was faced with a problem. According to all he had been taught, neither the dead nor all the other categories he discussed were legal persons. But reality refused to fit his ideal model of classical justice. He was therefore forced to explain why and how the dead should be tried. In so doing, he

---

[35] Kornmann, *De miraculis mortuorum* pars V, chs. 5-10. A reverse manifestation of the same belief may be found in the recurring motif of miracle stories concerning the wrongfully executed, whose feet were supported by a protective saint until they were taken down unharmed from the gallows. See, for example, *Liber exemplorum ad usum praedicantium*, ed. A.G. Little (Aberdeen, 1908), p. 24; *Liber Sancti Jacobi*, ed. and trans. A. Moralejo et al. (Santiago de Compostela, 1951), pp. 349-50, and Caesarius, *Dialogus*, 2:130-31, 142.

[36] Adrian Beier, *An detur resuscitatio mortuorum: problema iuridicum* (Jena, 1665).

[37] Pierre Ayrault, "Des procès faicts au cadaver, à la memoire, aux bestes brutes, aux choses inanimées et aux contumaux," in *L'ordre, formalité et instruction iudiciaire, dont les anciens Grecs & Romains ont usé és accusations publiques (sinon qu'ils ayent commencés l'execution) conferé au stil & usage de nostre France*, 2 vols. (Paris, 1615), 1:572-646. The treatise was composed already in 1591 (*Ibid.*, pp. 572-73). The author was the lieutenant-criminal of the high court of Angers during the wars of religion.

lumped them in one category together with all other non-human defendants in trials whose aim was symbolic rather than practical, such as the trial and execution of effigies and animals. Consequently, the explanation was also on a symbolic level. The most cogent argument for trying the defunct was that if one could not condemn a dead person, neither could one posthumously exonerate one found innocent. Conversely, a criminal who had died untouched and uncondemned by the law should not be allowed to bear an unsullied memory. In the case of such notorious heretics as Wycliff a refusal to condemn the dead could easily lead to mistaken veneration by future generations.

Still, claimed Ayrault, trials and executions of dead people were to be allowed only in cases of crimes so horrible that the very memory of the criminal had to be condemned and his corpse still punished as a lesson to the living. Such were cases of treason, parricide or sodomy, *cas tres-grief et tres-enorme*. Even then, they should be held only in three cases: if the criminal got killed while resisting arrest, if he killed himself in order to avoid the public penalty, or if he died during the trial. One could try a dead person only if the proceedings against him had commenced while he was still living, and his premature death had simply cheated the gallows.[38] What bothered the learned jurist most of all was that the trial concerned neither the memory nor the legal personality of the dead, but his actual corpse. He would have preferred, stated Ayrault, to see the execution of the dead performed in effigy, but unfortunately effigies were employed only for the contumacious. Where the body, dead or alive, was available for punishment, legal practice insisted that no substitutes be employed. Corpses were condemned, corpses were exonerated, and corpses were strung up on the gallows.

The preoccupation with the problem of the dead's legal identity was a purely early modern problem. Late medieval jurists were confronted neither with the growth of post-mortem beliefs nor with their judicial implications. Two centuries earlier, Jacques d'Ableiges had summarily dismissed the problem. If a confessed criminal died during the trial, all proceedings were stopped at that stage. The dead criminal was merely buried in the fields rather than a cemetery as a measure of disgrace, but "because the body can never feel punishment, it will never be executed."[39] It is highly doubtful that anyone in the sixteenth century, jurist or laymen, would have agreed with him.

[38] Ayrault, "Des procès faicts au cadaver," pp. 584-97.
[39] GC, p. 658.

Whatever the folkloric substratum of belief underlying the legal practices concerning the dead and the doubtfully dead, their punishment was part and parcel of the perception of punitive justice as a universal force. To refrain from punishing a criminal's corpse would have been an upset of the universal balance of justice. It mattered little that the suicide's soul undoubtedly burned in hell. If one did not wreak justice upon that part of him still available upon the earth, the authority of the judicial system would be undermined. Just as local seigneurs made sure to execute a criminal from time to time largely so as not to let their privilege of high justice fall into desuetude, so they insisted upon their right to execute justice upon the dead in order to preserve the universal character of their own judicial structure. The same was true also on a larger scale: whether regional, urban or royal, the justice practiced by living people had staked by the early modern era a claim to universality. A system committed to trying animals could not abdicate its powers when it came to dead human beings.

The most striking aspect of the trials of the dead was the church's attitude. Though predicated upon a Germanic belief in the continued life of the body and categorically opposed to the Christian dogma of the soul, the trials and punishment of cadavers received the wholehearted support of the church. Far from condemning them as superstition, preachers did their best to foster the belief in the life of the corpse by attributing miraculous bleeding and posthumous motion to martyrs and saints. Thus an ancient pagan tradition fostered by Christian preaching and promoted by early modern circumstances coalesced into a legal practice.

THE CONTEXT OF AUTHORITY

CHAPTER NINE

THE INTERACTIVE VOCABULARY OF JUSTICE

The origins of legal rituals range all the way from academic learning to peasants' beliefs, from Roman law to tales and fables. But first and foremost, they were ceremonies of government and power. Unlike the popular justice of the *charivari*, there was nothing spontaneous about them. Inside the courthouse or out of it, legal ritual behavior was explicitly prescribed by judicial authorities.

In a system based upon legislation, the conduct of legal rituals would naturally form part of posited law. But the problem is far more complex in customary law structures. Who was to decree the manner in which murderers, for example, were to be put to death? Was it a deliberate, conscious decision of a ruler, or simple adherence to custom? To what extent did judicial authorities employ these ceremonies as displays of power, and up to what point were their hands tied by traditional forms? Furthermore, were judges indeed interested in altering those forms to suit their own ideas? Or indeed, were they perhaps most anxious to merge the traditional and the innovative in one framework?

Legal rituals are secular ceremonies, functioning in many ways like political and other public rites. In a seminal essay devoted to this subject, Moore and Myerhoff have posited the most basic functions and forms of secular rites. In the first place, such rituals cannot be detached from their social context. They are embedded in a specific socio-cultural setting, and the statements they make are usually far more specific than the universal assertions articulated by religious rituals. Nevertheless, the connection between the ceremony and its cultural context is very often implicit rather than explicit.

Not only are secular ceremonies structured within a certain matrix, they also play an important role in the formation of the same. They present certain doctrines, dramatize social and moral imperatives, and all without recourse to supernatural forces. They lend authority and legitimacy to particular persons, occasions, and values. In fact, "ritual... can be construed as an attempt to structure the way people think about social life." The structuring has many facets. Traditional values, ties and social roles are legitimized and reinforced. At the same time, new values, ideas and relationships can be introduced and shaped by the ritual. Once these innovations are presented within the ritualized, repetitive framework of the ceremony, they become integrated in the traditional material. Finally, the very holding of the ceremony is a means of propagating certain specific messages.

No ceremony is necessarily univalent. Like religious ceremonies, secular ritual also "shows... ideas or values which are inherently invisible most of the time. It objectifies and reifies them. It displays symbols of their existence and by implicit reference postulates and enacts their 'reality'." Beyond the simple, explicit message acted out in public rituals there lies an entire spectrum of implicit societal perceptions and values. Secular ceremonies display certain specific formal properties. They are repeated, usually in the same format, time and again. Their performance entails deliberate acting in word and gesture, incorporating extraordinary actions and symbols, or ordinary ones used in an unusual manner. Thus, ceremonies are ordered events, with very little room for spontaneity. The repetition and order "imply permanence and legitimacy of what are actually evanescent cultural constructs."[1]

All these insights are applicable and important for understanding the social and cultural dimensions of medieval legal rituals. They were ordained by authorities combining both political and judicial power, using one force to bolster the other. They were also meant to transmit certain messages to all participants in an intelligible manner. It is therefore important to study these rituals from both points of view: that of their traditional content, and that of the stage directors, the judges who decreed which public punishment each criminal should suffer.

Public executions and other punitive rituals were very carefully planned and staged. Practically every capital sentence spelled out the exact sequence of the punishment and its meanings. For example, in 1441 a Norman criminal was sentenced to be dragged as a murderer, beheaded as a traitor, quartered for several other crimes, and hung on the gibbet as a thief and brigand.[2] Similarly detailed sentences appear

---

[1] Sally F. Moore and Barbara G. Myerhoff, "Introduction: Secular Ritual, Forms and Meanings," in Moore and Myerhoff, eds., *Secular Ritual* (Assen, 1977), pp. 3-24.

[2] BN, ms. fr. 7645, No. 50.

in trial protocols of most serious criminals. Behind this profusion of penalties stood a twofold principle. The basic tenet of contemporary punitive justice insisted that people, and not actions, stand trial. If a recidivist came up again for trial, it was perfectly acceptable in customary procedure to try him twice for the same crime. A criminal brought to the dock for one offense was often tortured, not so much to gain a confession concerning the formal charge, but mostly in order to elicit a full list of his earlier misdeeds. Court sentences followed the same principle. They penalized the person as a total legal fact, not one or another of his actions. Consequently, fitting the separate penalties to the crimes of hardened recidivists was important. A traitor, murderer and thief was thus chastised in three different ways to symbolize the three different types of crimes.

But exacting the precisely correct retribution for each crime was not the only aim of punitive justice, nor even its main purpose. Though contemporary judicial sources rarely dealt with the issue of abstract aims, the few who did try to define the purposes of punishment made it clear that retribution was at best only one of several aims. Beaumanoir, an eminently practical jurist, stressed the deterring force of example as a primary aim:

> It is well that someone should run in front of the malefactors [i.e., as a herald] and that they should be harshly punished and executed according to their misdeeds, so that others, for fear of justice, should observe the example and beware of committing any crimes.[3]

While stopping short of declaring deterrence the aim of justice, the *bailli* of the Beauvaisis clearly considered the educational impact of public punitive rituals of paramount importance. The author of the *Coutumez, usaigez et stillez... ou pais d'Anjou* gave a more detailed consideration, consisting of four reasons. Though his first consideration was indeed retribution for evil deeds, the other three were strictly utilitarian. The second argument for punishing criminals, predicated upon the obvious assumption that all such discipline took place in public rituals, was to serve the rest of society as a cautionary example. The last two considerations formed the essence of punitive justice until the eighteenth century: the removal of evil men from the community, and the prevention of further evil.[4] More than a century later, Pieter Breughel the Elder used a similarly teleological definition of justice as

---

[3] *CB*, art. 883, 1:446.

[4] Written ca. 1440. In *CIAM*, 4:308.

the caption of his engraving *Justitia*: "The aim of law is either to correct him whom it punishes, or that his punishment should improve others, or that, once the evil ones are removed, the rest should live in greater safety."[5] While Breughel (or whoever wrote out the Latin caption) chose to condense removal and prevention into one motive, he left the first two aims as distinct entities. Significantly, he substituted correction for retribution, presaging a new approach to criminal justice. The pure exaction of revenge no longer mattered, but the improvement of the criminal through means of punishment did. The one purpose to remain unchanged was the improvement of the spectators in the ritual. And this element continued constant as long as punitive justice stayed public.

The aim of punitive justice, then, was both intrinsic and extrinsic. Beyond the criminal and his judges—guardians of law and society's vengeance—it involved a third element, the public. It is unclear whether the authorities' main anxiety was directed towards protecting this public from further harm or to educating it. When François Villon claimed that, were his death of any benefit to the public weal, he would gladly condemn himself to die a criminal, he was making a purely rhetorical statement.[6] In claiming that his, or any criminal's death was useless, Villon was running counter to all governmental views of the time. But even his challenge to authority had a certain basis in common perceptions. Criminals' deaths could serve the common weal by way of a public moral statement. It is no accident that Breughel chose to describe *Justitia* as a compendium of criminal trials and public penalties. None of the horrors of punitive justice are missing from the picture. Torture, followed by confession and subsequently the appropriate punishments—so much more cruel and drawn-out in the sixteenth century than before—are all set out in minute detail. Some are whipped, others have their hands lopped off, are decapitated, hanged, or burned on the stake. Finally, as was typical for German sixteenth-century justice, several criminals are shown slowly dying on the wheel. All this, in the presence of great crowds of spectators meant morally to benefit from the sight. Justice, then, was both punishment and lesson, but while one suffered the penalty, others benefited from the lesson.

---

[5] "Scopus legis est, aut ut eum quem punit emendet, aut poena eius caeteros meliores reddet, aut, sublatis malis, caeteri securiores vivant." See frontispiece.

[6] "Se, pour ma mort, le bien publique/ D'aucune chose vaulsist mieulx,/A mourir comme ung homme inique/Je me iugasse, ainsi m'ait Dieux!" *Le Testament*, c. 16.

In order to understand the painstaking detail devoted to the staging of public executions and rituals of infamy it is necessary to preface the analysis with some general comments concerning late medieval perceptions of the human body and its sensations, specifically physical pain. In addition, one must take into account the symbolic functions of the body and of physical gestures in particular. One cannot dismiss public executions as expressions of sadism and barbarity alone.[7] The deliberate causation of physical suffering can qualify as barbarism only if one accepts modern perceptions of and attitudes towards pain.

The idea that physical pain was harmful, and hence undesirable, evolved very slowly and recently. Until the thirteenth century, noble society considered pain, *dolor*, as the concomitant of *labor*, associated with women and working lower classes. "A man worthy of the name does not suffer; in any case he must not show that he suffers, otherwise he will find himself unmanned, degraded, lowered to the female condition... also, physical pain, because it is associated with the idea of labor, appears especially unfit for the free man."[8] The change in attitudes towards pain emerged in the thirteenth century, with the growing perception of Christ as the 'man of suffering' and the increasing identification mystics sought with his physical sensations. The appearance of the stigmata on the body of Saint Francis was one of the first indications of this emerging sensitivity.

At the same time, the reality of physical suffering as an integral part of everyday life made it acceptable simply because it was inevitable. Though the pain-killing properties of many plants were known from antiquity, anesthesia in surgery was not employed until the nineteenth century. Henri de Mondeville, a sophisticated fourteenth-century surgeon, openly discouraged the use of pain-killers, arguing that they were dangerous. His description of the operation necessary for removing an arrow from a wounded limb does not take the factor of pain into account, though the procedure must have been agonizing.[9]

---

[7] On this point, see James A. Sharpe, "'Last Dying Speeches': Religion, Ideology and Public Execution in Seventeenth-Century England," *Past and Present* 107 (1985), 146-47, and Michel Bée, "Le spectacle de l'exécution dans la France d'Ancien Régime," *Annales E.S.C.* 38 (1983), 843-62. Though dealing with a later period, much of their analyses is valid also for the later middle ages.

[8] Georges Duby, "Réflexions sur la douleur physique au moyen âge," in *Mâle moyen âge* (Paris, 1988), p. 206.

[9] This attitude was regarded as barbaric by eastern physicians, who asserted that western surgical practices often caused death of shock. See for example Ousama Ibn Mounkidh, *The Autobiography of Ousama (1095-1188)*, trans. G.R. Potter (London, 1929), pp. 172-73.

Mondeville was not being callous or unfeeling. He was a child of his time, and did not consider suffering something better avoided. Pain was often perceived not as a cause of harm, but as a healer. In fourteenth-century miniatures surgeons were identified with executioners as 'people of blood', for they both caused pain, and in both cases the aim of the pain was salutary.[10]

Beyond being beneficial for physical health, pain occupied an important place in the economy of grace and salvation during the later middle ages. Significantly, the suffering of the flesh, not of the spirit, was central to this perception. Le Goff has noted "the essential place of corporal symbolism within the cultural and mental system of the middle ages. The body not only reveals the soul, but is also the symbolic place in which the human condition, in all its forms, is accomplished."[11] The body was the essence of the human condition. Its very existence was ineluctably tied with symbolic and astrological perceptions, and each limb and part bore a different significance.[12] Its different forms both defined and manifested social gradations, so that noblemen appeared both in literature and in medical texts as well-formed and strong, while simple people bore an ugly, malformed appearance.[13] It was the most common metaphor for the body politic, for human society, and for the nuclear family.[14] The four elements of the human body both paralleled and symbolized the four elements of the universe. The human body was thus a multivocal symbolic microcosm, reflecting almost all the surrounding macrocosmic elements and spheres of the universe.[15]

Moreover, it was through physical sensations that one achieved the metaphysical. Far from seeking to transcend corporeal feelings (as eastern religions did), late medieval Christianity was an intensely corporeal experience, in which pain and pleasure intermingled. The dichotomy of body and soul had no place in this scheme. Late medieval spirituality, especially feminine religiosity, perceived transcendent

---

[10] Marie-Christine Pouchelle, *Corps et chirurgie à l'apogée du moyen âge: Savoir et imaginaire du corps chez Henri de Mondeville, chirurgien de Philippe le Bel* (Paris, 1983), pp. 127-28.

[11] Jacques Le Goff, "Le rituel symbolique de la vassalité," p. 359.

[12] *Le grand et le petit Albert*, pp. 84-91; Gustav Radbruch, "Planetarische Kriminalanthropologie," *Elegantiae Iuris Criminalis* (Basel, 1938), pp. 12-25.

[13] Jacques Le Goff, "Body and Ideology in the Medieval West," in his *The Medieval Imagination*, trans. Arthur Goldhammer (Chicago, 1985), p. 84.

[14] Pouchelle, *Corps et chirurgie*, pp. 180-204.

[15] Charles Singer, "The Visions of Hildegard of Bingen, " in *From Magic to Science: Essays on the Scientific Twilight* (New York, 1928), pp. 199-239.

experiences in physical forms. The human body was "the locus of the divine", mystical experiences often being felt through the medium of bodily perceptions and described in explicitly physical terms.[16]

The body was a vehicle of both intentionally-caused and unavoidable pain. Late medieval mystics, seeking to identify with the crucified Christ, deliberately inflicted upon themselves a routine of physical punishment. Self-flagellation, insertion of thorns, and various other means of self-torture were common ascetic practices.[17] It was only one step from self-inflicted pain as a means of identification with the crucifixion to the acceptance of pain inflicted by others. The thirst for martyrdom, the voluntary acceptance of pain as a means of salvation, permeated late medieval religiosity.[18] The parallels between judicial executions of early Christians and of contemporary criminals were not lost upon late medieval people. Death by execution was undoubtedly painful, but properly accepted, it could be turned into an elevated religious experience. The original model of positive suffering was thus reinforced, together with the connection between execution/crucifixion and purifying pain. The feeling of kinship between the criminal on his way to the gallows and the saint in search of God, both transcending and expiating sin through mortification of the flesh, surfaced often in late medieval literature, art, and sermons.[19]

Life was beginning to imitate art when real condemned criminals began transmuting their experiences into martyrdom. Nicholas Tuldo was a young nobleman from Perugia, sentenced to death in Siena for having spoken ill of the city's magistrates. Angry at the excessive severity of his punishment, he rejected all consolations of religion until visited by Saint Catherine. The famous mystic recorded in one of her

---

[16] Caroline W. Bynum, *Holy Feast and Holy Fast: The Religious Significance of Food to Medieval Women* (Berkeley, 1987), pp. 251-59. The physical experience of spiritual sensations existed already in early Christianity. See Peter Brown, *The Body and Society: Men, Women, and Sexual Renunciation in Early Christianity* (New York, 1988), pp. 222-23, 236-37.

[17] Bynum, *Holy Feast and Holy Fast*, pp. 209-11.

[18] André Vauchez, *La sainteté en Occident aux derniers siècles du moyen âge* (Rome, 1981), pp. 174-83.

[19] For late medieval literature identifying terrestrial with heavenly punishment, see Jerôme Baschet, "Les conceptions de l'enfer au XIVe siècle: Imaginaire et pouvoir," *Annales E.S.C.* 40 (1985), 183-205, and Cohen, "To Die A Criminal," pp. 296-97; for artistic expressions of the same idea, see Alberto Tenenti, *La vie et la mort à travers l'art du XVe siècle* (Paris, 1952), pp. 30-48. For sermons, see for example those of Jean Gerson, *Six sermons français inédits*, ed. Louis Mourin (Paris, 1946), and his *Oeuvres complètes*, ed. Mgr. Glorieux, 7 vols. (Paris, 1960-68); A. Lecoy de la Marche, *La chaire française au moyen âge* (Paris, 1886); Zink, *La prédication*.

letters the subsequent conversion and execution of the young dissident. In words charged with metaphors of fire, blood, tears, and food, Catherine's letter turned a commonplace execution into glorious martyrdom. "I have received one head already in my hands, and I have felt in it a sweetness that the heart cannot understand, the mouth cannot tell, the eye cannot see, and the ear cannot hear." Indeed, Catherine experienced a mystical vision while holding the severed head. For Nicholas himself the execution was even more of a journey to God. Before the execution, "his will was united and submissive to the will of God. His one fear was to be weak at the supreme moment." Due to Catherine's consolation and encouragement, he lost all fear. "See what a light he has received, since he called holy the place of justice [i.e., the gallows]!" Nicholas made a holy end, "like a peaceable lamb," comforted and supported all the way by Catherine.[20]

It is difficult to recall that Nicholas Tuldo was no martyr for the faith. He died for a secular crime against the state, not for a religious cause. And yet, his death became a momentous religious experience for him and for his spiritual guide. Through God's grace, the gallows had become holy to both of them—no longer a place of infamy and degradation, but a gateway to heaven. The merit of the execution resided in the religious conversion of the culprit and his wholehearted acceptance of his fate. But the tool that accomplished his salvation was the suffering and shame of a public execution.

In fact, Nicholas Tuldo died well. The late medieval preoccupation with making a good end is well-known. Dying well was an art to be learned, and death an occasion one carefully prepared for. The cosmic battle between angels and devils was fought at every deathbed, for every soul again, and the victory of the angels depended largely on how one comported oneself on that momentous occasion.[21] The cult of Saint Barbara, patroness of the good death and protector against sudden and unprepared demise, was extremely popular at the time.[22]

The idea that the good death was not reserved for those who had lived a good life, but was perhaps even more important for those who had not, took root in the fourteenth century. Repentance before exe-

---

[20] Catherine of Siena, *Les lettres de Sainte Catherine*, trans. E. Cartier (Paris, 1886), pp. 886-91.

[21] Mary Catharine O'Connor, *The Art of Dying Well: The Development of the Ars Moriendi* (New York, 1942); Roger Chartier, "Les arts de mourir, 1450-1600," *Annales E.S.C.* 31 (1976), 51-75; Tenenti, *La vie et la mort.*

[22] Emile Mâle, *L'art réligieux de la fin du moyen âge en France* (Paris, 1931), p. 186.

cution was far more dramatic than the usual deathbed scene. Here the duel over the human soul was magnified tenfold. The condemned criminal could still be saved at the price of physical suffering and contrition. It was then that the death of criminals on the gallows was incorporated into the framework of conversion, acceptance and salvation.[23] A good death was not a painless one necessarily.[24] It was a death which one accepted, and for which one had made ready. Undergoing physical pain and accepting it was a way of preparing for death. Physical agony was thus not something to be shunned or mitigated. Whether self-inflicted or caused by others, it was a reminder of the suffering of Christ and the martyrs, most of whom had died by execution of one type or another.

Pain was perceived also as a means of reaching the truth. The religious truth of the soul, which could be reached by pain-induced revelations, was affirmed by confession, but secular judicial truth was equally important. Reaching truth by means of bodily pain was not limited to executions. Albeit in different senses, both ordeals and judicial torture employed this means. While in the ordeal the truth of guilt or innocence was objectively revealed by the body's reaction to the inflicted test (almost invariably a painful one), judicial torture was a method of eliciting facts. Nevertheless, both were meant to reveal the truth by means of pain, and when ordeals were banned, torture replaced them. In a manner reminiscent of the transition from gestures to spoken formulae in court rituals, oral confession came to supersede the physical gesture of the ordeal.[25]

Torture came into use as a mode of proof only when ordeals were discredited and confession became the paramount proof of guilt.[26] Its introduction has been attributed to the legacy of Roman law, but the explanation is insufficient. Only slaves were liable to torture in Rome, while in medieval Europe almost any criminal suspect could suffer in

[23] An early sixteenth-century German woodcut, depicting a procession to the gallows, puts this sentiment in the mouth of the condemned: "If you bear your pain patiently/It shall be useful to you/ therefore, give yourself to it willingly." ("Wo du Gedult hast in der Peyn/ So wirt sie dir gar nutzlich sein/ darumb gib dich willig darein.") Woodcut by Wolfgang Katzenheimer, 1508, reproduced in Ch. Hinckeldey, ed., *Justiz in alter Zeit* (Rothenburg, 1984), p. 425.

[24] The idea that a peaceful death was evidence of a virtuous life and future salvation only became entrenched in the sixteenth century. See Claude Blum, "Le corps à l'agonie dans la littérature de la renaissance," in *Le corps à la renaissance. Actes du XXXe colloque de Tours, 1987*, ed. Jean Céard et al. (Paris, 1990), pp. 151-53.

[25] Talal Asad, "Notes on Body Pain and Truth in Medieval Christian Ritual," *Economy and Society* 12 (1983), 288-98.

[26] Ullmann, "Reflections on Medieval Torture."

the same way.[27] Furthermore, judicial torture was freely employed also in the lands of customary law, where Roman law had no authority. Judges in those areas could borrow at will from Roman law, ignoring whatever they found alien to their own system. If customary practice adopted torture as a fact-finding procedure, it was because the method fitted in with contemporary judicial perceptions of truth and the law. It is impossible to understand the adoption of judicial torture merely as a technical device of the inquisitorial mode of procedure. Like many other legal processes, it was rooted in a combination of ancient traditions and contemporary perceptions concerning the moral value of human suffering.

The idea that the human body and its agony were both a vehicle and an expression of truth did not die out when the ordeal disappeared. Judicial torture, carefully regulated and administered, could only have been accepted as a means of eliciting truth in a society that intimately connected pain, salvation, and truth. Torture was never administered unless there were substantial grounds for assuming guilt, and no other mode of proof was possible.[28] It was thus something of a prefatory punishment, used when the judge was convinced of the suspect's guilt, but lacked sufficient proof for condemnation.

This practice reflects a further dimension in the perception of pain: pain as punishment. Here the change in linguistic usage stands as witness to the perceptual process that came to identify suffering with retribution. While the blameless physical suffering of the martyrs took on the classical generic word *passio*, the term denoting punishment, *poena*, came to replace *dolor* in the sense of pain. *Poena* was both punishment and physical mortification, for the two were inextricably tied together. Meting out justice in the form of punishment could serve a variety of purposes, the correction of the offender certainly being one of them.

The infliction of suffering was thus anything but gratuitous cruelty. It was a combination of correction (both moral and physical), justice, search for truth, and salvation. In a period stressing above all the figure of Christ as the man of suffering, pain did not possess its present-day negative connotations. The execution of a criminal under these circumstances was not an act of barbarism. For the sake of all those involved—judges, criminals and spectators—it had to be con-

[27] John Langbein, *Torture and the Law of Proof* (Chicago, 1977), pp. 3-10.
[28] Ullmann, "Reflections on Medieval Torture," 124.

ducted as a public ritual charged with complex and interrelated messages.

Many of these messages were on a symbolic level. The use of liminality in punitive rituals has been viewed earlier within the context of socially and culturally marginal groups—women, Jews, the dead, and the non-human. But all these groups (with the exception of animals) were already liminal by their very nature. The rituals applied to them did no more than symbolically articulate an already existent status. In punitive rituals applied to living Christian men the process of liminalization stood out in sharper outline, for here an integral member of society underwent a ritual which, much like the *Chrenecruda*, excluded him forever. The symbolic functions of ejection, branding, and infamy were fairly clear. They banished the criminal from the normative community, either permanently when prefacing an execution, or temporarily when merely inflicting a transitory penalty. Many of the rites applied to integral members of society undergoing liminalization were identical to the vocabulary of permanently liminal groups.

Both moral and symbolic levels were overlaid with a complex of governmental messages. Like numerous other rituals staged by politico-judicial authorities, punitive rites and ceremonies were part of a deliberate set of symbols intended to impress upon the public the majesty and power of the law and its representatives. This fact is perhaps best illustrated in the multivalence of the term 'justice'. Beyond the abstract, moral meaning attributed to it, justice in contemporary parlance meant mainly two things. It was the authority inherent in any lordship—be it urban, royal, feudal, or ecclesiastical—to hold court and try criminals. One could own a justice (high, middle, or low), lose it, sell it, or bequeath it. At the same time, the term was inextricably tied to capital executions. *Faire justice* or *justicier* meant to execute, while the noun *la justice* simply denoted the gallows.

Justice was thus a perceptual crossroads of moral judgment, public capital punishment, and political authority. The connection between the coalescence of political structures and the growth of penal law is obvious.[29] Though these structures were not necessarily royal, in every case the power of jurisdiction was ineluctably tied to political authori-

[29] For a survey of the literature on this subject, see Pieter Spierenburg, *The Spectacle of Sufffering: Executions and the Evolution of Repression* (Cambridge, 1984), pp. 3-5. The clearest statement of the connection between state formation and punitive structures is Julius Goebel, *Felony and Misdemeanor: A Study in the History of Criminal Law* (Philadelphia, 1976).

ty. Again, the process was reflected in verbal usage. In the thirteenth century Beaumanoir could still speak of the 'vengeance' of authorities against malefactors, while later jurists, free from the feudal mentality, termed the state's actions punishment.[30] No wonder, therefore, that early modern states on their way to absolutism were responsible for comprehensive and stringent punitive codes. State formation and harsh punitive measures went hand in hand, as the *Constitutio Criminalis Carolina* in Germany, the Marian statutes in England and ordinance of Villers-Cotterets in France testify.[31]

Given the complexity and political importance of the messages encoded in punitive rituals, it was only to be expected that the stage directors would rely upon a rich vocabulary of pre-existent symbols and associations. All ceremonies are composed of sets of symbols, but these do not function in a vacuum. "Symbols are matters of relationships which must in some way be publicly recognized and remembered—they are not absolutes, but function entirely within social life," wrote Mary Carruthers in her study of memory.[32] As individual memory relies upon symbols, so does the collective memory.

Any public authority wishing to use effectively a set of symbols in ritual has to make sure they are understood by all participants. There are two possible strategies for achieving this end. One can explicitly indoctrinate the audience as to the specific meaning of each symbol, as Christian preachers did when explaining the meaning of the eucharistic host or the baptismal water in their sermons. But it is simpler and more effective to rely upon a pre-existent set of symbols and cultural associations embedded in the collective memory. And the spectatorship of punitive rituals constituted such a collective repository of symbolic associations.

This indeed was the strategy adopted by French royal authorities in the later middle ages. The remarkable part of this usage lies not so much in the choice, probably imposed by necessity, but in the form it took. Lacking both a pulpit and a corps of preachers, civil authorities in a partially-literate society could not afford to create an entirely new set of punitive symbols. Broadsheets and gallows' speeches (pronounced by the criminals themselves) introducing a strong verbal ele-

30 *CB*, ch. 30, *passim*.

31 John Langbein, *Prosecuting Crime in the Renaissance* (Cambridge, Mass. 1974).

32 Mary J. Carruthers, *The Book of Memory: A Study of Memory in Medieval Culture* (Cambridge, 1990), p. 260.

ment into punitive rituals, appeared only in the seventeenth century.[33] Until then, the message had to rely upon pictures, gestures, and symbols. The provenance of the latter is the most noteworthy element in the whole interactive vocabulary of justice.

In the first place, it might be well to survey the possibilities which remained unexploited. Though the Salic code abounded with symbolic legal rituals, none of them was revived in the later middle ages. This despite French jurists' awareness of the existence of this code, which they claimed as the fundamental law of the realm. The famous misuse of Salic law in the matter of the inheritance of the French crown in the early fourteenth century is proof not only of a certain familiarity, but also of respect towards what was seen as the oldest law of France. The contemporary growth of the cult of Clovis (an unlikely saint by any standard) must have increased the awareness of Salic law tradition.[34] But the Salic law remained a concept, a myth of origin. Not a single jurist attempted to put any of its historical ceremonies to practice.

One could possibly argue that nobody in the fourteenth century possessed sufficient familiarity with the provisions of the Salic law to be able to copy them. But newer traditions, rituals of shame and punishment common in the twelfth century, also fell into desuetude later on. It was not merely forgetfulness, but occasionally deliberate suppression of certain traditional legal rituals. Rites based upon oral, rather than written elements, or stemming from obsolete cultural tenets at variance with contemporary judicial culture were deliberately omitted from late medieval sentences and formal customals.

If ancient traditions commanded no emulation, one might have turned to contemporary or near-contemporary customary literature. Though these writings possessed no legislative authority, they presumably reflected local usages. Nevertheless, there is very little correlation between customary texts and actual punitive practice. Most of the customals were remarkably succinct when it came to this subject. Their words did not reflect more than a fraction of the rich variety of punitive symbols in actual use. Though Beaumanoir noted that "... certain crimes should be punished by different deaths, just as the types of crime committed by criminals are in different manners..." he distinguished only the executions of heretics, counterfeiters, and

[33] Sharpe, "Last Dying Speeches."

[34] Colette Beaune, "Saint Clovis: Histoire, religion royale et sentiment nationale à la fin du moyen âge," in Bernard Guenée, ed., *Le métier d'historien au moyen âge. Etudes d'historiographie médiévale* (Paris, 1977), pp. 139-56.

criminals in general.[35] D'Ableiges avoided the subject almost completely, only exhorting judges to adopt a more lenient stance. His one comment upon modes of punishment is revealing of the complexity of the problem: "There are diverse kinds of punishment, [varying] according to the crimes, but you should adhere to what is usual in the land in which you find yourself and to the customs of the place, for it is well to guard them, though temperately, for the judgments are in doubt..." [36] His perplexity is typical of thirteenth- and fourteenth-century jurists who, at a loss to explain practice, avoided the subject as far as possible.

With the passage of time punitive rituals became more varied and complex, and jurists began paying more attention to the different types of punishment. The fifteenth-century authors of the various Angevin customals were probably the first to do so. The *Coutumes et stilles observez et gardez ès pays d'Anjou et du Maine,* dating from 1411, was the first to provide a detailed list of criminal acts with the corresponding penalties, a list copied by subsequent Angevin authors.[37] Chassenée, reflecting the Renaissance preoccupation with detailed punitive rites, did state that all mutilations should affect a functional member of the body, and be symbolically related to the crime which they were meant to punish. Thus, one should not pull out the eyes of a blind person as punishment. Nevertheless, he had no answer when querying why thieves were hung, while murderers received the easier death of decapitation. The best he could argue was that hanging a thief was ancient custom, both French and universal, and that the French manner of hanging was no more cruel than a beheading.[38]

Chassenée's work, typical of Renaissance jurisprudence, displayed an ever-growing interest bordering upon a morbid fascination with types of punishment. The interest was not limited to France. It culminated in the anecdotal and hair-raising catalogue of suffering compiled by Jacob Döpler, *Theatri poenarum suppliciorum et executionum criminalium, oder Schau-platzes derer Leibes- und Lebens- Strafen.*[39] Undoubtedly, this type of literature was closely related to the early

[35] *CB*, arts. 823, 831-34, 1:428-29, 430-31.

[36] *GC*, p. 650.

[37] *CIAM*, 1:430-40; cf. Liger, *Les coustumes d'Anjou et du Maine intitullées selon les rubriches du Code* (1437), *Ibid.*, 2:502-506; *Les coustumes des pays d'Anjou et du Maine* (1463), *Ibid.*, 3:21-380, *passim.*

[38] Chassenée, *In consuetudines ducatus Burgundiae*, fols. 43a, 46b.

[39] Leipzig, 1697.

modern growth in the complexity and cruelty of public executions. In line with the intellectual trends of the time, most Renaissance jurists tried to find classical precedents for contemporary practices in the customs of the Romans, Greeks, or even Persians. Nevertheless, their work contained no further insight as to the symbolic meanings of executions.

So old legal traditions were not invoked, and new ones could not be invented. All the same, the vocabulary of justice showed a remarkable consistency. Sentences from all over northern France indicate that roughly the same penalties were meted out for similar crimes. Thieves were hung, murderers beheaded, sodomites burned. More intriguingly, with very few variations the same vocabulary was employed all over Europe.[40]

Where did it come from? The vocabulary of justice is not hard to trace. It forms part of the extra-legal cultural context of the period. The colors condemned men and women wore to the gallows, their degree of dress or undress, the gestures they performed, and the words they spoke were all culled from the general public culture of the time. The routes traversed by criminals during whippings or on the way to the gallows consisted of a symbolic use of urban space echoing other public ceremonies. And whenever a pre-existent symbol was lacking, we find the earliest beginnings of written dissemination of information: the placard.

On the whole, judicial authorities devoted a great deal of thought and planning to public executions, staging them most deliberately and expensively. The price of an execution in fifteenth-century Rouen, for example, could vary from 11 *sous tournois* (10 for a simple hanging and 1 for new gloves for the hangman) to 53 *sous* for dragging, beheading and displaying various portions of the criminal's body in various parts of the city.[41] The execution of a great personage in Paris was a far more spectacular affair. The city of Paris spent £94 19s. 6d. *parisis* for the execution of the constable of St.-Pol, the price including such expenses as payment to the companies of soldiers keeping the

[40] Esther Cohen, "Symbols of Culpability and the Universal Language of Justice: The Ritual of Public Executions in Late Medieval Europe," *History of European Ideas* 11 (1989), 407-16. For the remarkable longevity of this principle, see Anton Blok, "The Symbolic Vocabulary of Public Executions," in June Starr and Jane F. Collier, eds., *History and Power in the Study of Law: New Directions in Legal Anthropology* (Ithaca, N.Y., 1989), pp. 31-54, dealing with eighteenth-century crime.

[41] BN, ms. fr. 7645, Nos. 9, 25.

route clear of spectators and the cost of candles for the dead man's soul, to be lit in various churches.[42] On other occasions special gallows, platforms or galleries were erected for specific executions or rites of degradation and punishment. Obviously, whoever planned and financed such deliberate ceremonies, meticulous to the last symbolic detail, had a specific purpose in mind. As the purpose was multiple, so was the symbolism used to convey it. As the purpose was largely extra-judicial, so was the symbolism. Both formed part of the cultural matrix of the time.

The effectiveness of such spectacles depended to a large extent upon the shared background of all participants, be they judges, criminals, or spectators. As the sources describing these ceremonies are most often the chronicles of the time, we have no record (barring the laconic criminal sentences) for those punishments that failed to impress the public. Obviously, writers would record executions of greatest impact upon observers, including the writer. Nevertheless, there are certain indications that on the whole these rituals were understood by their target audiences very well indeed. Occasionally chroniclers noted quite specifically that this or that spectacle made a deep impression upon the people. But perhaps the clearest evidence is the very elliptic style of the chroniclers. They described in minute detail the dress of the condemned man and his behavior on the way to the gallows, but they did not bother to explain the meaning of either. Seemingly, this type of information was so obvious as to need no elucidation.

The present-day reconstitution of the vocabulary of justice may sometimes suffer from this elliptic style, but as a rule it is possible to reconstruct it. The most obvious piece of evidence is that salient feature of most ritual symbols: the constant repetition which embeds the meaning within the rite. Throughout the later middle ages in France there was a constant usage, closely resembling that of other European countries at the time and little altered until the sixteenth century. It is this constant repetition that provides the main key to the vocabulary of justice.

[42] Jean de Roye, *Chronique scandaleuse*, 1:362.

CHAPTER TEN

POWER AND DISGRACE: RITUALS OF INFAMY

1. Defamation by Marking

The vocabulary of justice found expression in rituals of infamy. They were extremely varied ceremonies, rich in symbolic and cultural associations. The extra-legal, cultural origins of the vocabulary were evident in all punitive rituals. The pillory, the stocks, the whipping-cart and the gallows all carried a dual significance: based upon the most fundamental perceptions and ideas of contemporary culture, they were designed to show the power of political authority in a universally intelligible language. In the search for common understanding, authorities borrowed modes of expression born and used in the ostensibly disparate contexts of carnivals, religious rites and popular feasts.

Rituals of infamy could be either mere scenes of shame or executions. While both types resorted to the same vocabulary, there were some inherent differences between capital and non-capital rituals. The interconnection of justice, lordship, and punishment was largely lacking in the latter. While the authority of government explicitly doing justice was the central motif of executions, the moral content played a major role in defamatory rites. No wonder that the church, which kept carefully away from non-capital ceremonies, gradually worked its way into the ritual of executions, for there lay the messages of power over bodies and souls.

Rituals articulating norms rather than authoritative messages were apt to display a far richer and more varied popular content than capital executions. Every judicial authority possessing even the right of middle or low justice could erect a pillory and stage punitive ceremonies. Consequently, these were held even in the smallest of urban centers, often away from the watchful eyes of central authorities, their staging a matter of local decisions and local perceptions of justice. Thus a great deal of ceremonial matter excised from executions by judges of central courts remained in defamatory rites, especially those held outside the centers of power.

Non-capital punitive ceremonies had various aims. Usually they were meant to shame the culprit by exposing him to pain and public derision for a prescribed period of time. Such were the public whippings, the exposure on the pillory or in the stocks, and the *amende honorable*. All of these punishments publicly labelled the offender for the duration of the ceremony. Once the term of punishment was over, there were two alternatives. For trivial offenses defamation constituted the entire penalty, but in notoriously severe cases it was merely a prologue to an ultimate sentence of banishment or execution.

As these penalties, either alone or in conjunction with a severer sequel, could be applied to a very wide spectrum of offenses and offenders, they were necessarily as explicit as possible. It served no purpose merely to place a man upon the pillory for a few hours if the spectators could not know whether he was a nefarious traitor on his way to the gallows or merely a workman caught with a few bunches of illicitly culled grapes on his way home. Consequently the reasons for defamation were invariably spelled out. The action which had caused public exposure was proclaimed by word, gesture, picture or writing for all to see.

In some ceremonies self-condemnation formed an integral part of the sentence. People sentenced to an *amende honorable* were to accuse themselves loudly throughout the term of their punishment. This ceremony, so common as to be performed almost daily, was the cornerstone of shame and atonement rituals. Criminals could be sentenced to perform it, alone or in conjunction with other penalties, for almost any type of crime. The culprit knelt barefoot and bare-headed, either clad in his shirt or naked, holding aloft a candle of specified weight, proclaiming his guilt and begging pardon of God, king, and justice. Thus he was to remain until the candle had burned down.

This ritual was carried out as far as possible at the place of the crime. A wife-murderer performed it in the street next to his house, the attacker of a Parlement councillor did it in the very same chamber, a sacreligious priest in front of the cathedral, and royal sergeants who had maltreated some monks performed their ritual atonement in front of the monastery.[1] The insistence upon the locality of the ceremony was not specific to the *amende honorable*. Recognized as a principle of punitive customary law, it was common to many rituals of shame. Jean Boutillier in the fourteenth century and Jean Bacquet in the fifteenth

---

[1] *Quaestiones Johanis Galli*, pp. 171-72, 175-76, 180-82, 220-21; AN, X^{2a} 10, fol. 235; Y6^{1}, fol. 144; BN, ms. fr. 21731, fol. 52ro.

both stressed that "crimes should be punished where they are committed."[2] There is ample evidence that in this case both jurists were doing no more than describing a widely honored custom. The desecrators of a village church where whipped next to it; a child-deserter received the same punishment in front of the doorstep on which she had abandoned her baby, and the wife-murderer was hung upon a gibbet especially erected on the spot of the crime.[3]

The location of the punishment held a double meaning. On the symbolic level, punishment on the spot of the crime carried a hint of a talionic perception, a spectacle of justice visibly achieved. The contrast between the temporal discontinuity between crime and punishment and the spatial conjunction of the two by the subsequent righting of a wrong on the same spot heightened the retributive effect. From the point of view of the cautionary impact, the people most likely to witness a punishment on the spot would be those familiar with the crime and the criminal. The effect was undoubtedly stronger for the audience, while for the culprit the shame of suffering punishment among familiar people was all the greater. The rule of punishment on the spot was never applied to anonymous criminals, brigands or professional thieves. It was usually put into practice when the crime was a matter of family, neighborhood, or village relationships. In these cases the spectators' previous knowledge made punishment on the spot not only desirable, but also necessary.

The *amende honorable* could be imposed in conjunction with any other penalty. In a typical case, a forger was sentenced to make a full restitution to his victims, suffer a public humiliation, be banished and have all his property confiscated. The humiliation consisted first of being publicly whipped through the streets of Paris while a herald denounced his crime before him, then of being pilloried, and finally of performing an *amende honorable*: kneeling at a public spot naked, holding a four-pound burning candle in his hand and proclaiming he was an evil forger.[4]

In the *amende honorable* the culprit spoke his own lines, but far more often the task was entrusted either to the herald accompanying the whipping-cart on its route through the crossroads of the city, or to visual effects. An integral part of the culprit's costume was the placard

[2] "Où les crimes sont faits & perpetrez, là doivent estre punis." *SR*, p. 224; Bacquet, "Traicte des droicts de iustice," p. 61.

[3] *Registre criminel du Châtelet*, 2:246-47; AN, Y6^{6}, fol. 79; Y6^{4}, fol. 108ro.

[4] BN, ms. fr. 21731, fols. 78 ^{ro}-81vo.

stating his offense, either hanging upon his chest and back, or on the paper miter on his head. This form of proclamation was used mostly for criminals sentenced to public infamy on the pillory.[5] While the offense was usually spelled out in words, pictorial messages could be even more useful. Three perjurers stood on the pillory carrying pictures of a face with a long forked tongue on their chests and backs. Two women who had stolen and sold grapes were crowned on the pillory with grape-covered hats, and a man, similarly guilty, spent two hours at the city gates with a hat full of grapes hanging from his neck.[6]

On other occasions the visual message spelled out the penalty rather than the crime. It was common in France, as elsewhere in northern Europe, to parade the prisoner on his way to the gallows with the rope around his neck. Though in Germany this symbolism was reserved for criminals on their way to death, French practice, very much in the manner of the pillory placards, connected it with non-capital punishments. Two purse-cutters caught and condemned in Paris in 1488 were both "taken to the gallows, rope around their necks". Were it not for the fact that both sentences specified also beating, ear-cutting, and finally banishment, one would have assumed a death sentence.[7] Obviously, in these cases the execution was purely show. It was meant to display the spectacle of gallows-birds without actually inflicting the penalty, for the message was more important than the retribution. Both criminals were on their way to a social death as marked, banished men, and the social dimension was symbolized by the trappings of a physical death.

The show of execution could be taken farther. On occasion, ceremonies of shame borrowed from capital rituals the idea of an execution in effigy. This penalty, legally reserved for escaped criminals, could be applied as an act of defamation. When the future Charles the Bold rebelled against his father, Duke Philip the Good of Burgundy, the citizens of Dinant expressed their opinion of his acts in a very explicit manner:

> In their shamelessness and insanity, the inhabitants of Dinant rebelled, so that they dared to hang a figure of the said illustrious count of Charolais on a gallows in a public square of their town; they

[5] Hans von Hentig, "The Pillory: A Medieval Punishment," in *Studien zur Kriminalgeschichte*, p. 122, suggests that the paper miter "might go back to the crown of thorns applied in the execution of Jesus Christ."

[6] *Chronique parisienne anonyme*, p. 162; *Registre criminel du Châtelet*, 2:251, 254.

[7] AN, Y 5266, fols. 77ro, 83vo.

publicly proclaimed and sang derisive songs throughout the town, and offered prayers and intercessions for his soul, as though he had been hung on the Paris gallows called Montfaucon.[8]

Mock-executions were a form of popular justice borrowed from the formal ritual. But the pretended execution was a perfectly well-known and accepted legal rite for condemned criminals. Such people formed an intermediate category between those sentenced to temporary infamy and those about to die following the shame. They were criminals whose deeds had not merited death, but who were not destined to rejoin normative society once the punishment was over. Their sentences had another aim, not so much moral as utilitarian. The marking of recidivists as perennially dangerous to society was not merely the infliction of pain and retribution. Marking served as a warning to all those who in the future might meet a person lacking an ear, branded or mutilated. Such people were labelled for life as criminals and marginals. A killer who could claim that his victim "had had an ear lopped off" and was therefore a dangerous person could use this fact as grounds for gaining a remission.[9]

Marking and maiming hardly constituted public rituals. Though usually conducted in the open, they were carried out with very little ceremony or effect.[10] The best gauge of impact is the impressions contemporaries recorded in chronicles, and those almost never mentioned mutilation as a public ceremony. The only outstanding exceptions occurred when the mutilation formed part of an execution. Thus, when a number of forgers of the king's seal were caught, a special scaffolding was erected near Saint-Denis in order to have their hands cut off before the execution.[11]

Nor were the mutilations embedded within any kind of symbolic ritual. There was no need, for the message was simple, explicit, and

---

[8] "Qui etiam Dinatenses in tantum procacitatis et vesaniae proruperunt, ut ausi sint simulacrum praefati illustris comitis de *Charolois* in publica platea sui oppidi, erecto patibulo, suspendere; et publice proclamare et decantare irrisorie per totum suum oppidum; et orationes et suffragia pro ejus anima fierent, quasi in patibulo Parisiensi, dicto Mons-falconis, suspensus foret." Thomas Basin, *Histoire des règnes de Charles VII et de Louis XI*, ed. Jules Quicherat, 4 vols. (Paris, 1855-59), 2:134. See for a similar event elsewhere Angus MacKay, "Ritual and Propaganda in Fifteenth-Century Castile," *Past and Present* 107 (1985), 3-43.

[9] AN, JJ 154, No. 511, published in *Choix de pièces inédites rélatives au règne de Charles VI*, ed. L. Douët-d'Arcq (Paris, 1864), 2:94.

[10] Baye, *Journal*, 1:115; Hillairet, *Gibets, piloris et cachots*, pp. 21-22.

[11] *Les grandes chroniques de France*, ed. Jules Viard, 10 vols. (Paris, 1920-53), 9:244; *Chronique de Richard Lescot*, ed. Jean Lemoine (Paris, 1896), p. 62.

carried lifelong by the culprit. The act of infliction was therefore simply and expeditiously performed, without ceremony. It is thus that the records of the time abound with mentions of marked criminals, but in almost no case do we find a chronicler taking the trouble to describe the occasion of the marking. Nevertheless, just like other defamatory rituals, they were punitive rites embedded within contemporary cultural and physiological premises. And like other rituals of shame, they were meant to convey a certain message.

The problem of transmission was far more complex in big cities than in smaller communities, where every person passing the gallows knew the criminal and his deeds. In any big city, most criminals led either to the pillory or to their deaths were anonymous people, committers of nameless crimes. Any defamatory ritual with complex cultural symbolism and veiled references to the criminal and his life was meaningless in the context of a metropolis. In an extraordinary case, the Parlement ordered a corrupt official to undergo public whipping twice, once in Paris and once at Montferrand, the place of his birth where he was known to all spectators.[12] Much of the punitive matter in cities was thus concerned simply with imparting information to the public. When someone was sentenced to banishment in fourteenth-century Paris, the town crier announced:

> ...that such and such has been pronounced banished, and that henceforth no one should receive, accept, host, hide, or give aid and comfort to him, on pain of losing body and goods to the king; but whoever finds him outside a holy place should try to take him by assembling people, by hue and cry *(à cry, à haro)*, by the sounding of bells, by all possible means, and bring him to justice to receive punishment for his misdeeds.[13]

The announcement of banishment was perhaps the simplest, most direct way of marking a person. Unfortunately, the information imparted was of a partial nature. It meant something concrete only to those who knew the culprit already. In the anonymity of the big city banished outlaws could cheerfully return time and again. Unless arrested for another misdeed and recognized, chances were they would never be caught.[14] By contrast, branding and mutilation marked the person for life. Though Chassenée had insisted that mutilation must affect a functional member of the culprit's body, the most common

---

12 BN, ms. fr. 21731, fol. 78ro.
13 GC, pp. 655-56.
14 AN, Y 5266, fols. 14ro, 208ro; 29ro, 49ro, 62vo.

form of punishment touched symbolic, not functional members.[15] Recidivist blasphemers were to be branded on their lips (a punishment which did not cause mutism), while minor thieves and counterfeiters usually lost an ear, but not their hearing.

Ear-cutting did, however, have a purpose beyond simple marking. Already Hippocratic medicine had noted that man's generative powers depended upon the state of the 'juvenile veins' which passed behind his ears, leading sperm from the head to the sexual organs. With these severed, a man lost his power of procreation. The idea was common in the middle ages, often repeated in medieval medical treatises.[16] By the sixteenth century, popular tradition centered the generative powers of the ear only in the left one, and executioners were enjoined to lop off the left ear first, so as to prevent the propagation of criminals.[17] The left ear was considered a sexual organ of sorts; Gargantua was born through his mother's left ear, having climbed from the uterus via the same vein.[18]

Physical marking and mutilation thus served two functions. The pain they caused was both purifying and retributive, but the long-term result was to set the criminal apart from society for life and presumably sterilize him as well. Marking was a life-sentence of semi-outlawry, certainly of marginality.

2. Defamation by Inversion

Whether temporary or permanently shaming, defamatory rituals resorted to the same symbolic principles found in liminal figures. While the specific symbols obviously differed from case to case, the principle of inversion as derogation remained constant. Inversion was meant to deprive the culprit of both social and human identity. It was thus employed in all legal rituals, capital or non-capital, directed at liminal personalities or at common criminals. While the individual variations were endless, the constitutive elements were fairly stable.

---

[15] Chassenée, *In Consuetudines ducatus Burgundiae*, fol. 43a.

[16] Jacquart and Thomasset, *Sexualité et savoir médical*, p. 46, esp. n. 2.

[17] Henri Sauval, *Histoire et recherches des antiquités de la ville de Paris*, 3 vols. (Paris, 1724), 2:597; Hillairet, *Gibets, piloris et cachots*, p. 16.

[18] François Rabelais, *Gargantua*, in *Oeuvres complètes*, ed. Guy Demerson (Paris, 1973), ch. 6, p. 57. Though Gargantua was a known figure in French folklore before Rabelais, this curious form of his birth does not appear in other popular versions. See Paul Sébillot, *Gargantua dans les traditions populaires* (Paris, 1883). For the significance of left vs. right, see Robert Hertz, "The Pre-Eminence of the Right Hand: A Study in Religious Polarity," in Rodney Needham, ed., *Right and Left: Essays on Dual Symbolic Classification* (Chicago, 1973), pp. 7-21.

A. Nudity

Late medieval society attributed to costume a crucial role in denoting and defining hierarchical status. The contrast between the dressed (and hierarchically classified) and the naked and roleless was charged with dramatic symbolism.[19] Thus, the divestiture of clothing was probably the most common mechanism of status deprivation. But nudity was more than loss of social role. Nakedness was also associated with dehumanization and savagery. The naked man was equated with the wild man roaming the realms of medieval fantasy beyond the frontiers of civilization, with the madman outside the boundary of common human reason, and visibly, with the lawless who neither accepted communal norms nor was himself accepted as part of the community.

Hence, legal rituals resorted to ceremonial divestiture when appropriate, or, when there was nothing to remove but the simplest of garments, to the display of nudity. The advantage of social rather than physical nakedness was that it could be adjusted to specific degrees of guilt. Relative divestiture in group sentences denoted the subtle shades of responsibility among the culprits. Of three men performing an *amende honorable* together, one might be in nothing but his shirt (*en pure chemise*), while the others, though barefoot and bare-headed, were entitled to keep their doublets on.[20] The church also exacted divestiture on occasion: a thirteenth-century nobleman who had ordered a burial despite the interdict pronounced on his land was forced personally to disinter the body barefoot and in his shirt.[21] The prevalence of the *amende honorable* with its concomitant nudity in twelfth- and thirteenth-century society was reflected also in epic literature.[22] King Arthur performed a public act of contrition "naked and in breeches", and Renaud de Montauban walked barefoot as far as Mont-Saint-Michel in order to beg Charlemagne's pardon.[23]

---

[19] For the social importance of clothing, see Roland Barthes, "Histoire et sociologie du vêtement. Quelques observations méthodolgiques," *Annales E.S.C.* 12 (1957), 430-41.

[20] AN, X^{2a} 10, fol. 235; *Quaestiones Johannis Galli*, pp. 171-72, q. 148, concerning three royal sergeants who had broken the safeguard of the Paris Carmelites in 1386.

[21] Achille Luchaire, *La société française au temps de Philippe-Auguste* (Paris, 1909), p. 305.

[22] Charles Payen, *Le motif du repentir dans la littérature française médiévale (des origines à 1230)* (Geneva, 1967), pp. 196-211.

[23] *The Vulgate Version of Arthurian Romance*, ed. H. Oskar Sommer (Washington, 1910), p. 220; *Renaud de Montauban*, ed. Castets, (Montpellier, 1909), p. 463.

Divestiture and nudity were also an integral, preparatory stage for capital executions.[24] The social significance of costume was particularly stressed in cases concerning people of special status, whose position was symbolized by particular clothes. Rather than being a precedent, the divestiture then became part of the ceremony. The execution of two Augustinian monks who had pretended to cure Charles VI's madness began with the public stripping of their clerical garb, and the death of the constable of St.-Pol with the overt removal of his insignia of office. A councillor of the Parlement, condemned on several counts of forgery and official malfeasance, was made to hear his sentence kneeling in the Parlement chamber, wearing his councillor's gown. He was then taken to the courtyard, placed upon a stone and formally divested of his gown and honors. All this procedure was no more than a prelude to *amende honorable*, branding, and banishment.[25] The divestiture in these cases was social and symbolic rather than completely physical. Total nudity was usually reserved for lower-class criminals, as part of a whipping or pillory sentence. Frequently the text specified that the criminal should first be stripped completely naked prior to the execution of the defamatory sentence.[26]

Whether the garments removed were of ceremonial significance or not, the effect of divestiture and nudity was the same. It deprived the subjects of their status and their very social identity. Indeed, since all living humans were commonly clothed one way or another, nudity deprived them to a certain extent of their humanity. Nudity was thus a symbolic social death. Occasionally it foreshadowed the real event, while at other times it was a temporary phenomenon. But while naked, the subject of punishment formed no part of living human society.

B. Dehumanization: Spatial Inversion and Animalization

The tendency to dramatize abstract ideas by use of bodily postures was not limited to the realm of punitive law. Personified virtues, vices,

---

[24] The history of this custom goes back a long way. Every account and depiction of Christ's passion told of the stripping of his clothes, down to a loincloth, prior to the crucifixion procession. Indeed, punitive nudity was a common Roman pre-execution humiliation. P. Franchi de' Cavalieri, "Della furca e della sua sostituzione alla croce nel diritto penale Romano," *Nuovo bulletino di archeologia cristiana* 13 (1907), 101-109.

[25] *Chronique du rèligieux de Saint-Denys*, 2:662-69; Basin, *Histoire*, 2:376; Archives de la police, livre gris du Châtelet, fol. 62ro.

[26] *Registre criminel du Châtelet*, 2:247, 279, 520; AN, Y2, fols. 27ro (1491), 65ro (1495); Y6[1], livre vert neuf du Châtelet, fol. 79.

political entities and ideologies appeared in pictorial art and in the theater. Even death was a human body, though shorn of its skin and flesh. It was therefore quite natural for contemporary punitive dramas to manipulate the bodies of the culpable into symbolic postures in order to show their guilt. For this the law relied upon the simplest and most literal of inversions: the reversing of the normal human upright, forward-looking stance.

Physical directional inversion carried moral and cosmic overtones. The gestures of the human body and its proper positioning in space had always had symbolic significance.[27] The inversion of the common, normative stance of the human body had the effect of dehumanizing the subject. Unlike the 'world upside-down' symbolism, meant to establish a hierarchy of categories, individual inversion placed the subject outside the pale of the normative. Turning a person backwards was a statement of non-humanity. Practically every single criminal on his way to the gallows made the journey facing backwards, either tied to a hurdle or upon a cart.[28]

The same idea was also expressed in terms of animal symbolism. The rituals of animalization were based upon two conflicting premises. One was the standard hierarchy of being, regarding any identification of the human with an animal life-form as the greatest of degradations. The other was the belief in the existence of intermediate beings somewhere between the two absolute categories. The perceptual animal kingdom of the later middle ages was a much wider land than the modern, post-Linnean one. In it dwelt domestic and wild animals with fabulous beasts and creatures partaking of both the human and the animal. The categories of life merged in that borderland between the settled and the wild, reality and fantasy, to create the fabulous and the monstrous. According to late medieval travelers, the far reaches of the earth were inhabited by fantastic, semi-human monsters notorious for their ferocity, cruelty, and savagery.[29] Late medieval literature populated also the known geography of the West with mermaids, women-serpents, werewolves and child-swans, all beings who magically crossed the barriers between the human and the animal.[30] Some, like

[27] Schmitt, *La raison des gestes.*

[28] Von Hentig, "The Pillory," p. 121.

[29] Claude Kappler, *Monstres, démons et merveilles à la fin du moyen âge* (Paris, 1980), pp. 147-57; Peter Mason, "Half a Cow," *Semiotica* 85 (1991), 1-40.

[30] Daniel Poirion, *Le merveilleux dans la littérature française du moyen âge* (Paris, 1982), pp. 29-30, 110-15.

the serpent-woman Mélusine, were beneficent and maternal,[31] while others, like the werewolves, were extremely dangerous.

Not all of these monsters impinged upon daily life, though actual trials of werewolves were not unknown.[32] However, their presence in contemporary imagination did affect the attitude towards any human beings too closely associated with animals. When the Gypsies appeared in the West, their uncanny closeness to horses was one of the reasons for their rejection and stigmatization.[33] Though animals possessed no intrinsic demonic qualities, the breach of the barrier between human and animal endowed both sides with diabolic characteristics.[34] Werewolves, more frightening than any animal precisely because they underwent a metamorphosis, embodied this belief.

The human most closely identified with the animal world was the man deprived of reason. This particular perception of madness was closely tied with the belief in the existence of wild men—hairy, frightening, semi-humans who lived in wild places.[35] Some of them belonged to a special race of monsters, but others were merely temporarily deranged inhabitants of civilization. Kings and heroes ranging from Nebuchadnezzar to Chrétien de Troyes' Yvain lost their reason, fled to the forest or ate grass, and became temporarily wild men. [36]

> Wildness meant more in the Middle Ages than the shrunken significance of the term would indicate today. The word implied everything that eluded Christian norms and the established framework of Christian society, referring to what was uncanny, unruly, raw, unpredictable, foreign, uncultured, and uncultivated. It included the unfamiliar as well as the unintelligible.[37]

---

[31] Jacques Le Goff, "Mélusine maternelle et défricheuse," in *Pour un autre moyen âge*, pp. 307-31; Gaignebet, *Le Carnaval*, pp. 87-103.

[32] Charlotte F. Otten, ed., *A Lycanthropy Reader: Werewolves in Western Culture* (Syracuse, N.Y., 1986), pp. 69-76.

[33] Florike Egmond, "Gypsies: Crime, Stigmatization and Ambiguity. The Case of the Northern Netherlands, 1450-1780," Paper presented at the Third International Conference of the International Association for the History of Crime and Criminal Justice (Paris, 1988).

[34] Smith, "The Role of Animals in Witchcraft and Popular Magic," pp. 96-110.

[35] Kappler, *Monstres, démons et merveilles*, pp. 157-64; Richard Bernheimer, *Wild Men in the Middle Ages: A Study in Art, Sentiment and Demonology* (Cambridge, Mass., 1952).

[36] Gervase of Tilbury, *Otia Imperialia ad Ottonem IV imperatorem*, in G.W. Leibnitz, ed., *Scriptores rerum Brunsvicensium*, 3 vols. (Hanover, 1707-11), 1:1003; Bernheimer, *Wild Men*, pp. 8-17; Jacques Le Goff, "Lévy-Strauss in Brocéliande: A Brief Analysis of a Courtly Romance," in *The Medieval Imagination*, pp. 107-31.

[37] Bernheimer, *Wild Men*, p. 19.

The degradation into animal life could be viewed either as sin or as punishment. Audiences could sympathize with the literary plight of a man bewitched into lupine form or held by temporary madness, but any real-life encounter with hybrid creatures got short shrift. Whenever caught, werewolves were tried and executed. Monsters born in civilization were promptly exterminated, and an act of bestiality earned both human and animal participants the stake. People charged with animal metamorphosis by means of witchcraft suffered the same fate.[38]

The idea that the boundary between the human and the animal was far from absolute, in conjunction with the hierarchical view, lay at the foundation of the legal symbolism of animals. Insofar as one approximated a culprit to animals symbolically, one degraded and punished him. Furthermore, the specific choice of the animal employed, with all of its attendant cultural associations, could either aggravate the punishment (if the animal was a particularly infamous one) or elucidate to the public the nature of the crime by way of association with that animal's characteristic traits.

Both inversions were acted out in the backwards ride. Used in every execution, it was no more than a standard aspect of the ritual, articulating by the simplest of means the extra-societal, inverted status of the criminal. What changed the ordinary infamy into an extraordinary occasion was the addition of an animal as a beast of burden. The culprit in these cases was placed upon a disgraceful creature: an ass, a sick horse, or a ram (for licentious women). Often the sources stressed the scatological aspect of this ride, with the rider forced either to hold on to the animal's tail or lower his face into its anal cleft. But even when simply reversed, the ride carried an association of infamy. People guilty only of offending public norms usually suffered no worse than shame, but many traitors ended their backwards journey at the gallows.[39]

The animal motif was closely tied also to the most spectacular type of directional inversion, namely, the upside-down hanging. In the later

---

[38] Otten, *A Lycanthropy Reader*, pp. 99-134; W.M.S. Russell and Claire Russell, "The Social Biology of Werewolves," in *Animals in Folklore*, pp. 143-82; K.F. Smith, "A Historical Study of the Werewolf in Literature," *Publications of the Modern Language Association* 9 (1894), 1-42; Jodocus Damhouder, *Praxis rerum criminalium* (Antwerpen, 1562), ch. 96, art. 15, pp. 282-83. For witchcraft as inversion, see Stuart Clark, "Inversion, Misrule and the Meaning of Witchcraft," *Past and Present* 87 (1986), 98-127.

[39] Mellinkoff, "Riding Backwards," 154-66.

middle ages the custom of hanging a man upside-down with two dogs, or sometimes even wolves on either side, was reserved for Jews.[40] But long before the so-called Jewish execution achieved this doubtful honor, the punishment existed as an especially infamous death reserved for traitorous vassals who had killed their lords. The vassal and murderer of Count Thietmar of Hamburg was put to death in this way when caught by the dead count's son, and one of Charles the Good's murderers, according to Suger, died in a similar manner.[41] Unquestionably, the double inversion of direction and animal association both pointed to the heinousness of the offense and to the exclusion of the culprit from humanity.

The most famous animal-associated execution was also in punishment for a reversal of hierarchical structures. The Theodosian code had ordained that parricides should suffer the *poena culei*: to be sown into a sack together with a cock, a serpent, a monkey, and a dog. The penalty survived in the *Sachsenspiegel*, being fairly common in medieval and early modern Germany.[42] Johann von Buch, a fourteenth-century glossator of the *Sachsenspiegel*, explained the specific symbolic meaning of each animal in the ritual:

> The dog indicates that such a man has never shown honor to his parents, like the dog, who is blind the first nine days. The cock signifies the man's crime and unbridled presumption wreaked on his father or child. The adder signifies the misfortune of such parents. For of their procreation it is said that when they would mate, the male puts his head into the female's mouth, whereby she conceives, and thereupon she bites off the male's head from lust. Then when she gives birth to her young she, in turn, must die through them: for when they are about to be born, they bite their way out of the mother's body, of which she dies in that hour. The monkey signifies the likeness of man or the image of death without deed. For as the

[40] See above, chapter 6, pp. 92-94.

[41] Adam of Bremen, *Gesta Hammaburgensis ecclesiae pontificum*, ed. B. Schmeidler (Hanover 1917), *MGH, SS Rer. Germ. in usum scholarum*, p. 149; Ström, *The Sacral Origin*, p. 128 and n. 123. The event took place in 1048. Suger of Saint-Denis, *Vie de Louis VI*, ed. H. Waquet (Paris, 1964), pp. 248-49. Galbert of Bruges, who was an eye-witness to the events of 1127 in Flanders (*The Murder of Charles the Good, Count of Flanders*, trans. and ed. J.B. Ross, New York, 1967) mentioned no such death, while Suger, writing from a distance, did add this detail. Galbert spoke of an equally symbolic death for the traitors: that of being thrown from the top of a castle (*Ibid.*, pp. 250-54). The historicity of the execution is therefore highly doubtful, but the fact that Suger saw fit to punish the murderer of his lord in such a manner is indicative of his own views and those of his time.

[42] Florike Egmond, "Bijzondere beesten. Diersymboliek en strafvoltrekkingen," Paper presented at the Alterity Symposium, Amsterdam, 1989; Christina Bukowska-

> monkey is like a man in many things and yet is no man, so was this one similar to a man, but in deed and heart was not a man because he could act so inhumanly against his own flesh and blood.[43]

Legal symbolism perceived the animal in punitive law as the hierarchical opposite of the human being. When flesh-and-blood animals were placed in a human position on the dock and tried for homicide, this reversal of the natural order was righted by a second inversion, that of hanging the animal upside-down.

But the use of animal imagery, with or without directional inversion, in late medieval rituals of infamy applied also to far less heinous crimes. It was especially common in cases which the law could not formally penalize, but the community felt compelled to punish. Such cases were rarely recorded in formal proceedings. The backwards ride upon an ass of the beaten husband was a common form of *charivari*, but it never achieved the dignity of a legal procedure.[44] Professional jurists and governmental authorities usually recoiled from practices so deeply embedded within popular perceptions of humanity and the animal kingdom. Indeed, Count Thietmar's son who had hung his father's murderer upside-down with two dogs was exiled by the emperor for his recourse to informal justice in the form of animalization.[45] Formal records of animalization and inversion are thus difficult to find. The scarcity of legal documents makes it worthwhile to examine in detail one case which has survived by chance.

In March 1310 the *bailli* of Senlis brought suit before the Parlement of Paris against the mayor and aldermen of Compiègne. According to the complaint, the city officials had inflicted "many injuries and violence" upon one Jean de Fécamp, a royal sergeant exercising his function in the city, "which redounded greatly to our contempt." The defendants did not deny the facts, but pointed out that "whatever they had done to the said Jean, they had justly and properly executed justice upon him as his faults demanded." Whatever the sergeant had done, his penalty was extraordinary enough. Despite his official status and royal immunity, he had been captured, placed in jail, and refused release until he had agreed to accept and perform the penalty imposed upon him:

Gorgoni, "Die Strafe des Sackens—Wahrheit und Legende," *Forschungen zur Rechtsarchäologie und rechtlichen Volkskunde* 2 (1979), 145-162.

43 Quoted in Kisch, "The Jewish Execution," 2:78-79.

44 Vaultier, *Le folklore*, pp. 40-42; Melinkoff, "Riding Backwards," 172-73.

45 See above, p. 174.

... The mayor and aldermen, having duly deliberated upon this, ordered thus: they had the said Jean harnessed near the soldiers' prison between the shafts of a certain cart or garbage-tumbrel, in which the figure of a certain woman was placed, and hoisted the said shafts upon the shoulders of the same, he claiming all the time that he was our sergeant. From there [they made him] pull, in the manner of a horse, the said cart to a certain place, where they said that a certain woman had escaped their hands, either through the negligence or the fraud of the said Jean, and at that place they made him seize the said figure and throw it in a certain ford outside the city of Compiègne, at their instructions. Prior to her flight, they had intended to throw the escaped woman in that ford.

As might be expected, the Parlement found for the plaintiff. The proceedings of the Compiègne authorities were ruled illegal, and their action little better than simple assault upon a royal official.

...The said mayor, aldermen and commune were condemned to pay the said Jean de Fécamp, for the injuries and violence done to him, one hundred *livres tournois*, and for our fine, two thousand *livres tournois*, which sum will be imposed [i.e., divided] by the *bailli* of Senlis and another suitable person appointed by our court, so as to encumber those who had transgressed most in the above by deed, help, or counsel, each according to the fashion of his crime and his position, as the said *bailli* and deputy should see fit.[46]

The records of the Parlement are full of local sentences overruled by the central court. Often, as is in this case, the Parlement sentence is the only remaining source for the events taking place in the local assembly. Here the Parlement expressed no opinion whatsoever concerning the sergeant's guilt or innocence in the matter of the escaped woman. The issue was the indignity visited upon a royal functionary, and that indignity consisting of animalization during a mock-execution. While executions in effigy of escaped criminals were common practice, the placing of a royal sergeant in the position of horse was not.

The extraordinary sentence was probably caused by the problematic character of the original failed execution. We know neither the woman's name nor her crime, but her sentence was suggestive of an informal offense and a trial of doubtful legality. Drowning was an unusual sentence, certainly prescribed by none of the customals of the area. It was a common enough penalty for male traitors in late medie-

[46] *Olim*, 3:540-42; Esther Cohen, "Inversie en liminaliteit in de rechtspraktijk van de late Middeleeuwen," *Theoretische Geschiedenis* 16 (1989), 433-43.

val northern France, but never for women. French customs employed water in women's trials only in two cases: first for the dunking of errant wives and later, in the sixteenth and seventeenth centuries, for the detection of witchcraft.[47] The recourse to drowning probably indicates that the woman had so offended the sensibilities of the town that she was considered worthy of execution, but that her crime was not a legally defined one. Flagrant marital infidelity or something akin to witchcraft are therefore possible offenses. Were it not for the inclusion of a royal sergeant in the proceedings, one might even doubt that an execution, rather than a dunking was intended. But the commune of Compiègne did not possess the privilege of high justice, this right being reserved to the royal *bailli* of Senlis and his sergeant.[48] Were the woman's penalty a mere dunking, the city would have been able to dispense with the services of the reluctant sergeant. But if she was to be drowned—a sentence the city fathers were qualified neither to pronounce nor to implement—the presence of a royal sergeant was essential.

Several facts support this assumption. First, the Parlement record avoided any specific mention of the woman's crime, thus suggesting that it was not a legal offense. Furthermore, it fully exonerated the sergeant of any malfeasance. Finally he, a royal official ostensibly in charge of an execution, had allowed the woman to escape. There is no way of knowing whether his negligence was deliberate or not, but the city fathers of Compiègne evidently suspected that it was. They were thus faced with the need to penalize a second offense for which standard legal practices had no answer. They had resorted in the case of the woman to measures of popular justice. In the case of the sergeant, they delved into the common memory of long-obsolete rituals of shame and penance, coming up with a specific type of animalization. It was invariably tied with penalties imposed by no court, but associated with the breach of faith.

This ritual usually consisted of having the culprit walk a specific course carrying a horse's saddle upon his back. It first appeared in ninth-century capitularies as one type of *harmiscara*, or royal punish-

---

[47] See above, p. 96.

[48] See the Compiègne charter of privileges of 1153-54 in Achille Luchaire, *Etudes sur les actes de Louis VII* (Paris, 1885, repr. Brussels, 1964), p. 197. When the city tried to claim the privilege of high justice in 1261, the Parlement summarily rejected this claim. (*Olim*, 1:519).

ment.[49] It was then a penalty for theft, official malfeasance, or any other offense the king saw fit directly to chastise. By the eleventh century, however, it had vanished from legislation, only to reappear in chronicles and *chansons de geste* as the fate of rebellious vassals. Geoffrey I Martel of Anjou was forced to carry a saddle on his back for several miles after a failed rebellion against his father, Fulk Nerra, and to prostrate himself before his irate parent with the saddle still on his back.[50] The eleventh-century dukes of Normandy used the same procedure to good effect more than once. Robert of Bellême sought the mercy of Duke Robert after a failed rebellion barefoot and with saddle, and Hugh of Chalon carried the saddle on his head to the future Duke Richard III of Normandy after another rebellion.[51]

While all these cases clustered around the middle of the eleventh century, the custom still appeared, in a remarkably similar guise, in *chansons de geste* written a century later. Duke Naimes suggested to Girard de Vienne, in the poem of that name, that he should carry the saddle on his head barefoot for one league. Elsewhere in the same poem the demand for this humiliation was refined with the specification that the saddle should belong "to a broken-down warhorse or a poor pack-horse."[52] In *Raoul de Cambrai* a lord who had wronged his vassal offered a similar reparation, only to have it rejected.[53] The sources invariably stressed three elements. First, the saddle was to be carried, either on the head or hanging from the neck, for a prescribed distance, in formal procession from one place to another. Secondly, the culprit was to be barefoot, bareheaded, and 'naked' in his shirt. In one *chanson*, he was to carry a staff in his hand, "like a disgraced man."[54] All the old elements of shame were included

[49] "Quicumque caballum, bovem, friskingas, vestes, arma, vel alia mobilia tollere ausus fuerit, triplici lege componat, et liber cum armiscara, id est, sella ad suum dorsum, ante nos a suis senioribus dirigatur et usque ad nostram indulgentiam sustineat..." Ludovicus II, "Constitutio de expeditione Beneventana" (866), ch. 9, in *MGH, Capitularia regum francorum*, ed. A. Boretius and V. Krause, 2 vols. (Hanover, 1883), 2:96.

[50] William of Malmesbury, *De gestis regum Anglorum*, ed. William Stubbs, 2 vols. (London, Rolls Series, 1887-89), 2:292.

[51] William of Jumièges, *Gesta Normannorum ducum*, ed. J. Marx (Rouen and Paris, 1914), pp. 96, 101. For several other cases, see C. Ducange, *Glossarium mediae et infimae Latinitatis*, 7 vols. (Paris, 1840-50), 7:403-404, s.v. *sella*.

[52] "...La selle au col que tendra per l'estrier/ d'un roncin gasté ou d'un povre somier." Bertrand de Bar-sur-Aube, *Le roman de Girard de Vienne*, ed. Frederic G. Yeandle (New York, 1930), p. 79, lines 4030-31.

[53] *Raoul de Cambrai*, p. 59.

[54] "La verge el poing, comme homme escoupé." *Le Roman de Garin le Loheran*, quoted in Ducange, *loc. cit.*

in this public penance, with the addition of the saddle. Finally, in no case was this ritual prescribed as a legal sentence, following a proper trial. It was usually suggested as a voluntary act of reparation and contrition for rebellion, rather than a punitive sentence.[55]

The history of the saddle ceremony stresses once more the non-legal character of the sergeant's offense. Had he really neglected his duty, allowing a convicted criminal to escape, he would have been punished by the *bailli* according to the law. As it was, he probably refused to play a part in an illegal procedure, an act for which the city fathers could not legally penalize him. They therefore resorted to a modified version of an old public disgrace, that of turning a man into a horse in a public procession. They placed him between the shafts of a cart, forcing him to participate in the mock-execution of the effigy (while he had refused to take part in the real one), not as a royal official, but as a cart-horse.

The case of the royal sergeant forced to drag a garbage-cart is a tantalizing hint of an entire level of local justice that has vanished unrecorded. Given the traditional character of legal ceremonies, it is more than unlikely that the city fathers of Compiègne should have been unique in their choice of public humiliation. Their sentence was archaic, unknown to any written customal of the area, and offensive to the Parlement of Paris. But in all probability it was not unheard-of in local courts, for it relied upon a long tradition of legal animalization.

The reaction of the Parlement in this case was equally significant. The professionally-trained jurists of the central court were offended not only by the slight to royal authority, but also by the archaic, semi-obsolete form of the slight. The carrying of the saddle stood contrary to all ideas of humanity and the animal kingdom accepted in elite circles since the thirteenth century. The more popular level of justice enacted at Compiègne took an all-inclusive view of its subject, regarding justice as a universal attribute. The *parlementaires*, by contrast, saw it as a royal prerogative. Paradoxically, the universe of justice as viewed from Paris was a much narrower one than the one seen from Compiègne. In Parisian eyes, it was quite proper to animalize a criminal on his way to the gallows, for he was shortly destined to leave the normative human community for good. But temporary infamy could not so degrade a human being, arbitrarily crossing and recrossing boundaries. The saddle ceremony did precisely that, and was therefore

[55] A parallel ceremony of shame, that of carrying a dog (see Ducange, 2:90, s.v. *canis*), seems to have been employed exclusively in Germany.

intolerable to fourteenth-century educated sensibilities. The associations attendant upon animalization in the minds of the Paris jurists were undoubtedly far graver than those present in the minds of the city fathers of Compiègne. For the latter, it was presumably no worse than time spent on the pillory. For the former, it was an unforgivable degradation.

The suppression of such ceremonies was therefore both a judicial and an intellectual necessity. Indeed, all the remaining evidence to animalization rites as temporary infamy stems from literary and narrative sources. The emergence of trial protocols coincided with the imposition of new norms and practices allowing no room for certain traditional punitive rites. Temporary animalization was almost invariably meted out for social rather than legal offenses. Most of the penalties associating humans with animals concerned betrayal of some sort. In almost every case, the culprit had stepped out of his or her social role—the son and the vassal by being faithless to their natural or social lord, the sergeant by being negligent, the husband by allowing his inferior to rule him. By doing so they had already created a small world upside down, and the way to right it was by another inversion.

The association of the guilty with an animal life-form was an ancient and enduring punitive inversion. It was based upon a rich complex of attitudes towards the animal world dictating the relative place of humans and animals within the universe. Many of those attitudes had nothing to do with law, punitive or otherwise, but nevertheless they did affect legal attitudes towards humans. Animalizing human beings was the mirror image of animal trials. Whether one turned man into animal in a legal ritual of infamy, or treated animals like human beings in another, the result was the same. The order and balance of justice were restored, not just within one courtroom, but within the universe comprising both human and animal.

That was in fact the concern of all rituals of infamy. Though retributive in nature like all punishments, their essential aim was the imparting of a moral and cautionary lesson to the public. It was a lesson of justice in the most abstract sense of the word: not power, nor jurisdiction, nor lordship but the correct balance of the universe, in which each one got his due.

CHAPTER ELEVEN

POWER AND DEATH: PUBLIC EXECUTIONS

Much has been written in recent years about public executions within the process of state-building. Historians perceived them as spectacles of justice making visible the public order and openly restoring the balance of society, upset by crime.[1] "The execution is therefore a deterrent, not only because it shows the downfall and suffering of the condemned, but also, and perhaps mostly, because it stages the frightening omnipotence of justice and the state."[2] With few exceptions, all other elements of public executions have been ignored.[3] True, judicial authorities (though not necessarily the state) deliberately staged executions, but their messages, like those of all public ceremonies, had to be couched in a language both intelligible and acceptable to the recipients. Authorities had to rely upon a traditional vocabulary of symbols and perceptions while imbuing much of the old forms with a new content. The careful acting out of relationships between government, spectators, and culprits, eventually heightened by the mediating role of established religion, could only work by integrating elements and beliefs derived from all relevant spheres.

Yet the governmental content of public capital executions was undoubtedly far weightier than that of simpler rituals of infamy. Justice was synonymous with political lordship, and doing justice meant putting to death. But death meant more than a display of political power. Its application carried an entire spectrum of religious and folkloric perceptions of life, afterlife, and the role of the human body in the transition from one to the other. In addition, religious authorities invariably had their say in matters concerning the human soul, especially at its separation from the body. Thus the balance of components

[1] See, for example Spierenburg, *The Spectacle of Suffering*, pp. 200-207.

[2] Chiffoleau, *Les justices du Pape*, p. 241.

[3] As exceptions, see Richard van Dülmen, "Das Schauspiel des Todes: Hinrichtungsrituale in der frühen Neuzeit," in *Volkskultur zu Wiederentdeckung des vergessenen Alltags (16.-20. Jahrhundert)*, ed. Richard van Dülmen and Norbert Schindler (Frankfurt, 1984), pp. 203-245, 417-423, and Anton Blok, "Openbare strafvoltrekkingen als rites de passage," *Tijdschrift voor Geschiedenis* 97 (1984), 470-81.

grew far more complex in the symbolism of public executions than the folkloric vocabulary employed in non-capital defamatory rites.

Penal death was of all legal rituals perhaps the most heavily charged with religious associations. The centrality of the crucifixion and of martyrdom to late medieval spirituality made both the inherent contrast and the formal parallels between criminal and holy death a natural basis for the shaping of the execution ceremonies. It was thus quite natural for public executions to make use of religious elements within an essentially secular context. The formal distinction of secular and religious rituals is hardly applicable to the later middle ages, especially to legal rituals. Though the church was officially debarred from taking an active role in any procedure shedding blood or terminating human life religious ideas, symbolism and authority permeated executions as they did all public ceremonial.[4] The modern dichotomy of secular and religious spheres is anachronistic in this context. Human life and death, justice, authority and the normative boundaries of society were all tied together in one integrated world view.

All narrative descriptions of executions dwell upon the active role of the spectators in the drama unrolling before their eyes. People watching the death of criminals were hardly a passive audience. They reacted, as they were expected to, with a variety of emotions. The care chroniclers took to record these reactions is an index both of their intensity and of their importance to the authorities. Undoubtedly, executions were mass events. The number of spectators varied according to place, time, and the culprit's status and deed. One chronicler estimated an audience of 200.000 people at the 1475 execution for treason of the count of Saint-Pol, constable of France.[5] While this number is undoubtedly inflated, other sources support the picture of an enormous mass of people. The fact that two companies, one of sergeants and one of archers, had to be employed to keep the press of people out of the route and the square, adds to the impression of a considerable crowd.[6]

---

[4] It is enlightening to compare the imposition of religious contents in executions and in royal coronations. See Ernst Kantorowicz, *Laudes Regiae: A Study in Liturgical Acclamations and Medieval Ruler Worship* (Berkeley, 1958); Richard A. Jackson, *Vive le Roi: A History of the French Coronation from Charles V to Charles X* (Chapel Hill, N.C., 1984).

[5] Jean de Roye, *Chronique scandaleuse,* 1:361.

[6] "Nam ad spectaculum contuendum, cui simile multis retro aetatibus minime visum seu auditum ferebatur, innumerabilis paene omnis ordinis, aetatis et sexus multitudo concurrebat." Basin, *Histoire,* 2:376; cf. the bill for the execution in Jean de Roye, *Chronique scandaleuse,* 1:361-62, n. 3.

The same insistence upon the "great multitude of people" recurred time and again in descriptions of spectacular executions.[7]

The presence of the public and its reactions on those occasions was very much on the authorities' minds. Sometimes the crowd acted in a bloodthirsty manner, crying out that no last-minute pardon should deprive them of the show. This was especially true when the condemned was universally hated.[8] On such occasions, the execution was deliberately tailored to satisfy the demands of a vengeful crowd: "It is wonderful indeed," said Thomas Basin of Saint-Pol, "how the hatred of all the region's people was excited against him. Therefore, in order to satisfy both their desires and their hatred, and to instill both example and terror in all others, the king wished his execution to be highly visible."[9] The admonitory element was ever-present in public executions, but even the most high-minded of chroniclers had to concede the role of human passions and their political manipulation in a manifest drama. On more ordinary occasions the audience was less likely to demand blood, but its reaction was invariably on the minds of the authorities. So much so, that erroneous executions had to be publicly and ceremoniously rectified. The university of Paris insisted upon such a procedure in 1407, when two clerks were put to death by mistake, lest the people conclude that henceforth civil authorities had the power to execute clergymen: "The open and public way in which they suffered the ultimate punishment [caused] people from all over the city to come, as usual, to the ignominious spectacle, and all that was heard on everyone's lips was 'this is an incontrovertible sign that henceforth scholars and monks shall be punished like secular people.'"[10]

The case was typical of the tension between the two powers holding authority over life and death. The secular and religious messages of executions often stood in mutual opposition, an opposition that was to become all the stronger as both state emphasis upon punitive rites and religious sensibilities sharpened. The inclusion of folkloric elements within the same rituals further exacerbated the struggle over the shaping of an increasingly important public rite. It was essentially a struggle over the ultimate power: dominion over people's souls.

---

[7] "Grant multitude de peuple," *Chronique parisienne anonyme*, pp. 53, 127, 167.

[8] *Grandes Chroniques de France*, 9:16-19; the *Chronique parisienne anonyme*, pp. 50-53 records the crowds shouting at Henri de Taperel's execution "Let him be hanged, thus he will pronounce no more false judgments!"

[9] Basin, *Histoire*, 2:377.

[10] *Réligieux de Saint-Denys*, 3:724-25; Baye, *Journal*, 1:229-31.

1. Secular Power and Death

In 1398 two Augustinian monks claiming to possess supernatural healing powers were brought in to cure the Charles VI's madness. When they not only failed, but made the mistake of accusing the king's brother of having bewitched the patient, they were unmasked and tried by the bishop as "idolaters, invokers of demons, apostates and sorcerers." Their execution was a spectacular event. At sunrise, the two were taken from the bishop's prison, hands tied, heads crowned with paper miters bearing their names, and two parchments sown on their shoulders, back and front, bearing the legend of their crimes. They were placed on a cart drawn by four horses and taken to the Place de Grève, in the middle of the city.[11] There, the bishop of Paris, in full regalia, assisted by six other bishops and many important people, stood on a specially erected and magnificently decorated scaffolding, faced by the condemned on a lower scaffold across the square. Thereupon a doctor of theology read a long indictment, describing all their various crimes. At the end, the bishop pronounced their ecclesiastical sentence: to be deprived of all clerical office and defrocked, the sentence to be executed on the spot. The condemned were then dressed in the clerical garb of their ordination, in which they confessed their crimes before the bishop. Then a chalice was presented to each, and formally withdrawn, together with their right to use it in the celebration of the Mass. Next, they were stripped of their chasubles, and presented with a missal, which was also taken away. At this stage, their dalmatics and subdeacon tunics were stripped off. Having been physically, as well as formally defrocked, their fingers were scrubbed to remove the chrism used at their ordination, and they were declared devoid of all ecclesiastical authority.

The transition from clerical to lay status was achieved first by the formal handing over of the culprits to the sergeants of the law, and then by the solemn shaving of their heads to eradicate their tonsures. The secular part of the ceremony, beginning at this point, did not greatly differ from other public executions. The former monks were promenaded throughout the streets of the city, the procession halting at each crossroads for the herald to proclaim aloud their crimes. Every time the condemned assented to this list "with signs and words",

[11] The prison of For-l'évêque was situated on the right bank of the Seine, somewhat to the west of the Pont-aux-Meuniers. The journey to the Place de Grève would therefore have taken the culprits across the busiest part of the city. See H. Legrand, *Paris en 1380* (Paris, 1868), map.

before the procession continued. This scene was enacted again and again, until they arrived at the place of execution at the ninth hour of the day (around three o'clock). There the two were confessed and beheaded. The hangman placed their heads on lances on a high spot, their cut-off limbs in front of the principal gates of Paris, and their trunks on the gibbet. The chronicler concluded: "Thus these two miserable men atoned for their iniquities, serving as an example to traitors and criminals."[12] Atonement and caution were once more the central aims of the punishment, not retribution.

Formally, the ceremony fulfilled all the requirements of public ritual. All participants consciously acted in a stylized, formal manner, prescribed specifically to set the occurrence apart from mundane life. Under the circumstances the symbolism in use had to be religious, but the context was extremely unusual. All the emblems of sacral priestly power were present in the inverse. Chalice, missal, liturgical apparel, and chrism were used and invoked in this context in a deliberately extraordinary manner. The whole affair was conducted according to a strict temporal, spatial, and thematic order. As the day progressed, the culprits moved from clergy to laity to penal death, from prison to a central public area, thence to the city streets and finally out of the walls, to the gallows. The message conveyed to all watchers endowed the execution with a collective dimension. It set the criminals apart, while binding all spectators together in a tacit community of consent against them.

The case of the apostate Augustinians was described in great detail by the monk of Saint-Denis. As might be expected, the chronicler devoted far more space to the highly uncommon religious ceremony than to the final secular part. Nevertheless, by his own admission the secular ceremony lasted longer and covered more space than the preceding religious degradation. Furthermore, it was far more explicit, reaching and impressing a far wider audience than the select group viewing the defrocking with its intricate theological symbolism. Still, the two formed one integral ceremony in which each part complemented the other. All the elements present in the defrocking were part of the symbolic inventory of secular defamatory rites: labelling by placards and miters, ceremonial divestiture of clothes, and inversion of the ordination ritual. The transition from religious to secular meant only a passage from the hands of one authority, debarred from shed-

[12] *Réligieux de Saint-Denys*, 2:662-69.

ding blood, to another possessing no such scruples. In symbolism and spirit it was essentially one ceremony in which both forces combined to present a single, coherent message.

Public penalties being above all cautionary in nature, they were bound to present the audience with a great deal of information concerning the criminal and the crime. The culprit's status was invariably represented by a number of methods, most obviously by his clothes. Since common criminals wore at best their shirts and at worst nothing on such occasions, any man going to his death fully clothed was immediately labelled a person of rank. Four sons of Paris *bourgeois* were taken to death wearing "robes of Saint-Marcel woollens," while another official was allowed to retain his cotte, stockings and shoes on the gibbet.[13] The higher the rank, the more noteworthy and noted were the costumes. Jehan de Montagu, grand master of the king's residence, went to his death in his own livery, wearing a red-and-white cloak and hat, one white and one red shoe, and golden spurs.[14] The *prévôt* who arrested him, Pierre des Essarts, wore a checkered black-and-white fur-lined cloak, white stockings and black shoes to his own execution.[15] Often disgraced functionaries wore colors proclaiming their familial or political allegiance. The count of Saint-Pol was led to the gallows wearing all his insignia of office, including the collar of the royal order of Saint-Michel.[16] The robber baron Jourdain de L'Isle, executed in 1323 for a long list of crimes, wore the colors of Pope John XXII, whose niece he had married.[17] Clothing could also convey political allegiance and, with certain modifications, the state's opinion of that allegiance. The messengers bringing Pope Benedict XIII's excommunication bull to the university of Paris were sentenced to public infamy, wearing black dalmatics displaying the Pope's personal arms inverted and paper miters describing them as disloyal to church and king.[18]

The use of red-and-white, or black-and-white combinations had nothing fortuitous about it. Nor was it a matter of personal taste, an

---

[13] *Chronique parisienne anonyme*, pp. 16, 167.

[14] *Journal d'un bourgeois de Paris*, p. 6; Jean Lefevre, *Chronique de Jean le Fevre, seigneur de Saint-Remy*, ed. François Morand, 2 vols. (Paris, 1876-81), 1:19 and Enguerrand de Monstrelet, *Chronique*, ed. L. Douët-d'Arcq, 6 vols. (Paris, 1857-62), 2:44, report the execution with less details.

[15] *Journal d'un bourgeois de Paris*, p. 33.

[16] Basin, *Histoire*, 2:376.

[17] *Grandes chroniques de France*, 9:18.

[18] A. Le Roux de Lincy and L.M. Tisserand, eds., *Paris et ses historiens au XIVe et XVe siècles* (Paris, 1867), pp. 406-407; Félibien, *Histoire de la ville de Paris*, 2:744.

assertion of individuality. Like all other personal elements, the colors chosen by Jehan de Montagu and Pierre des Essarts carried a specific meaning of status. Those were, within the context of late medieval chivalric culture, the basic heraldic colors denoting power, royalty, and death. Their ostentation in this context was an explicit statement of pride, noble status, even of hope in the face of death.[19] The usage obviously meant a great deal to contemporary chroniclers, invariably careful to record what culprits of rank wore to their deaths. Furthermore, the meaning was so clear as to require no comment or elucidation. They had all seen these colors worn at numerous royal ceremonies, not only in France, but wherever chivalric culture held sway.[20]

Another means of denoting status, usually determined by the authorities, was the mode of transportation from jail to gallows in the punitive procession. There were two main forms of transport. Noblemen were usually carried on a cart, while simple folk were dragged on a hurdle behind it. The use of a dung-cart for additional infamy was reserved for heretics.[21] The count of Saint-Pol—an unusually noble criminal—was actually allowed to ride his own horse from the courthouse to the place of execution, but his was an exceptional execution in this as in many other senses. The fact that criminals were moved, rather than moving by their own force, made clear the interplay of power and submission. The culprit might have been the chief actor of the drama, but not the producer.

One highly dramatic way of denoting guilt and infamy was the deliberate disjunction between various sets of symbols. Jourdain de l'Isle was executed in his individual nobleman's outfit, but was dragged to the gallows at the horses' tails like a common criminal. Furthermore, the third status symbol of the execution also pertained to common criminals, for Jourdain was hung like a common thief. Noblemen were usually beheaded in the town square, while simple folk hung on the gibbet. "The common gibbet of thieves" was a current description of the extra-mural gallows.[22] While death in town was more honorable,

[19] For the symbolic importance of customes and their colors in public ceremonies, including executions, see Johan Huizinga, *The Waning of the Middle Ages*, trans. F. Hopman (Harmondsworth, 1965), pp. 42-43. For the specific meaning of red, black and white see Michel Pastoureau, "Les couleurs médiévales: Systèmes de valeurs et modes de sensibilité," in *Figures et couleurs* (Paris, 1986), pp. 35-49, esp. p. 40.

[20] Cf. Teofilo F. Ruiz, "Festivités, couleurs et symboles du pouvoir en Castille au XVe siècle," *Annales E.S.C.* 46 (1991), 521-46.

[21] "...ung tumbereau ou l'en porte les immondices de la ville," BN, ms. fr. 21730, fol. 55ro.

[22] *Chronique parisienne anonyme*, pp. 16, 21, 54.

the culprit's body or some of it, regardless of his status, was usually displayed on the gallows. The deliberate execution of a properly-clad nobleman in a plebeian manner was an additional infamy.

Status was only one element of information. The facts of the crime and the ultimate sentence were undoubtedly of far greater importance for cautionary ceremonies. Information of guilt and condemnation was conveyed by deliberate gestures and words spoken either by a herald preceding the execution procession or by the culprit himself. As in the *amende honorable*, it was often the role of the accused to declare his own crime and beg forgiveness for it. Indeed, an *amende honorable* could also be held as part of an execution. In a typical case, the bigamous Robert Bonneau was sentenced to perform this rite be-ore the main gate of Notre-Dame kneeling on the pavement barefoot, bare-headed, clad only in his shirt with a rope around his neck. Robert held in his hand a two-pound torch, and while it burned he repeatedly proclaimed his offense, begging pardon of God, king, and justice. When the torch had burnt down, the offender was taken across the Seine to the cemetery of Saint-Jean on the right bank and hung. His body was only removed to the gibbet of Montfaucon twenty-four hours later.[23]

Public recantation was an essential part of the spectacle. Henri de Taperel, another *prévôt* of Paris condemned in 1320, cried along his route: "Good people, pray for my soul; I die because of hatred." Similar sentiments were voiced a century and a half later by the count of Saint-Pol on the gallows.[24] Such exemplary behavior was undoubtedly demanded only of illustrious felons, for no chronicler described common criminals uttering speeches on their final way. Occasionally, though, the leading actor refused to play. During the *Cabochien* revolt of 1413, the *prévôt* of Paris Pierre des Essarts was granted upon request the grace of being spared a public lecture of his crimes at the scene of execution. Another victim of the same revolt, Jacques de la Rivière, was rumored to have committed suicide in jail so as to avoid seeing "the mobs of Paris rejoicing at my shameful death."[25] Com-

---

[23] AN, Y6[6], Livre noir neuf du Châtelet, fol. 97. For similar ceremonies, see BN, ms. fr. 21731, fols. 84ro, 87ro.

[24] "Bonnes gens, pries pour l'ame de moy; je meur par haynne," *Chronique parisienne anonyme*, p. 53; Jean de Roye, *Chronique scandaleuse*, 1:361.

[25] "... quod villani Parisienses gaudeant super ignominiosa morte mea..." *Réligieux de Saint-Denys*, 5:56; both the monk of Saint-Denis and Lefevre, *Chronique*, p. 86, though, claim that Jacques de la Rivière was actually murdered in jail. Cf. also Monstrelet, *Chronique*, 2:370, 6:119, 217, and *Journal d'un bourgeois de Paris*, p. 32.

mon criminals could also refuse their role, remaining defiant to the end. Some, claimed the preachers, took it for granted that they would end on the gallows, being quite philosophical about it. Others so enjoyed their position and notoriety high above the crowd that it counted more for them than the expected end.[26]

Public acts of contrition were performed during the procession leading to the final place of execution along precisely set-out routes. Most sources merely stated that criminals were paraded through the crossroads of the city, only specifying the exact itinerary in extraordinary cases. These routes of infamy were also used for public whippings of common criminals, and did not necessarily lead to the gallows. Nevertheless, spectacular executions were often planned to cover as much space as possible. From prison to the site of the crime (when possible), to the market-place for pillory or beheading, to an extra-mural gibbet for hanging or burning.[27]

The symbolic spatial arrangement of a city as a microcosm, emerging through other public rituals as well,[28] was both enunciated and used in public executions. The center, where power and justice resided, was embodied in the prison, the market-place, and the church. The execution procession usually led from this center to the periphery, the extra-mural site of the gallows or the pyre. When Olivier de Clisson (father of the constable of the same name) was executed for treason in 1343, his procession began at the Temple, where he had been kept prisoner. He was first taken towards the center of town, to the Châtelet "bare-headed and hatless" to hear his sentence. Thence he was dragged to the market-place (a common spot for beheadings), placed upon a high scaffolding "where he could be seen by all," and decapitated. From that point his body was dragged out of the walls to the gibbet, where it was hung at the top. But the journey did not end at this spot. Clisson's head was taken to Nantes, the city he had

[26] "Item similes sunt irrisores bonorum et simplicium latroni, qui dum duceretur a bedellis multis ad suspendium super equum maximum et videret incedentes in via pedites simplices, irridebat eos non curans de proximo interitu vilissimo suo." Welter, *Tabula exemplorum*, p. 36.

[27] For places of execution in Paris, see Hillairet, *Gibets, piloris et cachots*, pp. 15-29. For a detailed description of Montfaucon, see E. Viollet-le-Duc, *Dictionnaire raisonné de l'architecture française du XIe au XVIe siècle*, 10 vols. (Paris, 1861), 5:553-63. Cf. Samuel Y. Edgerton, *Pictures and Punishment: Art and Criminal Prosecution During the Florentine Renaissance* (Ithaca, N.Y., 1984), pp. 139-42, for contemporary Italian gallows architecture.

[28] Bryant, *The King and the City*, esp. pp. 169-94.

planned to betray, for final display. The end of the justice journey brought the criminal once more to the place of the crime.[29]

The importance of this interplay of center and periphery could best be seen in the cases where authorities took the trouble to eject the offender or offenders simultaneously in all directions. Following a drastic rise in rents in 1306, the Paris populace had rioted, looted and destroyed the house of Etienne Barbette, a leading *bourgeois*, finally besieging the king at the Temple and destroying his food supplies. Twenty-eight ringleaders were arrested and executed for the riot. First imprisoned, they were subsequently divided into four groups and led from the Châtelet to the four main gates of the city. Seven were hung outside the Porte Saint-Denis (North), seven outside the Porte Saint-Antoine (East), six at the western Porte Saint-Honoré, and eight at the southern Porte Saint-Jacques. The effect on the cowed people of Paris was both vivid and memorable: "This event caused great sorrow to the simple people of Paris...."[30]

The spacing of executions around the four cardinal points of the city was a common symbolic act. In cases of notorious criminals, such as the Augustinian monks, their bodies were dismembered after death so as to 'adorn' each of the four main gates with a different limb.[31] The city was thus perceived as a nucleus of justice extruding offensive elements in all directions. The universe of the city and the universe of justice coincided in those rituals, endowing the human and evanescent with a measure of universal sanction and justification.

The central, though not necessarily final event of these rituals was the actual putting to death. Here both status and guilt played a role in determining the exact form. The sentence of Mérigot Marchès, the famous noble *routier* who had terrorized the Auvergne during the 1370s, exemplifies the careful balancing of status, crime, public lesson and ceremony:

> ... due to his nobility and noble lineage, he deserves a solemn execution; and in order to preserve a perpetual memory and that all others take warning [it should be conducted] in the following fashion: that the said Mérigot, prisoner, be dragged on a hurdle as a gentleman and then, seated high on a shield placed across the side railings of a cart, be carried to the sound of trumpets through the market-place of Paris and elsewhere past the main gates of the city of

---

[29] *Grandes chroniques*, 9:241-42.

[30] "Laquelle chose envers le menu peuple de Paris chey en grant douleur..." *Chronique parisienne anonyme*, pp. 18-20.

> Paris, and that at the market-place the aforesaid Mérigot should be beheaded, his head placed on the point of a lance upon the scaffold, his four limbs hanged at the four gates of the city of Paris, and the trunk hanged at our lord the king's gibbet in Paris.[32]

Though Marchès' body remained on display, he did not suffer the disgrace of a common hanging. Hanging, considered an ignominious death, was associated with thieves. Common murderers merited a similar fate, though they were usually dragged first to the place of execution. While the display of the body argued infamy, the total disposal of the same was an even greater disgrace. The burning of heretics, witches, and sodomites totally eradicated the body. In these cases, the rules exhorted authorities to burn not only the culprit, but also his animal accomplice (in the case of bestiality) and the very trial records. This was done, in the words of one French jurist, in order to erase all memory of the act.[33] Thus executions which left the body on display were considered less arduous a penalty than those destroying the body. When a thief and rapist was sentenced to drowning in the Seine in 1344, his sentence was commuted to a less shameful death.[34] In general, drowning was reserved for traitors. Counterfeiters were supposed to die in the most horrible of manners, by boiling, though in reality they were often granted death by hanging.[35] Finally, all women sentenced to death died, by virtue of their sex, in a manner that left no visible body—either by burning or by live burial. While giving justice a maximum of publicity, authorities were also anxious to display very clearly the total eradication of the crime and the criminal.

Both traditions, publicity and eradication, go back a very long way. Tacitus already noted in the *Germania* two peculiarities of the Germanic punitive system. First of all, the Germans had different penalties for different crimes. Secondly, he asserted, the difference lay between crimes which should be publicized by hanging, and shameful crimes,

---

[31] This symbolic practice was not limited to northern France; it was also noted in Avignon by Chiffoleau, *Les justices du Pape*, p. 241.

[32] *Registre criminel du Châtelet*, 2:207-8; for a miniature depicting this execution, see British Museum, ms Harl. 4379, fol. 64vo (Froissart's Chronicles).

[33] Jean Duret, *Traité des peines et amendes* (Paris, 1573), p. 36.

[34] Sauval, *Antiquités*, 2:597. By the early modern period, the shame of publicity was considered greater than the disgrace of drowning. In 1531 the king commuted a hanging sentence to drowning in a sack at an hour when as few people as possible might see it, in order to spare the family's honor. AN, Y4, fol. $1^{ro\text{-}vo}$.

[35] *Registre criminel du Châtelet*, 1:492-93; *Chronique parisienne anonyme*, p. 41; AN, $Y6^1$, fol. 107ro, $Y6^4$, fol. 79vo; BN, ms. fr. 21731, fol. 68ro; Sauval, *Antiquités*, 3:274, 362, 368.

for which the culprit was buried under a hurdle in a swamp.[36] Tacitus provided the governmental interpretation of the two types, but in fact Germanic religion knew another explanation. As Dumézil has shown, both hanging and drowning were deaths charged with religious significance. One lifted the body upwards, the other pushed it downwards.[37] By the later middle ages in France this tradition had been lost, but not the dichotomy of high and low, upwards and downwards gestures. To the contrary: this symbolic spatial distinction seems to have supplanted the old Roman left-right symbolism during the middle ages.[38] Also, apotropaeic beliefs played a central role in the treatment of criminals' corpses. The total eradication of a particularly maleficent corpse, or the severance of a less dangerous one from the ground by hanging were not merely matters of justice, but of protection against revenants. Undoubtedly, the extra-legal element played a major role in the preservation of ancient punitive forms.

Practically none of these ideas remained in any explicit form in late medieval French jurisprudence. What did remain was the consciousness, shared by judges and jurists alike, that the vocabulary of justice was an ancient and enduring cultural form, and that any tampering with it was liable to cause the loss of shared communication between authorities and spectators in execution ceremonies. Thus, the forms of execution were undoubtedly the oldest and most popular of all constitutive elements in the entire ceremony. Practically all other elements—dress, route, speech, gestures, and texts—could be controlled by judicial authorities, or even by the culprits themselves. But the actual deed of punishment belonged to a common European substratum of custom which was quite deliberately kept unaltered. Even if the reasons were no longer known, the results most certainly were.

So strong was the perception that executions were symbolic as well as purely punitive rites that it made little difference whether the criminal was present or not. Escaped criminals were still brought to justice, though in the form of an effigy. While in no way affecting the body of the punished person, the execution in effigy put to death his

---

[36] "Distinctio poenarum ex delicto: proditores et transfugas arboribus suspendunt, ignavos et imbelles et corpore infames caeno ac palude, iniecta insuper crate, mergunt. Diversitas supplicii illuc respicit, tamquam scelera ostendi oporteat, dum puniuntur, flagitia abscondi." Cornelius Tacitus, *Germania*, ed. and trans. M. Hutton, Loeb series (London and New York, 1914), ch. 12, p. 149.

[37] Georges Dumézil, "Le noyé et le pendu," in his *La Saga de Hadingus: Du mythe au roman* (Paris, 1953), pp. 135-59.

[38] Le Goff, "Body and Ideology," p. 85.

or her public *persona*. It enunciated punitive death in the most graphic of forms, explicitly articulating the community's condemnation.

There was one way, however, in which the ruler's power could affect traditional symbolic structures: by reversing the entire ceremony at the last moment. Audiences watching the spectacle of execution were not necessarily conscious of the careful staging behind the ritual. A conspicuous intervention of the authorities in an ostensibly autonomous process provided the clearest and most dramatic manifestation of lordship. Last-minute reprieves were uncommon, thus heightening their dramatic effect. The prospect of such a reversal was a built-in possibility of spontaneity within a rigidly prescribed ritual. The constable of Saint-Pol went calmly and cheerfully to his death partly because he was convinced that the king, content with a gesture of warning and repentance, would pardon him at the last moment. The chance existed also for less notable criminals in a rather unique form of pardon. According to a custom common throughout northern France, an unmarried condemned man could be claimed at the very foot of the gallows by an honest woman prepared to marry him.[39] The phenomenon is well-documented in legal sources, eye-witnesses recording its highly dramatic effect. Following the hunger-riots of 1430, the authorities held a mass execution:

> ... and on the tenth [of January] following, eleven men were taken to the Paris market, and ten were beheaded. The eleventh was a very handsome young man, approximately twenty-four years old. He was undressed and ready to have his eyes bound when a locally-born young girl boldly came to claim him, and so insisted in her good intention that he was taken back to the Châtelet, and they were later married.[40]

[39] Monstrelet, *Chronique*, 2:373; Basin, *Histoire*, 2:376-77. Chassenée, *In consuetudines ducatus Burgundiae*, title I, art. 5; P. Lemercier, "Une curiosité judiciaire au moyen âge: La grâce par mariage subséquent," *Revue d'histoire du droit* 33 (1955), 464-74; Vaultier, *Le folklore*, p. iv; Jacques Foviaux, *La rémission des peines et des condamnations: Droit monarchique et droit moderne* (Paris, 1970), p. 36.

[40] "... et le Xe [janvier] ensuivant on en mena XI es halles de Paris, et leur coppa on les testes a tous dix. Le unziesme estoit ung tres bel jeune filx d'environ XXIIII ans, il fut despoullie et prest pour bander ses yeulx, quant une jeune fille nee des Halles le vint hardiement demander et tant fist par son bon pourchas qu'il fut remene ou Chastellet, et depuis furent espousez ensemble." *Journal d'un bourgeois de Paris*, p. 250. The custom existed also in Germany and the Netherlands. See von Dülmen, "Das Schauspiel des Todes," pp. 203-45. Popular French tales record cases of men who preferred to die rather than marry the volunteer. See P. Saintyves, "Le folklore juridique," in *Etudes de sociologie et d'ethnologie juridiques*, pp. 74-75. For

Apparently women who claimed criminals at the foot of the gallows made an eloquent plea on behalf of their chosen husbands. When Perrot Pechon, a carter, was sentenced to death for the rape of a prostitute,

> A certain woman named Raoulete, living in the same parish of Breuil, moved by great pity and knowing that the said Perrot was a man of good reputation and life, came before the said squire, very humbly requesting him that he should please to give her the said Perrot in marriage, and that for such a case, instigated by a woman of such evil reputation, he should not wish to make him die; promising that if he agreed, she would marry him and take him for husband; and to this the said Perrot agreed....[41]

The custom was indeed prevalent all over France, from Bayonne to Laon. The earliest mentions date from 1274, but it was still practiced in the sixteenth century.[42] Typically, late medieval jurists provided no explanation for the custom. Chassenée, writing in the sixteenth century, reflected Renaissance misogyny rather than late medieval judicial practice. According to him, the foot-of-the-gallows marriage was not a reprieve, but a punishment worse than death—good women, following Juvenal's dictum on the matter, being as rare as black swans. "And certainly, it is not without cause that a man condemned to death is pardoned if he is claimed by a woman, for he falls into perpetual torment...."[43]

The tension between ejection and reconciliation permeated the entire procedure. The very authorities that so carefully staged the whole drama were often ambivalent about the total rejection of any human from society. The foot-of-the-gallows marriage was a realization of the

---

an actual case of such a refusal in Holland, see J.M. Fuchs, "De keuze tussen beul en bruid," in *De hond aan de galg* (Amsterdam, 1957), p. 115.

[41] "... et en voulant enteriner ladite condempnation a este menez a la justice dudit escuyer, a laquelle une femme nommee Raoulete, demourante en la paroisse dudit Breuil, meue de grant pitie, saichant ledit Perrot de bonne renommee & vie, vint devant ledit escuyer en luy requerant tres humblement quil voulsist donner en marrage [*sic*] ledit Perrot, et pour un tel cas, amist meue a femme de si mauvaise renommee il ne le voulsist pas faire mourir, promettant que si le vouloit faire de lespouser et prendre en mary, & a ce saccordoit ledit Perrot..." AN, JJ 142, fols. 22^{ro-vo}. Though pardoned by local authorities by virtue of his marriage, Perrot needed a formal remission from the king to ratify this pardon.

[42] A. Floquet, *Histoire du privilège de Saint Romain* (Rouen, 1833), p. 36; M. Melleville, "De l'usage au moyen âge de permettre à une jeune fille de sauver un criminel en l'épousant," *Bulletin de la société académique de Laon* 3 (1854), 383-85.

[43] "Et pro certo, non sine causa huic condemnato ad mortem parcitur, si a muliere petatur, cum incidat in tormentum perpetuum..." Chassenée, *In consuetudines ducatus Burgundiae, loc. cit.*

ever-present possibility of reintegration. Marriage as a basis for grace made sense in terms of contemporary secular perceptions of societally marginal and threatening people. Marriage to an honest woman reintegrated the criminal within society by forcing him to use its mechanisms. It was grace by virtue of prospective rehabilitation, not grace by exoneration.

Secular executions thus integrated and balanced a number of elements: ancient punitive perceptions, explicit contemporary symbolic structures, and above all, governmental power as a coercive judicial force. The one element they ignored was the fact that these rituals severed Christian souls from their bodies. Recognition of this fact brought into these rituals a new, religious content destined to change their meaning. By the end of the middle ages, secular authorities no longer possessed the absolute lordship over penal death: religion, the force controlling all transitions from life to death, had come to intervene also in the death of criminals.

2. Ecclesiastical Power and Death

Secular capital rituals were essentially rites of severance. The culprit was carried from the city to its outskirts, from society to beyond its boundaries, from life to death. All these measures were meant to mark the criminal as different from the community, an outsider on his way to permanent ejection. This expulsion was religious as well as social, for the denial of confession and shriving until the end of the fourteenth century translated the exclusion from the physical to the metaphysical plane. In an age very much preoccupied with the economy of the afterworld, sentencing a criminal to die unconfessed and unshriven meant eternal damnation and banishment from the community of the faithful. The eternally restless soul was symbolically represented by the unburied, exposed body, whose grisly remains were eventually dumped under the gallows rather than buried in a Christian grave.[44]

In a religion that had always kept its dead as an integral part of the community of the living, the exclusion of criminals' souls from this shared destiny was perhaps the harshest penalty of them all. It was only by extraordinary, miraculous grace that a criminal could escape this punishment. Caesarius of Heisterbach told of a knight hung by Emperor Frederick who, thanks to his zealous daily prayers through-

[44] Sauval, *Antiquités*, 3:278, described the repairs of the Montfaucon gallows in 1421, which involved the disinterring of bones.

out life, remained alive on the gallows until the last rites had been administered to him.[45] But run-of-the-mill delinquents could expect no divine intervention to save their souls. François Villon gave in his *Ballade des pendus* the most poignant expression of the loss of individuality and humanity suffered by those dying on the gallows. The poet spared his readers none of the grisly details of the sun-blackened, rain-drenched corpses dancing endlessly in the wind, eyes and hair plucked out, flesh decaying and bones disintegrating. But in the face of all this, Villon affirmed the bonds common to the living and the dead by addressing his readers as "brothers in humanity," begging their prayers and stating that the dead were on their way to Christ.[46]

Villon might have been the voice of the criminals, he was also a child of the fifteenth century. By then, the attitude towards delinquents and their death had undergone a remarkable change, closely associated with the growth of late medieval piety. In this process one may see the first glimmerings of the re-humanization of criminals.

The beginnings of the change lay in the traditional power struggles over clerical immunity. Ecclesiastical authorities were not prepared to accept any miscarriage of justice in which a clerk might wrongly suffer death at lay hands. Rectification, they claimed, was not meant primarily to soothe the wounded sensibilities of prelates and university rectors; first and foremost, amendment was the reintegration of the wrongly excluded clerks in the society of the Christian dead. The church insisted upon the post-mortem reintegration of wrongly executed criminals by means of an inverted ceremony.

The public taking down from the gallows and ceremonial burial procession, duplicating in reverse the execution, was a rare occurrence, all the more powerful in its impact because of its rarity. In 1304 four clerks, sons of Parisian *bourgeois*, were condemned for various crimes, properly degraded, handed over to the civil arm and executed. Unfortunately, a fifth and innocent clerk was also put to death. He had indeed fought and wounded a certain Lombard, but the man had subsequently recovered. Worse, he had never been tried, but merely appended to the group of condemned clergymen. The university of Paris, always protective of clerical immunities, complained to the king and excommunicated the *prévôt*. The argument lasted from May, when the multiple execution had taken place, until October 1304, when Philip the Fair decided in the university's favor. The clerk's body

[45] Caesarius, *Dialogus*, 2:204-205.
[46] Villon, *L'epitaphe Villon*, p. 215.

was consequently taken down from the gibbet in procession to its proper, Christian, in-town burial-place. The culprit in the unhanging procession, fulfilling the role of the condemned in a usual execution, was the guilty *prévôt*. He proclaimed aloud his crime along the route, begging the spectators for their prayers. The procession went from the gibbet outside the northern gates of Paris all the way to the burial-place in the Dominican church near the southern gate of Saint-Jacques, crossing the entire city. It stopped at every crossroad and the *prévôt*, laying his hand on the bier, declaimed "Good people, here is the clerk that I have caused to die wrongly and without reason; pray for him." In a similar case a century later (1407-8), the univer-sity threatened to leave Paris unless the *prévôt* personally take down two unlawfully-executed clerks, kiss the bodies (which had been hanging for five months) on their lips, and literally hand them over to the ecclesiastical authorities, begging pardon on his knees. Though the king balked at the gruesomely symbolic kiss, they were indeed taken down and buried with great ceremony and procession.[47]

The right to post-mortem reintegration, first limited to clergymen, slowly spread to the entire community of believers, be they innocent or guilty. The process gained impetus with the spreading consciousness that all humans were sinners, likely to suffer in afterlife as criminals suffered on earth. Late medieval religiosity used the symbolism of the gallows to articulate its own perceptions of sin and punishment. Many fifteenth-century sermons and popular texts equated sinners with gallows-birds, promising them a hell that resembled the instruments of execution at their city's gates. Jean Gerson, the famous preacher and rector of the university of Paris, filled his own sermons with criminal imagery: sins were false traitors, thieves, cutthroats and pillagers; the sinner's soul was a thieves' lair, hell was a gibbet and the devil its hangman.[48] An entire sermon was built around the simile of purgatory as a temporary prison and hell as a permanent death sentence.[49] Other popular preachers sounded a similar note. The heretical Franciscan Brother Richard, whose sermons have not survived, preached his own version of hell-fire at the gates of the cemetery of Saints-Innocents in Paris, with the paintings of the *danse macabre* as

[47] *Chronique parisienne anonyme*, pp. 16-17; *Réligieux de Saint-Denys*, 3:722-29.
[48] Louis Mourin, *Jean Gerson, prédicateur français* (Bruges, 1952), pp. 446, 462; Jean Gerson, "Mansionem apud eum faciemus," in *Six sermons*, p. 81.
[49] Jean Gerson, *Beati qui lugent*, in *Six sermons*, pp. 219-44

background.[50] Collections of *exempla* often made use of this parallel, equating the devil with thieves and robbers. The latter, notorious for their matter-of-fact acceptance of their own and their friends' eventual and inevitable executions, were also favorite similes for hardened and unrepentant sinners.[51]

Villon's poem reflected a new trend in late medieval attitudes towards the dying criminal. The allowance of good deaths and the possibility of a posthumous grace to criminals marked the beginnings of a new sensitivity towards those dying on the gallows. The right of the condemned to remain a part of the Christian community after their death and reach ultimate salvation began emerging as part of the same preoccupation with a good death so central to late medieval religiosity.

The first step was the granting of the foot-of-the-gallows confession to the condemned. The confession, a public event and integral part of the execution ceremony, served a double purpose. It ensured true repentance and the salvation of the criminal's soul, while providing a dramatic spectacle of God's power and grace. In 1493 a heretical priest was sentenced to defrocking and burning as punishment for desecrating the host during Mass at the cathedral. Jean Lenglois expressed under interrogation a variety of 'Jewish' ideas (or so his judges claimed), arguing that the Mass was a sham. His execution ceremony was highly dramatic and extremely painful, taking him from the Châtelet prison to the Notre-Dame, and thence to the pig-market outside the western gates of the city, and involving various pre-execution mutilations of his separate offending limbs. The most dramatic part, however, was his recantation:

> And on the afternoon of the same day, after the pronunciation of the sentence, the said Jehan Lenglois, by the grace of God, reconciled himself to God, confessed and repented his crime, and like a good Christian... suffered the execution of the said sentence sweetly and patiently. Of this the people later praised God and rejoiced.[52]

The move to allow confession to dying criminals began with the papacy. In 1312 Clement V forbade the denial of penitence to the

---

[50] Le Roux de Lincy and Tisserand, *Paris et ses historiens*, pp. 404-12.

[51] "Item, nota dyabolus sicut fur vel latro...", "Et sunt similes latronibus, qui cum vident suspendi aliquem de sociis suis, non propter hoc dimittunt furta sua, sed videntes eum suspensum, dicit unus alteri: hoc est territorium inherencium." Welter, *Tabula exemplorum*, p. 35.

[52] AN, Y4, fol. 39ro.

condemned.[53] Towards the end of the fourteenth century Jean Gerson spearheaded in France an ecclesiastical campaign to allow the hitherto denied criminals' confession. Gerson's arguments were both theological and emotional. His theology contained nothing revolutionary, merely stressing the universal obligation of final confession and the sin in preventing it. But his emotional appeal was remarkable in its originality, sounding a new note of identification with the future corpse. Preventing confession was "great harshness and cruelty",[54] terms often used in criminal sentences to describe the culprit's own actions. The "poor condemned" suffered sufficient punishment without the additional spiritual agony of despair. An accomplished orator and preacher, Gerson did not hesitate to use the gallows that had stood at the very heart of Christianity, reminding his reader (King Charles VI) that Christ had also died as a criminal for the sake of these same condemned men and women: "...the poor Christians our brothers, for whose salvation, as for that of others, he had died..." [55] The confession thus identified the dying criminal with other Christians attempting to achieve a good death. The recurrent theme of Christ dying among criminals imbued the death of late medieval malefactors also with a sense of validity.

In consequence, felons were granted their foot-of-the-gallows confession. Pierre de Craon, Gerson's collaborator in his campaign, had a stone cross erected near the Paris gallows of Montfaucon for this purpose.[56] The confessor became both a physical and a spiritual guide to the condemned. He accompanied them all the way to the end, holding a cross before their eyes, so that the sufferers could concentrate upon their coming death without fear.[57] The same Jean Lenglois, a hardened and convinced heretic, was converted and accompanied on his long route to the gallows by no less a personage than Jean Standonck, rector of the university of Paris and notable ascetic. So

[53] Fernand M. Delorme and Aloysius L. Tàutu, eds., *Acta Clementis PP. V (1303-1314)* (Rome, 1955), p. 95, no. 62 (6 May 1312); *Clementis Papae constitutiones* (Rome, n.d.), Bk. 5, tit. 9, c. 1; Huizinga, *The Waning of the Middle Ages*, p. 23.

[54] "... grant durté & cruauté"

[55] "... les povres crestiens nos freres, pour les quelx sauver il ha receu mort comme pour les autres..." Jean Gerson, "Requeste pour les condamnes a mort" in his *Oeuvres Complètes*, 7/1:341-43.

[56] *Ordonnances des roys de France*, 8:122, 12 February 1397; Félibien, *Histoire de la ville de Paris*, 2:717.

[57] E.g. Jean de Roye, *Chronique scandaleuse*, 2:349, 358-61; Basin, *Histoire*, 2:377. For a similar role of confessors in Renaissance Florence, see Edgerton, *Pictures and Punishment*, pp. 165-221.

powerful was this experience for the confessor, that he abstained ever after from eating meat, observing a perpetual Lent.[58]

The confession at the foot of the gallows was only the first of several religious rituals introduced into an essentially secular ceremony. Once the theme of salvation for criminals had been sounded, it echoed in many forms. As the involvement of Gerson indicates, the movement was closely tied to the reforming trends of the later middle ages. While in France the very granting of confession was a newly-won victory, across the border in Alsace it was a long-standing custom. Strasbourg possessed two special chapels for this purpose, one near the gallows and another on the bridge from which drownings took place. Towards the end of the fifteenth century the reforming preacher Geiler von Keisersberg attacked this custom, demanding also the Eucharist for the dying. Having first secured the opinion of the Heidelberg theology faculty to the effect that repentant criminals requesting communion should not be denied, he embarked upon a campaign to pressure the city fathers. His arguments relied largely upon the writings of his own disciple and friend, Peter Schott. The latter pointed out that secular punishments were meant to inflict bodily pain both in order to purge the soul and to avenge the wrongs of society, but that they were not to punish souls as well by denying salvation. Criminals were reintegrated into the mystical body of Christ by virtue of their penitence, thus earning the right to his sacramental body. Just as secular judges were debarred from mutilating the face of the condemned, made in God's image, all the more so were they bound to respect his soul.

Schott's arguments and Geiler's pressure together won the day, and in 1485 the condemned of Strasbourg were granted communion following their confession and prior to their execution.[59] The new custom never won popularity in France proper, though many quasi-sacramental customs became entrenched there too. The constable of Saint-Pol was denied the Eucharist, but permitted to hear the Mass

---

[58] Jean Molinet, *Chroniques*, ed. G. Doutrepont and O. Jordogne, 3 vols. (Brussels, 1935-37), 2:373-76; BN, ms. lat. 15049, fol. 23vo-24ro; for a full account of the affair, see Augustin Renaudet, *Réforme et humanisme à Paris pendant les premières guerres d'Italie (1494-1517)*, 2nd ed. (repr. Geneva, 1981), pp. 110-11, 178-83; Idem, "Jean Standonck, un réformateur catholique avant la réforme," *Bulletin de l'histoire du protestantisme français* 57 (1908), 25-26.

[59] L. Dacheux, *Un réformateur catholique de la fin du XVe siècle: Jean Geiler de Kaysersberg, prédicateur à la cathédrale de Strasbourg, 1478-1510* (Paris, 1876), pp. 45-49.

and consume blessed water and bread before his death.[60] Simple criminals in Paris enjoyed a less formal, but more public version of this final grace. By 1500 the *Filles-Dieu* had erected a chapel on the rue Saint-Denis, the most common execution route in the city.[61] There they performed a ceremony-within-ceremony closely akin to the sacrament of the Mass. The nuns gave the condemned a cross to kiss, sprinkled holy water on them, and offered them blessed wine and bread. The condemned, responding with another symbolically religious gesture, took three bites of the bread before proceeding out of the city and out of humanity.[62]

The introduction of religious sacraments and quasi-sacramental gestures into a ritual originally intended to exclude and differentiate created an internal tension within the ceremony. By allowing criminals a Christian death (though rarely a Christian burial), the religious elements of the ceremony negated the secular symbolism. The first to go was the social hierarchy of the dying. The message of the *danse macabre* was quite explicit: death was the ultimate equalizer. It made no distinction between rich and poor, noble and commoner. All that counted was the merit of the soul and its ultimate destiny in the afterworld. Though souls were depicted in late medieval paintings as little bodies, they were bodies stripped of all insignia of rank and position. People whose souls were about to be forcibly divested of their bodies were expected to have little concern with the outer trappings of status. Thus, while the state did its best to stress the dying criminals' status and deeds, religion made both irrelevant by introducing the elements of repentance and good death as a counterbalance to just retribution. The use of the Eucharist or a similar sacramental, so central to late medieval spirituality, reintegrated them within Christian society. Though the criminal was set apart from the normative community, he was emphatically not set outside the *corpus Christianorum*.

[60] Jean de Roye, *Chronique scandaleuse*, 2:358.

[61] The rue Saint-Denis was the main route from either the Châtelet prison or the Halles to the Porte Saint-Denis and the Montfaucon gallows.

[62] "La Chappelle des Filles-Dieu, où il y a des religieuses qui donnent aux malfaicteurs la croix à baiser, l'eaue béniste, pain et vin bénis, dont ilz mengent trois morceaulx quant on les maine pendre ou ardoir à la Justice." Anonymous, *Les rues et églises de Paris vers 1500*, ed. Alfred Bonnardot (Paris, 1876), p. 31. The fact that this ceremony was performed by the *Filles-Dieu*, founded by Saint Louis as a refuge for repentant prostitutes, might also be significant, though already by the late fourteenth century the convent accepted only reputable novices. See *GC*, p. 182.

CONCLUSION

Late medieval law was a cultural crossroads, an intersection of perceptual trends. Scholastic and humanist philosophy, theology, literature, folklore, anatomy and zoology (both learned and popular)—one is hard put to name a field of human knowledge and experience which did not find expression in legal proceedings, in or out of the courthouse.

Given the location of this cultural pluralism, such interaction was only to be expected. The law in the middle ages, as Frederick William Maitland put it, was "the point where life and logic met."[1] Practice and theory, jurists and plaintiffs, ideas and interests all jostled each other for room and mastery in the realm of law. While such a situation might be true for all legal systems, two factors specific to the time and the place made it stand out in sharper outline. First, the intrinsically lay character of high medieval jurisdiction, which together with orality took a very long time in dying out, allowed a great deal of popular matter to creep in. Secondly, the fact that jurisdiction and political lordship were inextricably tied together made the governmental content of practical justice loom large. If all legal processes are modes of social interaction, in late medieval customary law this trait was magnified tenfold.

Perhaps the most obvious result of this melding is the existence of a perceptual infrastructure which was neither learned nor popular, neither governmental nor ecclesiastical, but common to all those who had use of and access to legal procedures—which meant practically all strata of society. The symbolic vocabulary of punitive justice can be traced to specific sources, but not so the underlying central beliefs. Those formed a bedrock foundation of general consensus which could be expressed in a few simple, axiomatic sentences. Just kings dispensed justice to all, regardless of status. Their justice derived from a law which was ancient, customary, and good. The belief that the king was the guardian of the good old law, and therein lay his justice, was shared by jurists and story-tellers, theologians and simple folk alike.

---

[1] F.W. Maitland, *Collected Papers*, ed. H.A.L. Fisher, 3 vols. (Cambridge, 1911), 3:xxxvii.

The normative community thus shared the most basic perceptions of justice and law throughout its strata. This consensus perhaps best explains the very strong reaction, on all levels, against those who transgressed the rules of this community either by nature or by their actions. A legal system resting upon shared beliefs could also be used to express communal identity and its boundaries. And this communal identity found its expression in legal rituals stressing the extra-societal character of certain types of transgressors. Justice, though applied to all—human or animal, living or dead—was anything but indiscriminate. The manner of doing justice clearly separated the different groups under its aegis.

Such a picture suggests a misleading impression of an almost monolithic stability. But above the stable infrastructure, all was changing. A legal system so deeply influenced by extraneous forces must necessarily be a cultural and political seismograph, recording changes in all other spheres. The growth of literacy, the coalescence of the state, the sharpening of religious sensibilities and of intolerance all constantly influenced and changed the law. The 'Jewish execution' could never have come to be applied to Jews without the concomitant appearance of two totally disparate cultural strands: the rise in Anti-Semitism and the development of the 'world upside-down' motif. Similarly, the trials of dead people cannot be understood outside the context of the late medieval and early modern preoccupation with death and the dead. In fact, every phenomenon and development of late medieval law can be traced to a more general context.

Nowhere is the dynamic character of customary practice more obvious than in the contradictory fate of courtroom and public legal rituals. The history of legal rituals as a whole presents a certain dilemma. Courthouse rituals died out during the later middle ages, largely due to the pressure of royal government. By contrast, punitive legal rituals continued to be used well into the modern era with the full support of royal authorities. It is therefore impossible to ascribe the change to any alteration in contemporary attitudes towards legal ritualism. Rather, the difference lies in contemporary views of what the purpose of the court was and what the purpose of punishment was. If ritual had ceased to serve one procedure and continued in another, it is possible that the perception of the two rituals was different.

This difference in the contemporary views of the two spheres of justice can be seen in the juxtaposition of their ritual functions. At the most basic level, the function was essentially the same. Both courthouse and execution articulated certain traditions, legal or otherwise, in order to create a community of consent. But beyond this basic level, different functions required a different form, different contents and different messages.

This dissimilarity can clearly be seen in the role political and judicial authorities played in both legal spheres. The governmental message was clearly spelled out in the public executions. The social order was maintained in the face of death, for even the greatest leveller of all did not alter the fact that commoner and noblemen went to their end in different manners and clothes, dying by different means. The manner of death also corresponded to specific crimes, thus articulating a system of punishment based not only upon order, but also upon justice. It meant giving each one his due not only according to his station, but also according to his deeds.

Courtroom rituals also dealt with justice, but of a different type. The courthouse was hardly the expression of an egalitarian community, but a community nevertheless. Whether expressed in ordeals or in spoken formulae and gestures, the ritualistc aspect of court procedures expressed a belief in the immanence of justice in nature. The water that rejected a guilty person, the fire that burned his hand, the stammered speech—all of them expressed a form of justice that transcended the merely human. It was not justice of punishment necessarily, but justice as an indicator of truth.

This entirely different type of justice was grounded in customs believed to be both ancient and traditional. By definition, customs were not legislated, but handed down. Their authoritative character was inherent, part of their very observance and constantly reinforced by it. In fact, every court, seigneurial or royal, that ruled according to custom was reaffirming its validity in the process. Hierarchy and status were certainly observed in courtroom proceedings, but more as a matter of legality than as a political statement. In a system that made the judge personally liable for a wrong sentence and enabled the disaffected party to challenge jurors to a duel, neither the power nor the authority of justice were paramount. Even in royal courts, whose power stemmed from above, the *bailli* was bound by custom, as defined by local jurors.

The same distinction applies to the folkloric element in manifest justice. Apotropaeic measures and the use of ancient modes of humiliation and execution do not constitute a ritual in the sense that their efficacy did not hinge upon the performance of specific, formally acted stages. They did not enunciate principles of either justice or order, but a world view that attempted to use human means to exclude hostile supernatural forces. Their application by judicial authorities, however, reinforced their legitimacy. These forms were employed by authorities because they constituted a bedrock of shared perceptions upon which one could superimpose more explicit messages, but the very usage kept the folkloric, extra-judicial element alive.

Courtroom practices evince no such tradition. As far as their lineage can be traced, court rituals had no extra-judicial roots. The oath, the ordeal, and the formula were born in the courthouse, not outside its walls. There is no indication that customary rituals stemmed from any popular substratum of belief. Furthermore, though many of these rituals were born in pagan societies, there were absolutely no traces of paganism in their performance during the later middle ages. The rituals surrounding ordeals, judicial duels, and oaths, were all thoroughly Christian in form and content. While the immanence of justice appeared also in popular cultural expressions, it was certainly not characteristic only or especially of this sphere. When popular cultural elements did turn up in the courthouse, they were confined within the framework of accepted traditional legal rituals.

If indeed popular beliefs were used to convey specific messages, they were only necessary when the ritual was staged by one party for another's benefit. Until the fourteenth century courthouse rituals were commonly shared by all participants, litigants and judges alike. Participation in the ritual bound the actors to the community of the court and its rules. Whatever options one might choose to exercise, they had to be phrased in the accepted formulae and forms. Consequently, if there was an extra-judicial message involved, it was a social, not a governmental one, and it was a message tacitly accepted by all participants. There was therefore no need to employ an extra-judicial set of symbols in order to convey an external message.

And yet, in both courthouse proceedings and in public executions, the most powerful extra-judicial force was not an ancient tradition, but the religiosity of the time. Though the church deliberately distanced itself from courthouse ordeals as of 1215, it was impossible to exclude religion entirely from court proceedings. As we have seen, the oath continued depending upon sacral objects and duels were still held towards the end of the fourteenth century. Nevertheless, the active role of clergymen in the legal ritual disappeared. In this role, though, they had conveyed no independent message of their own. They had been tools of secular justice, very much after the fashion of a medium invoking spirits. Their role consisted largely of adjuring the natural elements to elicit the truth of the case and the administration of the necessary oaths. The belief in immanent justice did not depend upon their participation, and it certainly survived the church's abdication of its function in legal rituals.

The religious element that came into public executions almost two centuries later was entirely different. Unlike the earlier phenomenon, it was extra-judicial and closely tied to late medieval spirituality. Here was no mechanical means of ensuring the working of immanent justice, but a new voice that contradicted many of the traditional messages of justice. Despite the divergent messages, the religious element in public executions was fitted in without any friction, probably because the difference lay in the contents, not in the addition of any new forms. As long as the traditional forms were kept, they could accomodate also another message, and their symbolic meaning need not have been univocal.

Once the ability to die a good death was no longer beyond the criminal, secular justice lost its absolute character. Real justice was therefore translated from the world of the living to the afterworld, though very much in the same terms. The application of instruments of physical punishment in purgatory and hell served a double purpose. For people who received a formally similar message in church and in the street spectacle, the analogy was clear. Not only was the criminal part of the general community, suffering the same fate (if somewhat earlier than the rest), but the moral order was also articulated in terms intelligible to anyone who had ever witnessed an execution. Rather than using cultural concepts to bolster the efficacy of visible law, the church was using the law to enunciate religious concepts.

Thus, both rulers and church used popular perceptions and beliefs in order to present a new message. At the same time, both forces superimposed their own sets of symbols, hierarchical or religious, upon the older form. Not surprisingly, the net result was an extremely complex, multivocal ritual. By the end of the middle ages, three different symbolic vocabularies—governmental, popular, and religious—were used in punitive rituals. The language of power, hierarchy, and order, the old beliefs concerning the body, and the religious beliefs in the soul and its ultimate destiny all played a role in these dramas. The fact that they did not clash is partly due to the tacit nature of the popular content and, more so, to the very clear demarcation of the different spheres. The messages of authority were conveyed largely during the pre-execution ceremonies, *amendes honorables* and processions. The role of the church was enacted at the foot of the gallows, and after that the popular tradition took over. It was thus possible first to stress the culprit's social position and then to negate it by assimilating him within the general body of believers, or first to save his soul and then to consign his body to a traditional death.

Yet even within these demarcated spheres there was an interpenetration of usages. Criminals on the way to the gallows not only declared their guilt, they also begged for prayers for their souls. Symbolic punitive measures, such as amputating an offending limb, were also carried out during the procession. And it could not have been otherwise, for the executions were in essence one ceremony, different elements welded together by an interactive use of symbols.

No similar phenomenon existed in the courthouse. The religious element had deliberately been expunged, and the folkloric element had never existed. As a result, a single language of symbols was employed throughout the history of courthouse rituals and their transmutations. When gestures and formulae ceased to be intrinsically valid, the terminology of the legal profession replaced them. This vocabulary, however, belonged exclusively to the growing class of professional lawyers with their ever-increasing jurisprudential training.

Herein probably lies the answer to the death of the courthouse ritual. Ritual serves a binding, integrating function, and the courthouse was no longer the locus of communal integration. There is no evidence that the professionalization and deritualization of the courthouse ever aroused any regrets or protests. To the contrary: the proliferation of urban charters absolving communes from judicial duels, and the prevalence of appeals to the Parlement indicate that most of those resorting to courts preferred efficient and professional resolutions of their conflicts to any abstract community of consent. Royal courts could and did offer such an alternative. The fact that the kings of France deliberately used justice as a tool of government in no way impeded litigants both great and small from using it for their own ends.

Public legal rituals, however, were not resolutions of conflicts, but imposed solutions. Unlike the courthouse ritual, the ceremony of the execution could be and was indeed manipulated for governmental purposes. While it fostered a sense of community by contrasting the criminal with the spectators, this community was shaped and controlled by the forces that staged the ceremony. Whether identified as the body social or the body Christian, it was based upon a deliberately created sense of identity. The death and survival of legal rituals, therefore, were intrinsically tied to their function. Those that had had a purpose survived, while those that had lost their function died out.

In this transition, legal rites reflected a much wider and deeper change in late medieval societal perceptions. Much of the high medieval view of the world was based upon an assumption of reciprocity within the hierarchy. The vassalage contract, rightly seen by Le Goff as a reflection of much wider perceptions, epitomizes this reciprocity. And indeed, rituals followed the same perception. High medieval feudal oaths, wedding rituals, and even pre-duel ceremonies all reflected reciprocity of engagement. No wonder that adversary actions in court used the same symbolic elements as other reciprocal rituals.

By the later middle ages, reciprocity was gradually being replaced by a strictly authoritarian view. The cult of royalty and the weakening of feudal nobility and feudal justice were among the causes for this transition. Concomitantly, relationships of power and control became unilateral. On the legal plane, the transition was expressed in punitive rites relying upon a new system of justice. While high medieval law depended upon the accusatory system, which made even criminal prosecution a matter of reciprocal, adversary relations, the introduction of the inquisitorial mode firmly placed prosecution in the hands of the state, thus making it purely unilateral. The rituals expressing this relationship of subjection to authority were intrinsically different from the earlier reciprocal rites.

The changes affecting legal rituals were thus part of the wider changes late medieval French society underwent. The crossroads of justice possessed yet another intersection. A meeting-ground of cultural, political and religious spheres, it also connected the permanent with the processual and the dynamic, the traditional continuum of law with its constant changes.

BIBLIOGRAPHY

Manuscript Sources

Archives Nationales, Paris

I have consulted the series X^{1a} (Parlement civil) and X^{2a} (Parlement criminel) for the fourteenth and fifteenth centuries.

For ecclesiastical jurisdictions, I have used the Z^{10} series.

Of the series Y (Châtelet) I have used the *livres de couleurs* of the later middle ages, listing many notable cases. Those books lacking in the *archives nationales* are to be found in later copies in the *archives de la police.*

The court cases have been supplemented by the remissions (series JJ) of the period.

Bibliothèque Nationale, Paris

In addition to the manuscripts of the collection Delamare (fr. 21731-36), directly concerning criminal matters, I have consulted ms. fr. 4472 (*Style du Châtelet*), ms. fr. 7645 (*Peines et supplices de la justice criminelle de France aux cinq derniers siècles*) and ms. lat. 15049 (*Liber de origine reformationis canonicorum regularium in Francia.*)

Primary Printed Sources

Ableiges, Jacques d'. *Le Grand Coutumier de France*. Ed. E. Laboulaye and R. Dareste. Paris, 1868.

Abrégé du livre des assises de la Cour des Bourgeois. In *Assises de Jérusalem*, q.v. 2:227-352.

Actes du Parlement de Paris. Ed. E. Boutaric and H. Fourgeot. 4 vols. Paris, 1863-1960.

Adam of Bremen, *Gesta Hammaburgensis ecclesiae pontificum*. Ed. B. Schmeidler. *MGH, SS Rer. Germ. in usum scholarum*. Hanover, 1917.

Ancien Coutumier de Bourgogne. Ed. A.J. Marnier. Paris, 1858.

Ancien coutumier inédit de Picardie. Ed. A.J. Marnier. Paris, 1840.

Andosilla, Martín de Arles y. "De Superstitionibus." In José Goñi Gaztambide, ed. q.v. "El tratado *De superstitionibus* de Martín de Andosilla," 267-322.

Anselm of Canterbury. *Sancti Anselmi Cantauriensis Opera Omnia*. Ed. F.S. Schmitt. 6 vols. Stuttgart, 1968.

Assises de Jérusalem. Ed. Beugnot. 2 vols. *Recueils des historiens des Croisades, Lois*. Paris, 1841-43.

Ayrault, Pierre. "Des procès faicts au cadaver, à la memoire, aux bestes brutes, aux choses inanimées et aux contumaux." In *L'ordre, formalité et instruction iudiciaire, dont les anciens Grecs & Romains ont usé és accusations publiques (sinon qu'ils ayent commencés l'execution) conferé au stil & usage de nostre France.* 2 vols. 1:572-646. Paris, 1615.

Azpilcueta, Martín de. *Opera omnia.* 5 vols. Cologne, 1616.

Bacquet, Jean. *Les Oeuvres de Iean Bacquet, advocat du roy....* Paris, 1630.

Bailly, Gaspard. "De l'excellence des monitoires." in Evans, q.v. *The Criminal Prosecution*, pp. 287-306. London, 1906.

Bartholomeus Anglicus. *De rerum proprietatibus.* Frankfurt, 1601. Repr. 1964.

Basin, Thomas. *Histoire des règnes de Charles VII et de Louis XI.* Ed. Jules Quicherat. 4 vols. Paris, 1855-59.

Baye, Nicolas de. *Journal.* Ed. Alexandre Tuetey. 2 vols. Paris, 1885.

Beaumanoir, Philippe de. *Coutumes de Beauvaisis.* Ed. A. Salmon. 3 vols. Paris, 1899-1974.

Beier, Adrian. *An detur resuscitatio mortuorum: problema iuridicum.* Jena, 1665.

Bertrand de Bar-sur-Aube. *Le roman de Girard de Vienne.* Ed. Frederic G. Yeandle. New York, 1930.

Boguet, Henri. *An Examen of Witches.* Trans. E.A. Ashwin. Ed. M. Summers. London, 1929.

Bourbon, Etienne de. *Anecdotes historiques, légendes et apologues tirés du recueil inédit d'Etienne de Bourbon, dominicain du XIIIe siècle.* Ed. A. Lecoy de la Marche. Paris, 1877.

Boutillier, Jean. *Le grand coustumier general de praticque, aultrement appelle Somme rural.* Ed. L. Charondas le Caron. Paris, 1603.

Caesarius of Heisterbach. *Dialogus miraculorum.* Ed. Joseph Strange. 2 vols. Köln, 1851.

Capitularia regum francorum. Ed. A. Boretius and V. Krause. 2 vols. MGH. Hanover, 1883.

Cartulaire de l'église Notre-Dame de Paris. Ed. M. Guérard. 4 vols. Paris, 1850.

Catherine of Siena. *Les lettres de Sainte Catherine.* Trans. E. Cartier. Paris, 1886.

Chartier, Jean. *Chronique de Charles VII.* Ed. Vallet de Viriville. 2 vols. Paris, 1858.

Chassenée, Bartholomé. *Concilia D. Bartholomaei a Chasseneo, Burgundi iurisconsulti.* Lyon, 1588.

——. *In Consuetudines ducatus Burgundiae, fereque totae Galliae, commentarii amplissimi.* Paris, 1552.

Choix de pièces inédites rélatives au règne de Charles VI. Ed. L. Douët-d'Arcq. Paris, 1864.

Chronique parisienne anonyme du XIVe siècle. Ed. A. Hellot. Nogent-le-Rotrou, 1884.

La clef des Assises de la Haute Cour dou Royaume de Jérusalem et de Chypre. In *Assises de Jérusalem* q.v. 1:573-600.

Clementis Papae constitutiones. Rome, n.d..

Corpus iuris civilis. Ed. P. Krueger, T. Mommsen, and R. Scholl. 3 vols. Berlin, 1884-95.

Coustumes et stilles de Bourgoigne. In Giraud, q.v. *Essai sur l'histoire du droit.* Vol. 2.

Les coustumes des pays d'Anjou et du Maine. In *CIAM*, q.v., vol. 3.

Les coustumes générales et particulières du royaume de France et des Gaules. Ed. Charles du Moulin. 2 vols. Paris, 1581.

Coustumes glosées d'Anjou et du Maine. In *CIAM*, q.v., vol. 1.

Coutumes et institutions de l'Anjou et du Maine antérieures au XVIe siècle. Ed. C.J. Beautemps-Beaupré. 4 vols. Paris, 1877-97.

Coutumes et stilles observez et gardez ès pays d'Anjou et du Maine. In *CIAM*, q.v., vol. 1.

Coutumes locales du bailliage d'Amiens, Ed. A. Bouthors. 2 vols. Amiens, 1845.

Coutumez, usaigez et stillez... ou pais d'Anjou. In *CIAM*, q.v., vol. 4.

Coutumiers de Normandie. Ed. E.J. Tardif. 3 vols. Rouen, 1881-1903.

Crónica Najarense. Ed. Antonio Ubieto Arteta. Valencia, 1966.
Cuvelier, Jean. *Chronique de Bertrand du Guesclin*. Ed. E. Charrière. 2 vols. Paris, 1839.
La danse macabre de Guy Marchant (1406). Facs. ed. Paris, 1925.
Damhouder, Jodocus. *Praxis rerum criminalium*. Antwerpen, 1562.
Delorme, Fernand M. and Aloysius L. Tàutu, eds. *Acta Clementis PP. V (1303-1314)*. Rome, 1955.
Delrío, Martín. *Disquisitiones magicarum....* Mainz, 1603.
"Dialogus Salomonis et Marcolphi." Ed. Giulio Cesare Croce. *Le sotilissime astuzie di Bertoldo....*, pp. 169-206. Torino, 1978.
Döpler, Jacob. *Theatri poenarum suppliciorum et executionum criminalium, oder Schau-platzes derer Leibes- und Lebens- Strafen*. Leipzig, 1697.
Du Breuil, Guillaume. *Stilus curie parlamenti*. Ed. Félix Aubert. Paris, 1909.
Duret, Jean. *Traité des peines et amendes*. Paris, 1573.
Les Evangiles des quenouilles. Ed. P. Jannet. Paris, 1855.
Expilly, Claude. *Plaidoyez de... C. Expilly, conseiller du roy et son advocat général au Parlement de Grenoble*. 5th ed. Paris, 1631.
Eynatten, Maximilian d'. *Manuale exorcismorum*. In *Thesaurus exorcismorum atque coniurationum terribilium*, q.v.
Établissements de Saint Louis. Ed. Paul Viollet, 4 vols. Paris, 1881-86.
Fontaines, Pierre de. *Conseil*. Ed. M.A.J. Marnier. Paris, 1846.
Formulae Merowingici et Karolini aevi. Ed. Karl Zeumer. *MGH*, Hanover, 1886.
"Fragment d'un répertoire de jurisprudence parisienne au XVe siècle." Ed. G. Fagniez. *MSHP* 17 (1890) 1-94.
Garin le Loheran. Ed. Josephine Elvira Vallerie. Ann Arbor, 1941.
Gerson, Jean. *Oeuvres complètes*. Ed. Mgr. Glorieux, 7 vols. Paris, 1960-68.
——. *Six sermons français inédits*. Ed. Louis Mourin. Paris, 1946.
Gervase of Tilbury. *Otia Imperialia ad Ottonem IV imperatorem*. In G.W. Leibnitz, ed. *Scriptores rerum Brunsvicensium*, 3 vols. 1:881-1004. Hanover, 1707-11.
Godelmann, Iohannes Georg. *De magiis, veneficiis et lamiis recte cognoscendi et puniendi libri tres*. Frankfurt, 1591.
Goñi Gaztambide, José. "El tratado *De superstitionibus* de Martín de Andosilla." *Cuadernos de etnología y etnografía de Navarra* 9 (1971) 249-322.
Le grand et le petit Albert. Ed. Bernard Husson. Paris, 1978.
Les grandes chroniques de France. Ed. Jules Viard. 10 vols. Paris, 1920-53.
Le grant kalendrier et compost des Bergiers, avec leur astrologie et plusieurs aultres choses.... Troyes, n.d.
Hrabanus Maurus. *De universo*. In *MPL*, 111:9-612.
Ibelin, Jean d'. *Assises de la haute cour*. In *Assises de Jérusalem*, q.v., vol. 1, pp. 7-432.
Ibn Mounkidh, Ousama. *The Autobiography of Ousama* (1095-1188). Trans. G.R. Potter. London, 1929.
Joinville, Jean de. *Vie de Saint Louis*. Ed. M. Natalis de Wailly. Paris, 1868.
Journal d'un bourgeois de Paris. Ed. A. Tuetey. Paris, 1881. Repr. Geneva, 1975.
Kornmann, Henricus. *De miraculis mortuorum*. n.p., 1610.
Le Coq, Jean. *Quaestiones Johannis Galli*. Ed. Marguerite Boulet. Paris, 1944.
Lefevre, Jean. *Chronique de Jean le Fevre, seigneur de Saint-Remy*. Ed. François Morand. 2 vols. Paris, 1876-81.
Lescot, Richard. *Chronique*. Ed. Jean Lemoine. Paris, 1896.
Lex Salica. Leges nationum Germanicarum. Ed. K.A. Eckhardt. *MGH LL* 4:2. Hanover, 1969.
Li livre de jostice et de plet. Ed. Rapetti. Paris, 1850.
Liber exemplorum ad usum praedicantium. Ed. A.G. Little. Aberdeen, 1908.
Liber Sancti Jacobi. Ed. and trans. A. Moralejo et. al. Santiago de Compostela, 1951.

Liger, Claude. *Les coustumes d'Anjou et du Maine intitullées selon les rubriches du Code*. In *CIAM*, q.v. vol. 2.

"*Livre des constitucions demenées el Chastelet de Paris.*" Ed. Charles Mortet. *MSHP* 10 (1883) 1-99.

Le livre du roy Modus et de la reyne Racio. Chambéry, 1486.

Le livre Roisin: Coutumier lillois de la fin du XIIIe siècle. Ed. Raymond Monier. Paris, 1932.

Loisel, Antoine. *Institutions coutumières*. Ed. Michel Reulos. Paris, 1935.

Maître Pierre Pathelin, farce du XVe siècle. Ed. R.T. Holbrook. Paris, 1937.

Malleolus, Felix. *Variae oblationes, opuscula et tractatus*. Basle, 1497.

Marès, Jean de. *Coutumes tenues toutes notoires et jugées au Chastelet de Paris*. In Julien Brodeau. *Commentaire sur la coustume de la prévosté et vicomté de Paris*. Paris, 1658.

Masuer, Jean. *Practique*. Ed. and trans. Antoine Fontanon. Paris, 1576.

Mengo, Girolamo. *Flagellum daemonum*. In *Thesaurus exorcismorum atque coniurationum terribilium* q.v.

Meung, Jean de. *Roman de la Rose*. Ed. Félix Lecoy. 3 vols. Paris, 1966-70.

Molinet, Jean. *Chroniques*. Ed. G. Doutrepont and O. Jordogne. 3 vols. Brussels, 1935-37.

Monstrelet, Enguerrand de. *Chronique*, Ed. L. Douët-d'Arcq. 6 vols. Paris, 1857-62.

The Murder of Charles the Good, Count of Flanders. Trans. and ed. J.B. Ross. New York, 1967.

"Notes d'audiences prises au Parlement de Paris de 1384 à 1386, par un praticien anonyme." Ed. Fr. Olivier-Martin. *RHDFE*. 4th ser. 1 (1922) 513-603.

Nouveau coutumier général de France. Ed. C.A. Bourdot de Richebourg. 4 vols. Paris, 1724.

Olim, ou registres d'arrêts rendus par la cour du roi. Ed. Beugnot, 3 vols. Paris, 1844.

Ordonnances des rois de France de la troisième race. Ed. E. de Laurière et al. 21 vols. Paris, 1723-1849.

Otten, Charlotte F. ed. *A Lycanthropy Reader: Werewolves in Western Culture*. Syracuse, N.Y., 1986.

Pactus Legis Salicae. Leges nationum Germanicarum. Ed. K.A. Eckhardt. *MGH LL* 4:1. Hanover, 1962.

Pape, Gui. *Decisiones Parlamenti Dalphinatis Gratianopolitanis*. 2nd ed. Geneva, 1667.

Papon, Jean. *Recueil d'arrests notables des cours souveraines de France*. 2 vols. Paris, 1621.

Paris, Geffroi de. *Chronique rimée*. In *RHGF* 22:89-166.

Der Physiologus. Ed. Otto Seel. Zürich, 1967.

Pizan, Christine de. *Le livre de faits et bonnes moeurs du sage roi Charles V....* Paris, 1892.

Plinius Secundus. *Naturalis historia*. Ed. H. Rackham. London, 1961.

The Prose of Solomon and Saturn and Adrian and Ritheus. Ed. James E. Cross and Thomas D. Hill. Toronto, 1982.

Rabelais, François. *Oeuvres complètes*. Ed. Guy Demerson. Paris, 1973.

Raoul de Cambrai. Ed. P. Meyer and A. Longnon. Paris, 1882.

Raynaud, Théofile. *Opuscula moralia*. Lyon, 1665.

Recueil de jugements de l'échiquier de Normandie au 13e siècle, 1207-1270. Ed. Léopold Delisle. Paris, 1864.

Registre criminel de la justice de Saint-Martin-des-Champs à Paris au XIVe siècle. Ed. Louis Tanon. Paris, 1877.

Registre criminel du Châtelet de Paris. Ed. H. Duplès-Agier. 2 vols. Paris, 1861-64.

Renaud de Montauban. Ed. Castets. Montpellier, 1909.

Roye, Jean de. *Journal, ou Chronique scandaleuse*, 1460-1483. Ed. B. de Mandrot. 2 vols. Paris, 1894.

Les rues et églises de Paris vers 1500. Ed. Alfred Bonnardot. Paris, 1876.
Saint-Victor, Jean de. *Memoriale historiarum*. In *RHGF* 21:630-89.
Speculum spiritualium, in quo non solam vita activa et contemplativa.... Paris, 1510.
Sprenger, J. and H. Institoris, *Malleus maleficarum*. Trans. M. Summers. London, 1968.
Suger of Saint-Denis. *Vie de Louis VI le Gros*. Ed. and Trans. H. Waquet. Paris, 1964.
Summa de legibus Normandiae. In *Coutumiers de Normandie*, q.v.
Tacitus, Cornelius. *Germania*. Ed. and trans. M. Hutton. Loeb series. London and New York, 1914.
La Tabula exemplorum secundum ordinem alphabeti. Ed. L.-T. Welter. Toulouse, 1927. Repr. Geneva, 1973.
Taillepied, Noël. *Traicté de l'apparition des esprits*. Rouen, 1616.
Thesaurus exorcismorum atque coniurationum terribilium. Cologne, 1626.
Thomas Aquinas. *Summa Theologiae*. Rome, 1886.
Thomas of Cantimpré. *Miraculorum et exemplorum sui temporis libri duo*. Douais, 1605.
Thou, Auguste de. *Histoire universelle depuis 1593 jusqu'en 1607*. 16 vols. London, 1734.
Traictié des paines d'enfer et de purgatoire. Paris, 1492.
Très-ancienne coutume de Bretagne. Ed. M. Planiol. Rennes, 1896.
Vieux Coustumier de Poictou. Ed. R. Filhol. Bourges, 1956.
Villon, François. *Oeuvres complètes*. Ed. Auguste Longnon. Paris, 1941.
The Vulgate Version of Arthurian Romance. Ed. H. Oskar Sommer. Washington, 1910.
William of Jumièges. *Gesta Normannorum ducum*. Ed. J. Marx. Rouen and Paris, 1914.
William of Malmesbury. *De gestis regum Anglorum*. Ed. William Stubbs. 2 vols. London, 1887-89.

SECONDARY SOURCES

Affergan, Francis. *Exotisme et altérité*. Paris, 1987.
Agnel, E. *Curiosités judiciaires et historiques du moyen âge. Procès contre les animaux*. Paris, 1858.
Amira, Karl von. *Der Stab in der germanischen Rechtssymbolik*. München, 1909.
——. "Thierstrafen und Thierprocesse." *Mitteilungen des österreichischen Instituts für Geschichtsforschung* 12 (1891) 545-601.
Aptowitzer, V. "The Rewarding and Punishing of Animals and Inanimate Objects." *Hebrew Union College Annual* 3 (1926) 117-55.
Asad, Talal. "Notes on Body Pain and Truth in Medieval Christian Ritual." *Economy and Society* 12 (1983) 288-98.
Autrand, Françoise. *Naissance d'un grand corps de l'état. Les gens du Parlement de Paris, 1345-1454*. Paris, 1981.
Babcock, Barbara A., ed. *The Reversible World: Symbolic Inversion in Art and Society*. Ithaca, N.Y., 1978.
——. "Introduction." In Barbara A. Babcock, ed. q.v. *The Reversible World: Symbolic Inversion in Art and Society*, pp. 13-36.
Bandera, Cesáreo. "From Mythical Bees to Medieval Anti-Semitism." In *Violence and Truth: On the Work of René Girard*. Ed. and trans. Paul Dumouchel, pp. 209-26. Stanford, 1988.
Barber, Paul. *Vampires, Burial, and Death: Folklore and Reality*. New Haven, 1988.
Baron, Salo W. *A Social and Religious History of the Jews*. 2nd ed. 18 vols. New York, 1952.

Bart, J. and M. Petitjean. *L'influence du droit romain en Bourgogne et en Franche-Comté (XIIIe-XVe siècles)*. IRMA, V.4.e.

Barthes, Roland. "Histoire et sociologie du vêtement. Quelques observations méthodolgiques." *Annales E.S.C.* 12 (1957) 430-41.

Bartlett, Robert. *Trial by Fire and Water: The Medieval Judicial Ordeal*. Oxford, 1988.

Baschet, Jerôme. "Les conceptions de l'enfer au XIVe siècle: Imaginaire et pouvoir." *Annales E.S.C.* 40 (1985) 183-205.

Baudot, P. and P. Chaussin. *Vie des saints et des bienheureux selon l'ordre du calendrier avec l'historique des fêtes*. 13 vols. Paris, 1935-59.

Beaune, Colette. "Saint Clovis: Histoire, religion royale et sentiment nationale à la fin du moyen âge." In Bernard Guenée, ed. *Le métier d'historien au moyen âge. Etudes d'historiographie médiévale*, pp. 139-56. Paris, 1977.

Beriac, Françoise. *Histoire des lépreux au moyen âge*. Paris, 1988.

Berkenhoff, Hans A. *Tierstrafe, Tierbannung und rechtsrituelle Tiertötung im Mittelalter*. Strasbourg, 1937.

Bernheimer, Richard. *Wild Men in the Middle Ages: A Study in Art, Sentiment and Demonology*. Cambridge, Mass., 1952.

Berriat-Saint-Prix, J. "Rapport et recherches sur les procès et jugements rélatifs aux animaux." *Mémoires de la société royale des antiquaires de France* 8 (1829) 403-50.

Beyerle, Franz. "Über Normtypen und Erweiterungen der Lex Salica." *ZRG, GA* 44 (1924) 216-261.

Bédier, Joseph. *Les fabliaux: études de littérature populaire et d'histoire littéraire du moyen âge*. 6th ed. Paris, 1969.

Bée, Michel. "Le spectacle de l'exécution dans la France d'Ancien Régime." *Annales E.S.C.* 38 (1983) 843-62.

Bloch, R. Howard. *Medieval French Literature and Law*. Berkeley, 1977.

Blok, Anton. "Openbare strafvoltrekkingen als rites de passage." *Tijdschrift voor Geschiedenis* 97 (1984) 470-81.

——. "The Symbolic Vocabulary of Public Executions." In June Starr and Jane F. Collier, eds. *History and Power in the Study of Law: New Directions in Legal Anthropology*, pp. 31-54. Ithaca, N.Y., 1989.

Blum, Claude. "Le corps à l'agonie dans la littérature de la renaissance." In *Le corps à la renaissance. Actes du XXXe colloque de Tours, 1987*. Ed. Jean Céard et al. pp. 147-60. Paris, 1990.

Bongert, Yvonne. *Recherches sur les cours laïques du Xe au XIIIe siècle*. Paris, 1942.

Bossy, John, ed. *Disputes and Settlements: Law and Human Relations in the West*. Cambridge, 1983.

Boucher, Alain. *Le sacre corps du roi*. Paris, 1989.

Browe, Petrus. *De ordaliies*. 2 vols. Rome, 1933.

Brown, Elizabeth A.R. "Authority, the Family and the Dead in Late Medieval France." *French Historical Studies* 16 (1990) 803-32.

Brown, Peter. "Society and the Supernatural: A Medieval Change." *Daedalus* 104 (1975) 133-51.

——. *The Body and Society: Men, Women, and Sexual Renunciation in Early Christianity*. New York, 1988.

——. *The Cult of the Saints: Its Rise and Function in Latin Christianity*. Chicago, 1981.

Brunner, Heinrich. "Die Klage mit dem toten Mann und die Klage mit der toten Hand." *ZRG, GA* 31 (1910) 235-52.

——. "Wort und Form im altfranzösischen Prozess." *Sitzungsberichte der philosophisch-historischen Classe der kaiserlichen Akademie der Wissenschaften* 57 (1867) 655-780.

Bryant, Lawrence M. *The King and the City in the Parisian Royal Entry Ceremony: Politics, Ritual and Art in the Renaissance.* Geneva, 1986.

Bukowska-Gorgoni, Christina. "Die Strafe des Sackens—Wahrheit und Legende." *Forschungen zur Rechtsarchäologie und rechtlichen Volkskunde* 2 (1979) 145-162.

Büchner, Karl. *Die Frauenfrage im Mittelalter.* 2nd ed. Tübingen, 1910.

Bynum, Caroline W. *Holy Feast and Holy Fast: The Religious Significance of Food to Medieval Women.* Berkeley, 1987.

——. "Women's Stories, Women's Symbols: A Critique of Victor Turner's Theory of Liminality." In *Anthropology and the Study of Religion.* Ed. Robert L. Moore and Frank E. Reynolds, pp. 105-25. Chicago, 1984.

Caeneghem, R. van. "The Law of Evidence in the Twelfth Century: European Perspective and Intellectual Background." *Proceedings of the Second International Congress of Medieval Canon Law: Rome, 1965.* pp. 297-310. Ghent, 1966.

Camporesi, Piero. *The Incorruptible Flesh: Bodily Mutation and Mortification in Religion and Folklore.* Trans. T. Croft-Murray. Cambridge, 1988.

Carruthers, Mary J. *The Book of Memory: A Study of Memory in Medieval Culture.* Cambridge, 1990.

Cauwenbergh, Etienne van. *Les pèlerinages expiatoires et judiciaires dans le droit communal de la Belgique au moyen âge.* Louvain, 1922.

Chartier, Roger. "Les arts de mourir, 1450-1600." *Annales E.S.C.* 31 (1976) 51-75.

Cheyette, F. "La justice et le pouvoir royal à la fin du moyen âge français." *RHDFE.* 4e ser. 40 (1962) 373-94.

Chiffoleau, Jacques. *Les justices du pape. Délinquance et criminalité dans la région d'Avignon au XIVe siècle.* Paris, 1984.

Clanchy, Michael T. "Law and Love in the Middle Ages." In John Bossy, ed. q.v. *Disputes and Settlements: Law and Human Relations in the West,* pp. 47-67.

——. "Remembering the Past and the Good Old Law." *History* 55 (1970) 165-76.

Clark, Stuart. "Inversion, Misrule and the Meaning of Witchcraft." *Past and Present* 87 (1986) 98-127.

Cohen, Esther. "Inversie en liminaliteit in de rechtspraktijk van de late Middeleeuwen." *Theoretische Geschiedenis* 16 (1989) 433-43.

——. "Law, Folklore, and Animal Lore." *Past and Present* 110 (1986) 6-37.

——. "Symbols of Culpability and the Universal Language of Justice: The Ritual of Public Executions in Late Medieval Europe." *History of European Ideas* 11 (1989) 407-16.

—— and Elliott Horowitz. "In Search of the Sacred: Jews, Christians, and Rituals of Marriage in the Later Middle Ages." *Journal of Medieval and Renaissance Studies* 20 (1990) 225-50.

Cohen, Gustave. *Le Théâtre comique au moyen-âge.* 2 vols. Paris, 1941.

Dacheux, L. *Un réformateur catholique de la fin du XVe siècle: Jean Geiler de Kaysersberg, prédicateur à la cathédrale de Strasbourg, 1478-1510.* Paris, 1876.

Dagani, B. "Carnival Plays and Satyric Literature as a tool of Anti-Semitism in the Fifteeth and Early Sixteenth Centuries." [Hebrew] In M. Stern, ed. *Uma Ve-Toldoteha,* 245-80. Jerusalem, 1983.

Dahan, Gilbert. "Contre un Juif. Trois poèmes inédits du XVIIe siècle." *Archives juives* 16:1 (1980) 5-9.

Danet, Brenda and Bryna Bogoch. "From Oral Ceremony to Written Document: The Transitional Language of Anglo-Saxon Wills." *Language and Communication* forthcoming.

Darnton, Robert. "Workers Revolt: The Great Cat Massacre of the Rue Saint-Séverin." In *The Great Cat Massacre and Other Episodes in French Cultural History,* pp. 75-106. New York, 1984.

Davis, Natalie Z. "Women on Top." In *Society and Culture in Early Modern France,* pp. 124-51. Stanford, 1975.

——. *Fiction in the Archives: Pardon Tales and their Tellers in Sixteenth Century France.* Stanford, 1987.

Dawson, John P. *A History of Lay Judges.* Cambridge, Mass., 1960.

Dähmhardt, Oskar, ed. *Natursagen. Eine Sammlung naturdeutender Sagen, Märchen, Fabeln und Legenden.* 3 vols. Berlin, 1907-10.

Delisle, Léopold. "Des revenus publics en Normandie au XIIe siècle." *Bibliothèque de l'école des chartes* 3e ser. 3 (1851-52) 97-135.

——. "L'Auteur du Grand Coutumier de France." *MSHP* 8 (1882) 140-60.

Delumeau, Jean. *La peur en Occident (XIVe-XVIIIe siècles).* Paris, 1978.

Desjardins, A. *Saint Yves, avocat des pauvres et patron des avocats.* Paris, 1897.

Diamond, A.S. *Primitive Law Past and Present.* London, 1971.

Diamond, Stanley. "The Rule of Law Versus the Order of Custom." In C.E. Reasons and R.M. Rich, eds. *The Sociology of Law*, pp. 239-62. Toronto, 1978.

Dietrich, Gérard. *Les procès d'animaux du moyen-âge à nos jours.* Lyon, 1961.

Dievoet, Guido van. *Jehan Boutillier en de Somme Rural.* Louvain, 1951.

——. "Le *Roman de Renart* et *Van den Vos Reynaerde*, témoins fidèles de la procédure pénale aux XIIe et XIIIe siècles?" In E. Rombauts and A. Welkenhuysen, eds. q.v. *Aspects of the Medieval Animal Epic*, pp. 43-52.

Douglas, Mary T. *Purity and Danger.* London, 1966.

Dubois, A. *Justice et bourreaux à Amiens dans les XVe et XVIe siècles.* Amiens, 1860.

Duby, Georges. "Réflexions sur la douleur physique au moyen âge." In *Mâle moyen âge*, pp. 203-209. Paris, 1988.

Ducange, C. *Glossarium mediae et infimae Latinitatis.* 7 vols. Paris, 1840-50.

Dumézil, Georges. *La Saga de Hadingus: Du mythe au roman.* Paris, 1953.

Dülmen, Richard van. "Das Schauspiel des Todes: Hinrichtungsrituale in der frühen Neuzeit." In *Volkskultur zu Wiederentdeckung des vergessenen Alltags (16.-20. Jahrhundert).* Ed. Richard van Dülmen and Norbert Schindler, pp. 203-245, 417-423. Frankfurt, 1984.

Edgerton, Samuel Y. *Pictures and Punishment: Art and Criminal Prosecution During the Florentine Renaissance.* Ithaca, N.Y., 1984.

Egmond, Florike. "Bijzondere beesten. Diersymboliek en strafvoltrekkingen." Paper presented at the Alterity Symposium. Amsterdam, 1989.

——. "Gypsies: Crime, Stigmatization and Ambiguity. The Case of the Northern Netherlands, 1450-1780." Paper presented at the Third International Conference of the International Association for the History of Crime and Criminal Justice. Paris, 1988.

Esmein, Adhémar. *Histoire de la procédure criminelle en France et spécialement de la procédure inquisitoire depuis le XIIIe siècle.* Paris, 1882.

Evans, Edward P. *The Criminal Prosecution and Capital Punishment of Animals.* London, 1906. Repr. 1987.

Fabre-Vassas, Claudine. "Juifs et Chrétiens. Autour du cochon." *Recherches et travaux de l'Institut d'ethnologie (CH-Neuchâtel)* 6 (1985) 59-83.

Fehr, Hans. *Das Recht in Bilde.* Erlenbach-Zürich, 1923.

——. "Über den Titel 58 der Lex Salica (De Chrene cruda)." *ZRG, GA* 27 (1906) 151-72.

Félibien, Michel. *Histoire de la ville de Paris.* 5 vols. Paris, 1725.

Filhol, René. "La rédaction des coutumes en France aux XVe et XVIe siècles." In John Gilissen, ed. *La rédaction des coutumes dans le passé et dans le présent*, pp. 63-78. Brussels, 1962.

Finkelstein, J.J. *The Ox that Gored.* Philadelphia, 1981.

Floquet, A. *Histoire du privilège de Saint Romain.* Rouen, 1833.

Fontette, M. de. *Les religieuses à l'âge classique du droit canon.* Paris, 1967.

Foviaux, Jacques. *La rémission des peines et des condamnations: Droit monarchique et droit moderne.* Paris, 1970.

Franchi de'Cavalieri, P. "Della furca e della sua sostituzione alla croce nel diritto penale Romano." *Nuovo bulletino di archeologia cristiana* 13 (1907) 63-113.
Franklin, Alfred. *Paris et les parisiens au seizième siècle.* Paris, 1928.
Fuchs, J.M. *De hond aan de galg.* Amsterdam, 1957.
Gaignebet, Claude. *Le Carnaval.* Paris, 1974.
Garrett, Clarke. "Women and Witches: Pattern of Analysis." *Signs* 3 (1977) 461-70.
Gaudemet, Jean. "L'influence des droits savants (romain et canonique) sur les textes de droit coutumier en Occident avant le XVIe siècle." *Actas del II congreso internacional de derecho canónico, Pamplona, 1976.* Pamplona, 1979. pp. 165-94. Reprinted in *Eglise et société en Occident au moyen âge.* London, 1984.
——. "Les ordalies au moyen âge: Doctrine, législation et pratique canoniques." In *La Preuve: Moyen âge et temps modernes. Recueils de la société Jean Bodin* XVII/2, pp. 99-135. Bruxelles, 1965.
Gauvard, Claude. "L'Image du roi justicier en France à la fin du moyen âge d'après les lettres de rémission." *La faute, la répression et le pardon. Actes du 107e congrès national des sociétés savantes.* 2 vols. 1:165-92. Brest, 1982.
Geary, Patrick. "L'humiliation des saints." *Annales E.S.C.* 34 (1979) 27-42.
Gessler, J. "Mulier suspensa: à délit égal peine différente?" *Revue Belge de philologie et d'histoire* 18 (1939) 974-88.
Giesey, Ralph E. *Cérémonial et puissance souveraine: France, XVe-XVIIe siècles.* Trans. J. Carlier. Paris, 1987.
Gijswijt-Hofstra, Marijke. "Mens, dier en demon. Parallellen tussen dieren en heksenprocessen?" In *Geschiedenis, Godsdienst, Letterkunde: Festschrift S.B.J. Zilverberg.* Ed. E.K. Grootes and J. den Haan, pp. 55-62. Roden, 1989.
Ginzburg, Carlo. "Presomptions sur le Sabbat." *Annales, E.S.C.* 39 (1984) 341-54.
——. *The Night Battles.* Trans. J. & A. Tedeschi. Harmondsworth, 1985.
Giraud, Charles. *Essai sur l'histoire du droit français au moyen âge.* 2 vols. Paris, 1846.
Glanz, Rudolf. "The 'Jewish Execution' in Medieval Germany." *Jewish Social Studies* 5 (1943) 3-26.
Goebel, Julius. *Felony and Misdemeanor: A Study in the History of Criminal Law.* Philadelphia, 1976.
Goldmann, Emil. *Chrenecruda. Studien zum Titel 58 der Lex Salica.* Deutschrechtliche Beiträge 13:1. Heidelberg, 1931.
Grundmann, H. *Religiöse Bewegungen im Mittelalter.* 1935. Repr. Hildesheim, 1961.
Guenée, Bernard. *Tribunaux et gens de justice dans le bailliage de Senlis à la fin du moyen âge.* Strasbourg, 1963.
Gurevich, Aron. *Medieval Popular Culture: Problems of Belief and Perception.* Trans. J.M. Bak and P.A. Hollingsworth. Cambridge, 1988.
Hambroer, Johannes. "Der Hahn als Löwenschreck im Mittelalter." *Zeitschrift für Religions- und Geistesgeschichte* 18 (1966) 237-54.
Handoo, Jawaharlal. "Cultural Attitudes to Birds and Animals in Folklore." In *Signifying Animals: Human Meaning in the Natural World.* Ed. Roy Willis, pp. 37-42. London, 1990.
Hentig, Hans von. "Beseelung und Tabu des Galgens." *Studien zur Kriminalgeschichte,* pp. 131-48. Bern, 1962.
——. "The Pillory: A Medieval Punishment." In *Studien zur Kriminalgeschichte,* pp. 112-28. Bern, 1962.
Hertz, Robert. "The Pre-Eminence of the Right Hand: A Study in Religious Polarity." In Rodney Needham, ed. *Right and Left: Essays on Dual Symbolic Classification,* pp. 7-21. Chicago, 1973.
Herwaarden, Jan van. *Opgelegde bedevaarten: Een studie over de praktijk van opleggen van bedevaarten in de Nederlanden gedurende de late middeleeuwen.* Assen, 1978.

Hillairet, Jacques. *Gibets, piloris et cachots du vieux Paris.* Paris, 1956.
Hinckeldey, Ch., ed. *Justiz in alter Zeit.* Rothenburg, 1984.
His, Rudolph. *Der Totenglaube in der Geschichte des germanishen Strafrechts.* Münster, 1929.
Hoebel, E. Adamson. *The Law of Primitive Man: A Study in Comparative Legal Dynamics.* Cambridge, Mass., 1954.
Honegger, Claudia. "Comment: Women and Witches." *Signs* 4 (1979) 792-98.
Huizinga, Johan. *The Waning of the Middle Ages.* Trans. F. Hopman. Harmondsworth, 1965.
Jackson, Richard A. *Vive le Roi: A History of the French Coronation from Charles V to Charles X.* Chapel Hill, N.C., 1984.
Jacquart, Danielle and Claude Thomasset. *Sexualité et savoir médical au moyen âge.* Paris, 1985.
Jordogne, O. "L'anthropomorphisme croissant dant le *Roman de Renart.*" In E. Rombauts and A. Welkenhuysen , eds., q.v. *Aspects of the Medieval Animal Epic,* pp. 25-42.
Kantorowicz, Ernst. *Laudes Regiae: A Study in Liturgical Acclamations and Medieval Ruler Worship.* Berkeley, 1958.
Kantorowicz, Hermann. "Volksgeist und historische Rechtsschule." In H. Coing and G. Immel, eds. *Rechtshistorische Schriften,* pp. 435-56. Karlsruhe, 1970.
Kappler, Claude. *Monstres, démons et merveilles à la fin du moyen âge.* Paris, 1980.
Kaufman, Ekkehard. "*Quod paganorum tempore observabant.* Ist der Titel 58 der Lex Salica (Pactus) eine Neuschöpfung der Merowinger?" In Karl Hauck et al., eds. *Sprache und Recht. Festschrift für Ruth Schmidt-Wiegand.* 2 vols. 1:374-90. Berlin, 1986.
Kern, Fritz. *Kingship and Law in the Middle Ages.* Trans. and introd. S.B. Chrimes. New York, 1956.
Kisch, Guido. *Jewry-Law in Medieval Germany: Laws and Court Decisions Concerning Jews.* New York, 1949.
——. "The Jewish Execution in Medieval Germany." In *Studi in memoria di Paolo Koschaker.* 2 vols. 2:65-93. Milan, 1954.
Krause, Sigrid. "Le *Reinhart Fuchs,* satire de la justice et du droit." In Danielle Buschinger and André Crépin, eds. *Comique, satire et parodie dans la tradition renardienne et les fabliaux,* pp. 139-51. Goppingen, 1983.
Krygier, Martin. "Law as Tradition." *Law and Philosophy* 5 (1986) 237-62.
Kunzle, David. "World Upside Down: The Iconography of a European Broadsheet Type." In Barbara Babcock, ed. q.v. *The Reversible World,* pp. 39-94.
Kuttner, Stephan. "The Revival of Jurisprudence." In Robert L. Benson and Giles Constable, eds. *Renaissance and Renewal in the Twelfth Century,* pp. 299-338. Cambridge, Mass., 1982.
La Borderie, A. de. *Les monuments originaux et l'histoire de saint Yves.* Saint Brieuc, 1885.
Langbein, John. *Prosecuting Crime in the Renaissance.* Cambridge, Mass. 1974.
——. *Torture and the Law of Proof.* Chicago, 1977.
Laurent, Sylvie. *Naître au moyen âge. De la conception à la naissance: La grossesse et l'accouchement (XIIe-XVe siècle).* Paris, 1989.
Le Bras, Gabriel. "Quelques conséquences juridiques et sociales des idées romaines sur la mort." In René Maunier, ed. q.v. *Etudes de sociologie et d'ethnologie juridiques,* pp. 5-22.
Le Goff, Jacques. "Body and Ideology in the Medieval West." In *The Medieval Imagination.* Trans. Arthur Goldhammer. pp. 83-96. Chicago, 1985.
——. "Le rituel symbolique de la vassalité." In *Pour un autre moyen âge,* pp. 349-420. Paris, 1977.
——. "Lévy-Strauss in Brocéliande: A Brief Analysis of a Courtly Romance." In *The Medieval Imagination,* pp. 107-31. Chicago, 1985.

——. "Mélusine maternelle et défricheuse." In *Pour un autre moyen âge*, pp. 307-31. Paris, 1977.

Le Mappian, Jean. *Yves de Tréguier*. Paris, 1981.

Le Roux de Lincy, Antoine. *Le livre des proverbes français*. 2 vols. Paris, 1859. Repr. Geneva, 1968.

—— and L.M. Tisserand, eds. *Paris et ses historiens au XIVe et XVe siècles*. Paris, 1867.

Le Roy Ladurie, Emmanuel. *Le carnaval de Romans*. Paris, 1979.

Lebrun, Auguste. *La coutume. Ses sources—son autorité en droit privé*. Paris, 1932.

Lecouteux, Claude. *Fantômes et revenants au moyen âge*. Paris, 1986.

——. "Paganisme, Christianisme et merveilleux." *Annales, E.S.C.* 37 (1982) 700-16.

Lecoy de la Marche, A. *La chaire française au moyen âge*. Paris, 1886.

Legrand, H. *Paris en 1380*. Paris, 1868.

Leguay, J.-P. *Un réseau urbain au moyen âge: Les villes du duché de Bretagne au XIVe et XVe siècle*. Paris, 1981.

Lemercier, P. "Une curiosité judiciaire au moyen âge: La grâce par mariage subséquent." *Revue d'histoire du droit* 33 (1955) 464-74.

Levy, Ernst. *West Roman Vulgar Law: The Law of Property*. Philadelphia, 1951.

Lévy, Jean-Philippe. "La pénétration du droit savant dans les coutumiers angevins et bretons au moyen âge." *Tijdschrift voor Rechtsgeschiedenis* 15 (1957) 1-53.

Lot, Ferdinand. "Des frais de justice au XIVe siècle." *Bibliothèque de l'école des chartes* 34 (1873) 204-32.

—— and Robert Fawtier. *Histoire des institutions françaises au moyen âge*. 3 vols. Paris, 1957-62.

Lourie, Elena. "Complicidad criminal: un aspecto insolito de convivencia Judeo-Cristiana." *Actas del III Congreso Internacional, "Encuentro de las tres culturas" Toledo, 15-18 October, 1984*. Ed. Carlos Carrete Parrondo, pp. 93-108. Toledo, 1988. Repr. in *Crusade and Colonisation*. London, 1990.

Löfstedt, Leena. "Après une lecture des Coutumes de Philippe de Beaumanoir." *Neuphilologische Mitteilungen* 85 (1984) 19-32.

——. "Le verbe du droit français: Pléonasmes d'origine latine." *Neuphilologische Mitteilungen* 86 (1985) 89-99.

Luchaire, Achille. *Etudes sur les actes de Louis VII*. Paris, 1885. Repr. Brussels, 1964.

——. *La société française au temps de Philippe-Auguste*. Paris, 1909.

MacKay, Angus. "Ritual and Propaganda in Fifteenth-Century Castile." *Past and Present* 107 (1985) 3-43.

Maitland, F.W. *Collected Papers*. Ed. H.A.L. Fisher. 3 vols. Cambridge, 1911.

Malul, Meir. *The Comparative Method in Ancient Near Eastern and Biblical Legal Studies*. Alter Orient und altes Testament: Kevelaer, 1990.

Mason, Peter. "Half a Cow." *Semiotica* 85 (1991) 1-40.

Maunier, René ed. *Etudes de sociologie et d'ethnologie juridiques*. Paris, 1932.

Mâle, Emile. *L'art réligieux de la fin du moyen âge en France*. Paris, 1931.

McCulloch, Florence. *Medieval Latin and French Bestiaries*. Chapel Hill, 1962.

McKitterick, Rosamond. *The Carolingians and the Written Word*. Cambridge, 1989.

Meijers, E. M. "L'Université d'Orléans au XIIIe siècle." In R. Feenstra and H.F.W.D. Fischer, eds. *Etudes d'histoire du droit*. 4 vols. 3:3-148. Leiden, 1956-76.

——. "Cerquemanage." In Feenstra and Visser, eds. *Etudes d'histoire du droit*. 4 vols. 1:179-184. Leiden, 1956-76.

Melleville, M. "De l'usage au moyen âge de permettre à une jeune fille de sauver un criminel en l'épousant." *Bulletin de la société académique de Laon* 3 (1854) 383-85.

Mellinkoff, Ruth. "Riding Backwards: Theme of Humiliation and Symbol of Evil." *Viator* 4 (1973) 153-76.

Metzger, Emile. "La mutilation des morts. Contribution à l'étude des croyances et rites funeraires des Germains." *Mélanges Charles Andler*, pp. 257-67. Strasbourg, 1924.

Ménabréa, Léon. *De l'origine, de la forme et de l'esprit des jugements rendus contre les animaux.* Chambéry, 1846.

Miller, S.J.T. "The Position of the King in Bracton and Beaumanoir." *Speculum* 31 (1956) 263-96.

Moeller, Ernst v. "Die Rechtssitte des Stabbrechens." *ZRG, GA* 21 (1900) 27-115.

Molin, Jean-Baptiste and Protaïs Mutembé. *Le rituel du mariage en France du XIIe au XVIe siècle.* Paris, 1974.

Moore, Sally F. *Law as Process: An Anthropological Approach.* London, 1978.

—— and Barbara G. Myerhoff. "Introduction: Secular Ritual, Forms and Meanings." In Moore and Myerhoff, eds. *Secular Ritual*, pp. 3-24. Assen, 1977.

Mourin, Louis. *Jean Gerson, prédicateur français.* Bruges, 1952.

Muchembled, Robert. *Popular Culture and Elite Culture in France,* 1400-1750. Trans. Lydia Cochrane. Baton Rouge, 1985.

——. "Satan ou les hommes? La chasse aux sorcières et ses causes." In M.-S. Dupont-Bouchat, W. Frijhoff, and R. Muchembled. *Prophètes et sorciers dans les Pays-Bas, XVIe-XVIIIe siècle,* pp. 13-40. Paris, 1978.

Nottarp, Hermann. *Gottesurteilstudien.* München, 1955.

O'Connor, Mary Catharine. *The Art of Dying Well: The Development of the Ars Moriendi.* New York, 1942.

Olivier-Martin, Fr. *Histoire de la coutume de la prévôté et vicomté de Paris.* 3 vols. Paris, 1922-30. Repr. 1972.

——. "Le roi de France et les mauvaises coutumes." *ZRG, GA* 58 (1938) 108-37.

——. "La coutume de la prévôté et vicomté de Paris." *MSHP* 48 (1921) 174-89.

Pastoureau, Michel. "Les couleurs médievales: Systèmes de valeurs et modes de sensibilité." In *Figures et couleurs,* pp. 35-49. Paris, 1986.

Payen, Charles. *Le motif du repentir dans la littérature française médiévale (des origines à 1230).* Geneva, 1967.

Petot, P. "Le droit commun en France selon les coutumiers." *RHDFE* 38 (1960) 412-29.

Pissard, Hippolyte. *Essai sur la connaissance et la preuve des coutumes en justice, dans l'ancien droit français et dans le système romano-canonique.* Paris, 1910.

Platelle, Henri. "La voix du sang: Le cadavre qui saigne en présence de son meurtrier." *La piété populaire au moyen âge. Actes du 99e Congrès national des sociétés savantes (Besançon, 1974).* 2 vols. 1:161-79. Paris, 1977.

Poirion, Daniel. *Le merveilleux dans la littérature française du moyen âge.* Paris, 1982.

Porter, J.R. and W.M.S. Russel, eds. *Animals in Folklore.* Cambridge, 1978.

Pospisil, Leopold. *Anthropology of Law: A Comparative Theory.* New York, 1971.

Pouchelle, Marie-Christine. *Corps et chirurgie à l'apogée du moyen âge: Savoir et imaginaire du corps chez Henri de Mondeville, chirurgien de Philippe le Bel.* Paris, 1983.

Praag, A. van "Het strafproces tegen dieren." *Themis* 93 (1932) 345-75.

Radbruch, Gustav. "Planetarische Kriminalanthropologie." In *Elegantiae Iuris Criminalis,* pp. 12-25. Basel, 1938.

Radding, Charles M. "Superstition to Science: Nature, Fortune and the Passing of the Medieval Ordeal." *American Historical Review* 84 (1979) 945-69.

Raphaël, Freddy. "La répresentation des Juifs dans l'art médiéval en Alsace." *Revue des sciences sociales de France de l'Est* (1972) 26-42.

Renaudet, Augustin. "Jean Standonck, un réformateur catholique avant la réforme." *Bulletin de l'histoire du protestantisme français* 57 (1908) 1-81.

——. *Réforme et humanisme à Paris pendant les premières guerres d'Italie (1494-1517).* 2nd ed. Repr. Geneva, 1981.

Roberts, John M. "Oaths, Autonomic Ordeals, and Power." *American Anthropologist* 67/2 (1965) 186-212.
Roberts, Simon. "The Study of Dispute: Anthropological Perspectives." In John Bossy, ed. q.v. *Disputes and Settlements: Law and Human Relations in the West*, pp. 1-24.
Rombauts, E. and A. Welkenhuysen , eds. *Aspects of the Medieval Animal Epic.* Louvain, 1975.
Rousset, P. "La croyance en la justice immanente à l'époque féodale." *Le moyen âge* 54 (1948) 225-48.
Ruiz, Teofilo F. "Festivités, couleurs et symboles du pouvoir en Castille au XVe siècle" *Annales E.S.C.* 46 (1991) 521-46.
Russell, W.M.S. and Claire Russell. "The Social Biology of Werewolves." In J.R. Porter and W.M.S. Russell, eds. q.v. *Animals in Folklore*, pp. 143-82.
Sainéan, Lazar. *Les sources indigènes de l'etymologie française.* 3 vols. Paris, 1925. Repr. 1972.
Saint-Edmé, M.B. de. *Dictionnaire de la pénalité dans toutes les parties du monde connu.* 5 vols. Paris, 1824-28.
Saintyves, P. "Le folklore juridique." In René Maunier, ed. q.v. *Etudes de sociologie et d'ethnologie juridiques*, pp. 65-108.
——. *Les cinquante jugements de Salomon, ou les arrêts des bons juges d'après la tradition populaire.* Paris, 1933.
Sauval, Henri. *Histoire et recherches des antiquités de la ville de Paris.* 3 vols. Paris, 1724.
Schmidt-Wiegand, Ruth. "Chrenecruda. Rechtwort und Formalakt der Merowingerzeit." In *Festschrift für Gustaf Klemens Schmelzeisen.* Ed. Hans-Wolf Thümmel, pp. 252-73. Stuttgart, 1980.
Schmitt, J.-C. *Le saint lévrier. Guinefort, guérisseur d'enfants depuis le XIIIe siècle.* Paris, 1979.
——. *La raison des gestes dans l'Occident médiéval.* Paris, 1990.
——. "Les revenants dans la société féodale." *Le temps de la réflexion* 3 (1982) 285-306.
Schmitz, H.J. *Die Bussbücher.* 2 vols. Düsseldorf, 1898.
Schreuer, Hans. "Das Recht der Toten." *Zeitschrift für vergleichende Rechtswissenschaft* 33 (1916) 333-432, 34 (1916) 1-208.
Sergène, André. "Le précédent judiciaire au moyen âge." *RIIDFE* 39 (1961) 224-54, 359-70.
Sébillot, Paul. *Gargantua dans les traditions populaires.* Paris, 1883.
Shachar, Isaiah. *The Judensau: A Medieval Anti-Jewish Motif and its History.* London, 1974.
Sharpe, James A. "'Last Dying Speeches': Religion, Ideology and Public Execution in Seventeenth-Century England." *Past and Present* 107 (1985) 144-67.
Shennan, J.H. *The Parlement of Paris.* Ithaca, N.Y., 1968.
Singer, Charles. "The Visions of Hildegard of Bingen. " In *From Magic to Science: Essays on the Scientific Twilight*, pp. 199-239. New York, 1928.
Smith, J.A. Clarence. *Medieval Law Teachers and Writers.* Ottawa, 1975.
Smith, Kathryn C. "The Role of Animals in Witchcraft and Popular Magic." In J.R. Porter and W.M.S. Russel, eds. q.v. *Animals in Folklore*, pp. 96-110.
Smith, K.F. "A Historical Study of the Werewolf in Literature." *Publications of the Modern Language Association* 9 (1894) 1-42.
Soman, Alfred. "Deviance and Criminal Justice in Western Europe, 1300-1800: An Essay in Structure." *Criminal Justice History* 1 (1980) 1-28.
Sorel, A. "Procès contre les animaux et insectes suivis au moyen âge dans la Picardie et le Valois." *Bulletin de la Société historique de Compiègne* 3 (1876-77) 269-314.

Spierenburg, Pieter. *The Spectacle of Sufffering: Executions and the Evolution of Repression*. Cambridge, 1984.

Stein, Simon. "Lex Salica." *Speculum* 22 (1947) 113-34, 395-418.

Stevenson, Kenneth. *Nuptial Blessing: A Study of Christian Marriage Rites*. New York, 1983.

Stock, Brian. *The Implications of Literacy*. Princeton, 1983.

Stokvis, J. "Bijdrage tot de kennis van het wereldlijke dierenproces in de noodelijke Nederlanden." *Tijdschrift voor Strafrecht* 41 (1931) 399-424.

Stow, Kenneth R. *Alienated Minority: The Jews of Medieval Latin Europe*. New Haven, 1992, forthcoming.

——. "Hatred of the Jews or Love of the Church: Papal Policy Towards the Jews." [Hebrew] In S. Almog, ed. *Antisemitism Through the Ages*, pp. 91-111. Jerusalem, 1980.

——. *The "1007 Anonymous" and Papal Sovereignty: Jewish Perceptions of the Papacy and Papal Policy in the High Middle Ages*. Cincinnati, 1984.

Ström, Folke. *On the Sacral Origin of the Germanic Death Penalties*. Stockhom, 1942.

Tenenti, Alberto. *La vie et la mort à travers l'art du XVe siècle*. Paris, 1952.

Toaff, Ariel. *Il vino e la carne*. Bologna, 1989.

Tolmer, L. *Folk-lore et biologie: les oeufs de coq et basilic*. Bayeux, 1928.

Trachtenberg, Joshua. *The Devil and the Jews*. New Haven, 1943. Repr. Philadelphia, 1983.

Turner, Victor. *Dramas, Fields and Metaphors*. Ithaca, N.Y., 1974.

——. *The Ritual Process*. Chicago, 1969.

—— and Edith Turner. *Image and Pilgrimage in Christian Culture*. New York, 1978.

Ullmann, Walter. "Bartolus on Customary Law." In D. Segoloni, ed. *Bartolo da Sassoferrato: Studi e documenti per il VI centenario*, pp. 49-73. Milan, 1961. Repr. in *Jurisprudence in the Middle Ages*. London, 1980.

——. "Reflections on Medieval Torture." *Juridical Review* 56 (1944) 123-37.

——. *The Medieval Idea of Law as Represented by Lucas de Penna*. London, 1946.

Vauchez, André. *La sainteté en Occident aux derniers siècles du moyen âge*. Rome, 1981.

Vaultier, Roger. *Le folklore pendant la guerre de Cent Ans d'après les lettres de rémission du trésor des chartes*. Paris, 1965.

Viaene, H. "Kattedag te Ieper." *Biekorf* 45 (1939) 47-52.

Viollet, Paul. "Les établissements de Saint Louis dans le Beauvoisis." *MSHP* 8 (1881) 95-106.

Viollet-le-Duc, E. *Dictionnaire raisonné de l'architecture française du 11e au 16e siècle*. 10 vols. Paris, 1861.

Viscardi, J. *Le chien de Montargis: Etude de folklore juridique*. Paris, 1932.

Waelkens, L. *La théorie de la coutume chez Jacques de Révigny*. Leiden, 1984.

Watson, Alan. *Rome of the XII Tables: Persons and Property*. Princeton, N.J., 1975.

Wehrhan, K. "Ein Detmolder Tierprozess von 1644 und die Bedeutung des Tierprozesses überhaupt." *Zeitschrift des Vereins für rheinische und westfälische Volkskunde* 1 (1904) 65-77.

Wetter, Philip van. "Le droit romain et Beaumanoir." In E. Meynial, ed. *Mélanges Fitting*. 2 vols. 2:535-82. Montpellier, 1907-1908.

Wood, Ian. "Disputes in Late Fifth- and Sixth-century Gaul: Some Problems." In Wendy Davies and Paul Fouracre, eds. *The Settlement of Disputes in Early Medieval Europe*, pp. 7-22. Cambridge, 1986.

Wormald, Patrick. "*Lex Scripta* and *Verbum Regis*: Legislation and Germanic Kingship from Euric to Cnut." In P.H. Sawyer and I.N. Wood, eds. *Early Medieval Kingship*, pp. 105-38. Leeds, 1977.

Yasif, Eli. "King Solomon Proverbs." [Hebrew] *Mechkaré Yerushalayim be-Safrut Ivrit* 9 (1986) 357-73.

Zink, Michael. *La prédication en langue romane avant* 1300. Paris, 1976.

INDEX

BRILL'S STUDIES IN INTELLECTUAL HISTORY

1. POPKIN, R.H. *Isaac la Peyrère (1596-1676)*. His Life, Work and Influence. 1987. ISBN 90 04 08157 7
2. THOMSON, A. *Barbary and Enlightenment*. European Attitudes towards the Maghreb in the 18th Century. 1987. ISBN 90 04 08273 5
3. DUHEM, P. *Prémices Philosophiques*. With an Introduction in English by S.L. Jaki. 1987. ISBN 90 04 08117 8
4. OUDEMANS, TH.C.W. & A.P.M.H. LARDINOIS. *Tragic ambiguity*. Anthropology, Philosophy and Sophocles' *Antigone*. 1987. ISBN 90 04 08417 7
5. FRIEDMAN, J.B. (ed.). *John de Foxton's Liber Cosmographiae* (1408). An Edition and Codicological Study. 1988. ISBN 90 04 08528 9
6. AKKERMAN, F. & A.J. VANDERJAGT (eds.). *Rodolphus Agricola Phrisius, 1444-1485*. Proceedings of the International Conference at the University of Groningen, 28-30 October 1985. 1988. ISBN 90 04 08599 8
7. CRAIG, W.L. *The Problem of Divine Foreknowledge and Future Contingents from Aristotle to Suarez*. 1988. ISBN 90 04 08516 5
8. STROLL, M. *The Jewish Pope*. Ideology and Politics in the Papal Schism of 1130. 1987. ISBN 90 04 08590 4
9. STANESCO, M. *Jeux d'errance du chevalier médiéval*. Aspects ludiques de la fonction guerrière dans la littérature du Moyen Age flamboyant. 1988. ISBN 90 04 08684 6
10. KATZ, D. *Sabbath and Sectarianism in Seventeenth-Century England*. 1988. ISBN 90 04 08754 0
11. LERMOND, L. *The Form of Man*. Human Essence in Spinoza's *Ethic*. 1988. ISBN 90 04 08829 6
12. JONG, M. DE. *In Samuel's Image*. Early Medieval Child Oblation. (in preparation)
13. PYENSON, L. *Empire of Reason*. Exact Sciences in Indonesia, 1840-1940. 1989. ISBN 90 04 08984 5
14. CURLEY, E. & P.-F. MOREAU (eds.). *Spinoza. Issues and Directions*. The Proceedings of the Chicago Spinoza Conference. 1990. ISBN 90 04 09334 6
15. KAPLAN, Y., H. MÉCHOULAN & R.H. POPKIN (eds.). *Menasseh Ben Israel and His World*. 1989. ISBN 90 04 09114 9
16. BOS, A.P. *Cosmic and Meta-Cosmic Theology in Aristotle's Lost Dialogues*. 1989. ISBN 90 04 09155 6
17. KATZ, D.S. & J.I. ISRAEL (eds.) *Sceptics, Millenarians and Jews*. 1990. ISBN 90 04 09160 2
18. DALES, R.C. *Medieval Discussions of the Eternity of the World*. 1990. ISBN 90 04 09215 3
19. CRAIG, W.L. *Divine Foreknowledge and Human Freedom*. The Coherence of Theism: Omniscience. 1991. ISBN 90 04 09250 1
20. OTTEN, W. *The Anthropology of Johannes Scottus Eriugena*. 1991. ISBN 90 04 09302 8
21. ÅKERMAN, S. *Queen Christina of Sweden and Her Circle*. The Transformation of a Seventeenth-Century Philosophical Libertine. 1991. ISBN 90 04 09310 9
22. POPKIN, R.H. *The Third Force in Seventeenth-Century Thought*. 1992. ISBN 90 04 09324 9
23. DALES, R.C. & O. ARGERAMI (eds.). *Medieval Latin Texts on the Eternity of the World*. 1990. ISBN 90 04 09376 1
24. STROLL, M. *Symbols as Power*. The Papacy Following the Investiture Contest. 1991. ISBN 90 04 09374 5

25. FARAGO, C.J. *Leonardo da Vinci's 'Paragone'.* A Critical Interpretation with a New Edition of the Text in the *Codex Urbinas.* 1992. ISBN 90 04 09415 6
26. JONES, R. *Learning Arabic in Renaissance Europe.* 1992. ISBN 90 04 09451 2
27. DRIJVERS, J.W. *Helena Augusta.* The Mother of Constantine the Great and the Legend of Her Finding of the True Cross. 1992. ISBN 90 04 09435 0
28. BOUCHER, W.I. *Spinoza in English.* A Bibliography from the Seventeenth-Century to the Present. 1991. ISBN 90 04 09499 7
29. McINTOSH, C. *The Rose Cross and the Age of Reason.* Eighteenth-Century Rosicrucianism in Central Europe and its Relationship to the Enlightenment. 1992. ISBN 90 04 09502 0
30. CRAVEN, K. *Jonathan Swift and the Millennium of Madness.* The Information Age in Swift's *A Tale of a Tub.* 1992. ISBN 90 04 09524 1
31. BERKVENS-STEVELINCK, C., H. BOTS, P.G. HOFTIJZER & O.S. LANKHORST (eds.). *Le Magasin de l'Univers. The Dutch Republic as the Centre of the European Book Trade.* Papers Presented at the International Colloquium, held at Wassenaar, 5-7 July 1990. 1992. ISBN 90 04 09493 8
32. GRIFFIN, JR., M.I.J. *Latitudinarianism in the Seventeenth-Century Church of England.* Annotated by R.H. Popkin. Edited by L. Freedman. 1992. ISBN 90 04 09653 1
33. WES, M.A. *Classics in Russia 1700-1855.* Between Two Bronze Horsemen. 1992. ISBN 90 04 09664 7
34. BULHOF, I.N. *The Language of Science.* A Study of the Relationship between Literature and Science in the Perspective of a Hermeneutical Ontology. With a Case Study of Darwin's *The Origin of Species.* 1992. ISBN 90 04 09644 2
35. LAURSEN, J.C. *The Politics of Skepticism in the Ancients, Montaigne, Hume, and Kant.* 1992. ISBN 90 04 09459 8
36. COHEN, E. *The Crossroads of Justice.* Law and Culture in Late Medieval France. 1993. ISBN 90 04 09569 1

www.ingramcontent.com/pod-product-compliance
Lightning Source LLC
LaVergne TN
LVHW012051011026
849162LV00017B/135
* 9 7 8 9 0 0 4 0 9 5 6 9 4 *